PEARSON

ALWAYS LEARNING

Marilyn Stokstad • Michael W. Cothren

A View of the World

Custom Edition for Oregon State University

Taken from:

Art History: A View of the World: Part One, Book 3, Portable Edition, Fourth Edition
by Marilyn Stokstad and Michael W. Cothren

Art History: A View of the World: Part Two, Book 5, Portable Edition, Fourth Edition
by Marilyn Stokstad and Michael W. Cothren

Art History, Fourth Edition
by Marilyn Stokstad and Michael W. Cothren

ISBN 10: 1-256-78034-0
ISBN 13: 978-1-256-78034-2

CONTENTS

The various features of this book reinforce each other, helping the reader to become comfortable with terminology and concepts that are specific to art history.

Starter Kit and Introduction   The Starter Kit is a highly concise primer of basic concepts and tools. The Introduction explores the way they are used to come to an understanding of the history of art.

Captions   There are two kinds of captions in this book: short and long. Short captions identify information specific to the work of art or architecture illustrated:

> artist (when known)
> title or descriptive name of work date
> original location (if moved to a museum or other site)
> material or materials a work is made of
> size (height before width) in feet and inches, with meters
>   and centimeters in parentheses
> present location

The order of these elements varies, depending on the type of work illustrated. Dimensions are not given for architecture, for most wall paintings, or for most architectural sculpture. Some captions have one or more lines of small print below the identification section of the caption that gives museum or collection information. This is rarely required reading; its inclusion is often a requirement for gaining permission to reproduce the work.

Longer, discursive captions contain information that complements the narrative of the main text.

Definitions of Terms   You will encounter the basic terms of art history in three places:

> **In the Text**, where words appearing in boldface type are defined, or glossed, at their first use. Some terms are boldfaced and explained more than once, especially those that experience shows are hard to remember.
>
> **In Boxed Features**, on technique and other subjects, where labeled drawings and diagrams visually reinforce the use of terms.
>
> **In the Glossary**, at the end of the volume (p. 1137), which contains all the words in boldface type in the text and boxes.

Maps   At the beginning of each chapter you will find a map with all the places mentioned in the chapter.

Boxes   Special material that complements, enhances, explains, or extends the narrative text is set off in six types of tinted boxes.

Art and its Contexts and The Object Speaks boxes expand on selected works or issues related to the text. A Closer Look boxes use leader-line captions to focus attention on specific aspects of important works. Elements of Architecture boxes clarify specifically architectural features, often explaining engineering principles or building technology. Technique boxes outline the techniques and processes by which certain types of art are created. Recovering the Past boxes highlight the work of archaeologists who uncover and conservators who assure the preservation and clear presentation of art.

Bibliography   The bibliography at the end of this book beginning on page 1146 contains books in English, organized by general works and by chapter, that are basic to the study of art history today, as well as works cited in the text.

Learn About It   Placed at the beginning of each chapter, this feature captures in bulleted form the key learning objectives, or outcomes, of the chapter. They point to what will have been accomplished upon its completion.

Think About It   These critical thinking questions appear at the end of each chapter and help students assess their mastery of the learning objectives (Learn About It) by asking them to think through and apply what they have learned.

MyArtsLab prompts   These notations are found throughout the chapter and are keyed to MyArtsLab resources that enrich and reinforce student learning.

Dates, Abbreviations, and Other Conventions   This book uses the designations BCE and CE, abbreviations for "Before the Common Era" and "Common Era," instead of BC ("Before Christ") and AD ("Anno Domini," "the year of our Lord"). The first century BCE is the period from 99 BCE to 1 BCE; the first century CE is from the year 1 CE to 99 CE. Similarly, the second century CE is the period from 199 BCE to 100 BCE; the second century CE extends from 100 CE to 199 CE.

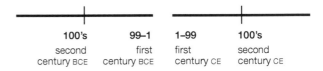

100's	99–1	1–99	100's
second century BCE	first century BCE	first century CE	second century CE

Circa ("about") is used with approximate dates, spelled out in the text and abbreviated to "c." in the captions. This indicates that an exact date is not yet verified.

An illustration is called a "figure," or "fig." Thus, figure 6–7 is the seventh numbered illustration in Chapter 6, and fig. Intro-3 is the third figure in the Introduction. There are two types of figures: photographs of artworks or of models, and line drawings. Drawings are used when a work cannot be photographed or when a diagram or simple drawing is the clearest way to illustrate an object or a place.

When introducing artists, we use the words *active* and *documented* with dates, in addition to "b." (for "born") and "d." (for "died"). "Active" means that an artist worked during the years given. "Documented" means that documents link the person to that date.

Accents are used for words in French, German, Italian, and Spanish only. With few exceptions, names of cultural institutions in Western European countries are given in the form used in that country.

Titles of Works of Art   It was only over the last 500 years that paintings and works of sculpture created in Europe and North America were given formal titles, either by the artist or by critics and art historians. Such formal titles are printed in italics. In other traditions and cultures, a single title is not important or even recognized.

In this book we use formal descriptive titles of artworks where titles are not established. If a work is best known by its non-English title, such as Manet's *Le Déjeuner sur l'Herbe (The Luncheon on the Grass)*, the original language precedes the translation.

Art history focuses on the visual arts—painting, drawing, sculpture, prints, photography, ceramics, metalwork, architecture, and more. This Starter Kit contains basic information and addresses concepts that underlie and support the study of art history. It provides a quick reference guide to the vocabulary used to classify and describe art objects. Understanding these terms is indispensable because you will encounter them again and again in reading, talking, and writing about art.

Let us begin with the basic properties of art. A work of art is a material object having both form and content. It is often described and categorized according to its *style* and *medium*.

FORM

Referring to purely visual aspects of art and architecture, the term *form* encompasses qualities of *line*, *shape*, *color*, *light*, *texture*, *space*, *mass*, *volume*, and *composition*. These qualities are known as *formal elements*. When art historians use the term *formal*, they mean "relating to form."

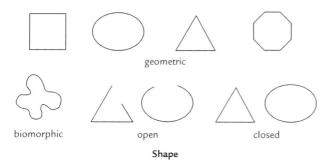

geometric

biomorphic   open   closed

Shape

Line and **shape** are attributes of form. Line is an element—usually drawn or painted—the length of which is so much greater than the width that we perceive it as having only length. Line can be actual, as when the line is visible, or it can be implied, as when the movement of the viewer's eyes over the surface of a work follows a path determined by the artist. Shape, on the other hand, is the two-dimensional, or flat, area defined by the borders of an enclosing *outline* or *contour*. Shape can be *geometric*, *biomorphic* (suggesting living things; sometimes called *organic*), *closed*, or *open*. The *outline* or *contour* of a three-dimensional object can also be perceived as line.

Color has several attributes. These include *hue*, *value*, and *saturation*.

Hue is what we think of when we hear the word *color*, and the terms are interchangeable. We perceive hues as the result of differing wavelengths of electromagnetic energy. The visible spectrum, which can be seen in a rainbow, runs from red through violet. When the ends of the spectrum are connected through the hue red-violet, the result may be diagrammed as a color wheel. The primary hues (numbered 1) are red, yellow, and blue. They are known as primaries because all other colors are made by combining these hues. Orange, green, and violet result from the mixture of two primaries and are known as secondary hues (numbered 2). Intermediate hues, or tertiaries (numbered 3), result from the mixture of a primary and a secondary. Complementary colors are the two colors directly opposite one another on the color wheel, such as red and green. Red, orange, and yellow are regarded as warm colors and appear to advance toward us. Blue, green, and violet, which seem to recede, are called cool colors. Black and white are not considered colors but neutrals; in terms of light, black is understood as the absence of color and white as the mixture of all colors.

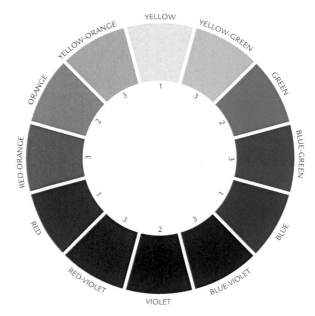

Value is the relative degree of lightness or darkness of a given color and is created by the amount of light reflected from an object's surface. A dark green has a deeper value than a light green, for example. In black-and-white reproductions of colored objects, you see only value, and some artworks—for example, a drawing made with black ink—possess only value, not hue or saturation.

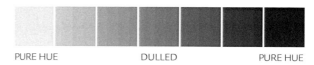

Value scale from white to black.

+ WHITE   PURE HUE   + BLACK

Value variation in red.

Saturation, also sometimes referred to as *intensity*, is a color's quality of brightness or dullness. A color described as highly saturated looks vivid and pure; a hue of low saturation may or look a little muddy or greyed.

PURE HUE   DULLED   PURE HUE

Intensity scale from bright to dull.

Texture, another attribute of form, is the tactile (or touch-perceived) quality of a surface. It is described by words such as *smooth*, *polished*, *rough*, *prickly*, *grainy*, or *oily*. Texture takes two forms: the texture of the actual surface of the work of art and the implied (illusionistically described) surface of objects represented in the work of art.

Space is what contains forms. It may be actual and three-dimensional, as it is with sculpture and architecture, or it may be fictional, represented illusionistically in two dimensions, as when artists represent recession into the distance on a flat surface—such as a wall or a canvas--by using various systems of perspective.

Mass and volume are properties of three-dimensional things. Mass is solid matter—whether sculpture or architecture—that takes up space. Volume is enclosed or defined space, and may be either solid or hollow. Like space, mass and volume may be illusionistically represented on a two-dimensional surface, such as in a painting or a photograph.

Composition is the organization, or arrangement, of forms in a work of art. Shapes and colors may be repeated or varied, balanced symmetrically or asymmetrically; they may be stable or dynamic. The possibilities are nearly endless and artistic choice depends both on the time and place where the work was created as well as the objectives of individual artists. Pictorial depth (spatial recession) is a specialized aspect of composition in which the three-dimensional world is represented on a flat surface, or *picture plane*. The area "behind" the picture plane is called the *picture space* and conventionally contains three "zones": *foreground*, *middle ground*, and *background*.

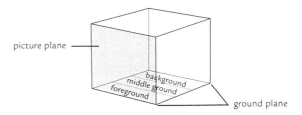

Various techniques for conveying a sense of pictorial depth have been devised by artists in different cultures and at different times. A number of them are diagrammed here. In some European art, the use of various systems of *perspective* has sought to create highly convincing illusions of recession into space. At other times and in other cultures, indications of recession are actually suppressed or avoided to emphasize surface rather than space.

TECHNIQUE | Pictorial devices for depicting recession in space

overlapping

In overlapping, partially covered elements are meant to be seen as located behind those covering them.

diminution

In diminution of scale, successively smaller elements are perceived as being progressively farther away than the largest ones.

vertical perspective

Vertical perspective stacks elements, with the higher ones intended to be perceived as deeper in space.

atmospheric perspective

Through atmospheric perspective, objects in the far distance (often in bluish-gray hues) have less clarity than nearer objects. The sky becomes paler as it approaches the horizon.

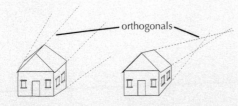

divergent perspective

In divergent or reverse perspective, forms widen slightly and imaginary lines called orthogonals diverge as they recede in space.

intuitive perspective

Intuitive perspective takes the opposite approach from divergent perspective. Forms become narrower and orthogonals converge the farther they are from the viewer, approximating the optical experience of spatial recession.

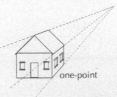 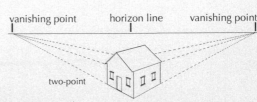

linear perspective

Linear perspective (also called scientific, mathematical, one-point and Renaissance perspective) is a rationalization or standardization of intuitive perspective that was developed in fifteenth-century Italy. It uses mathematical formulas to construct images in which all elements are shaped by, or arranged along, orthogonals that converge in one or more vanishing points on a horizon line.

CONTENT

Content includes *subject matter*, but not all works of art have subject matter. Many buildings, paintings, sculptures, and other art objects include no recognizable references to things in nature nor to any story or historical situation, focusing instead on lines, colors, masses, volumes, and other formal elements. However, all works of art—even those without recognizable subject matter—have content, or meaning, insofar as they seek to communicate ideas, convey feelings, or affirm the beliefs and values of their makers, their patrons, and usually the people who originally viewed or used them.

Content may derive from the social, political, religious, and economic *contexts* in which a work was created, the *intention* of the artist, and the *reception* of the work by beholders (the audience). Art historians, applying different methods of *interpretation*, often arrive at different conclusions regarding the content of a work of art, and single works of art can contain more than one meaning because they are occasionally directed at more than one audience.

The study of subject matter is called *iconography* (literally, "the writing of images") and includes the identification of *symbols*—images that take on meaning through association, resemblance, or convention.

STYLE

Expressed very broadly, *style* is the combination of form and composition that makes a work distinctive. *Stylistic analysis* is one of art history's most developed practices, because it is how art historians recognize the work of an individual artist or the characteristic manner of groups of artists working in a particular time or place. Some of the most commonly used terms to discuss *artistic styles* include *period style*, *regional style*, *representational style*, *abstract style*, *linear style*, and *painterly style*.

Period style refers to the common traits detectable in works of art and architecture from a particular historical era. It is good practice not to use the words "style" and "period" interchangeably. Style is the sum of many influences and characteristics, including the period of its creation. An example of proper usage is "an American house from the Colonial period built in the Georgian style."

Regional style refers to stylistic traits that persist in a geographic region. An art historian whose specialty is medieval art can recognize Spanish style through many successive medieval periods and can distinguish individual objects created in medieval Spain from other medieval objects that were created in, for example, Italy.

Representational styles are those that describe the appearance of recognizable subject matter in ways that make it seem lifelike.

> **Realism** and **Naturalism** are terms that some people used interchangeably to characterize artists' attempts to represent the observable world in a manner that appears to describe its visual appearance accurately. When capitalized, Realism refers to a specific period style discussed in Chapter 30.

> **Idealization** strives to create images of physical perfection according to the prevailing values or tastes of a culture. The artist may work in a representational style and idealize it to capture an underlying value or expressive effect.

Illusionism refers to a highly detailed style that seeks to create a convincing illusion of physical reality by describing its visual appearance meticulously.

Abstract styles depart from mimicking lifelike appearance to capture the essence of a form. An abstract artist may work from nature or from a memory image of nature's forms and colors, which are simplified, stylized, perfected, distorted, elaborated, or otherwise transformed to achieve a desired expressive effect.

> **Nonrepresentational (or Nonobjective) Art** is a term often used for works of art that do not aim to produce recognizable natural imagery.

> **Expressionism** refers to styles in which the artist exaggerates aspects of form to draw out the beholder's subjective response or to project the artist's own subjective feelings.

Linear describes both styles and techniques. In linear styles artists use line as the primary means of definition. But linear paintings can also incorporate *modeling*—creating an illusion of three-dimensional substance through shading, usually executed so that brushstrokes nearly disappear.

Painterly describes a style of representation in which vigorous, evident brushstrokes dominate, and outlines, shadows, and highlights are brushed in freely.

MEDIUM AND TECHNIQUE

Medium (plural, *media*) refers to the material or materials from which a work of art is made. Today, literally anything can be used to make a work of art, including not only traditional materials like paint, ink, and stone, but also rubbish, food, and the earth itself.

Technique is the process that transforms media into a work of art. Various techniques are explained throughout this book in Technique boxes. Two-dimensional media and techniques include painting, drawing, prints, and photography. Three-dimensional media and techniques are sculpture (for example, using stone, wood, clay or cast metal), architecture, and many small-scale arts (such as jewelry, containers, or vessels) in media such as ceramics, metal, or wood.

Painting includes wall painting and fresco, illumination (the decoration of books with paintings), panel painting (painting on wood panels), painting on canvas, and handscroll and hanging scroll painting. The paint in these examples is pigment mixed with a liquid vehicle, or binder. Some art historians also consider pictorial media such as mosaic and stained glass—where the pigment is arranged in solid form—as a type of painting.

Graphic arts are those that involve the application of lines and strokes to a two-dimensional surface or support, most often paper. Drawing is a graphic art, as are the various forms of printmaking. Drawings may be sketches (quick visual notes, often made in preparation for larger drawings or paintings); studies (more carefully drawn analyses of details or entire compositions); cartoons (full-scale drawings made in preparation for work in another medium, such as fresco, stained glass, or tapestry); or complete artworks in themselves. Drawings can be made with ink, charcoal, crayon, or pencil. Prints, unlike drawings, are made in multiple copies. The various forms of printmaking include woodcut, the intaglio processes (engraving, etching, drypoint), and lithography.

Photography (literally, "light writing") is a medium that involves the rendering of optical images on light-sensitive surfaces. Photographic images are typically recorded by a camera.

Sculpture is three-dimensional art that is *carved, modeled, cast,* or *assembled*. Carved sculpture is subtractive in the sense that the image is created by taking away material. Wood, stone, and ivory are common materials used to create carved sculptures. Modeled sculpture is considered additive, meaning that the object is built up from a material, such as clay, that is soft enough to be molded and shaped. Metal sculpture is usually cast or is assembled by welding or a similar means of permanent joining.

Sculpture is either free-standing (that is, surrounded by space) or in pictorial relief. Relief sculpture projects from the background surface of the same piece of material. High-relief sculpture projects far from its background; low-relief sculpture is only slightly raised; and sunken relief, found mainly in ancient Egyptian art, is carved into the surface, with the highest part of the relief being the flat surface.

Ephemeral arts include processions, ceremonies, or ritual dances (often with décor, costumes, or masks); performance art; earthworks; cinema and video art; and some forms of digital or computer art. All impose a temporal limitation—the artwork is viewable for a finite period of time and then disappears forever, is in a constant state of change, or must be replayed to be experienced again.

Architecture creates enclosures for human activity or habitation. It is three-dimensional, highly spatial, functional, and closely bound with developments in technology and materials. Since it is difficult to capture in a photograph, several types of schematic drawings are commonly used to enable the visualization of a building:

  Plans depict a structure's masses and voids, presenting a view from above of the building's footprint or as if it had been sliced horizontally at about waist height.

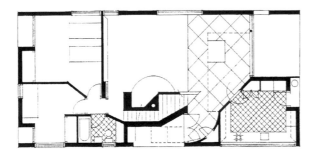

Plan: Philadelphia, Vanna Venturi House

Sections reveal the interior of a building as if it had been cut vertically from top to bottom.

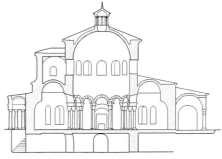

Section: Rome, Sta. Costanza

Isometric Drawings show buildings from oblique angles either seen from above ("bird's-eye view") to reveal their basic three-dimensional forms (often cut away so we can peek inside) or from below ("worm's-eye view") to represent the arrangement of interior spaces and the upward projection of structural elements.

Isometric cutaway from above: Ravenna, San Vitale

Isometric projection from below: Istanbul, Hagia Sophia

INTRODUCTION

INTRO-1 • Mark Rothko
NO. 3/NO. 13 (MAGENTA, BLACK AND GREEN ON ORANGE)
1949. Oil on canvas, 7'1⅜" × 5'5"
(2.165 × 1.648 m). Digital Image
© The Museum of Modern Art/Licensed
by SCALA/Art Resource, NY.

The title of this book seems clear. It defines a field of academic study and scholarly research that has achieved a secure place in college and university curricula across North America. But *Art History* couples two words—even two worlds—that are less well focused when separated. What is art? In what sense does it have a history? Students of art and its history should pause and engage, even if briefly, with these large questions before beginning the journey surveyed in the following chapters.

WHAT IS ART?

Artists, critics, art historians, and the general public all grapple with this thorny question. The *Random House Dictionary* defines "art" as "the quality, production, expression, or realm of what is beautiful, or of more than ordinary significance." Others have characterized "art" as something human-made that combines creative imagination and technical skill and satisfies an innate desire for order and harmony—perhaps a human hunger for the

LEARN ABOUT IT

I.1 Consider the criteria used to identify and characterize those cultural artifacts that are labeled as "art."

I.2 Survey the methods used by art historians to analyze works of art and interpret their meaning within their original cultural contexts.

I.3 Explore the methods and objectives of visual analysis.

I.4 Assess the way art historians identify conventional subject matter and symbols in a process called iconography.

I.5 Trace the process of art-historical interpretation in a case study.

HEAR MORE: Listen to an audio file of your chapter **www.myartslab.com**

beautiful. This seems relatively straightforward until we start to look at modern and contemporary art, where there has been a heated and extended debate concerning "What is Art?" The focus is often far from questions of transcendent beauty, ordered design, or technical skill, and centers instead on the meaning of a work for an elite target audience or the attempt to pose challenging questions or unsettle deep-seated cultural ideas.

The works of art discussed in this book represent a privileged subset of artifacts produced by past and present cultures. They were usually meant to be preserved, and they are currently considered worthy of conservation and display. The determination of which artifacts are exceptional—which are works of art— evolves through the actions, opinions, and selections of artists, patrons, governments, collectors, archaeologists, museums, art historians, and others. Labeling objects as art is usually meant to signal that they transcended or now transcend in some profound way their practical function, often embodying cherished cultural ideas or foundational values. Sometimes it can mean they are considered beautiful, well designed, and made with loving care, but this is not always the case, especially in the twentieth and twenty-first centuries when the complex notion of what is art has little to do with the idea of beauty. Some critics and historians argue that works of art are tendentious embodiments of power and privilege, hardly sublime expressions of beauty or truth. After all, art can be unsettling as well as soothing, challenging as well as reassuring, whether made in the present or surviving from the past.

Increasingly we are realizing that our judgments about what constitutes art—as well as what constitutes beauty—are conditioned by our own education and experience. Whether acquired at home, in classrooms, in museums, at the movies, or on the internet, our responses to art are learned behaviors, influenced by class, gender, race, geography, and economic status as well as education. Even art historians find that their definitions of what constitutes art—and what constitutes artistic quality—evolve with additional research and understanding. Exploring works by twentieth-century painter Mark Rothko and nineteenth-century quiltmakers Martha Knowles and Henrietta Thomas demonstrates how definitions of art and artistic value are subject to change over time.

Rothko's painting, **MAGENTA, BLACK AND GREEN ON ORANGE (FIG. INTRO–1)**, is a well-known example of the sort of abstract painting that was considered the epitome of artistic sophistication by the mid-twentieth-century New York art establishment. It was created by an artist who meant it to be a work of art. It was acquired by the Museum of Modern Art in New York, and its position on the walls of that museum is a sure sign that it was accepted as such by a powerful cultural institution. However, beyond the context of the American artists, dealers, critics, and collectors who made up Rothko's art world, such paintings were often received with skepticism. They were seen by many as incomprehensible—lacking both technical skill and recognizable subject matter, two criteria that were part of the general public's definition of art at the time. Abstract paintings

soon inspired a popular retort: "That's not art; my child could do it!" Interestingly enough, Rothko saw in the childlike character of his own paintings one of the qualities that made them works of art. Children, he said, "put forms, figures, and views into pictorial arrangements, employing out of necessity most of the rules of optical perspective and geometry but without the knowledge that they are employing them." He characterized his own art as childlike, as "an attempt to recapture the freshness and naiveté of childish vision." In part because they are carefully crafted by an established artist who provided these kinds of intellectual justifications for their character and appearance, Rothko's abstract paintings are broadly considered works of art and are treasured possessions of major museums across the globe.

Works of art, however, do not always have to be created by individuals who perceive themselves as artists. Nor are all works produced for an art market surrounded by critics and collectors ready to explain, exhibit, and disperse them, ideally to prestigious museums. Such is the case with this quilt **(FIG. INTRO–2)**, made by Martha Knowles and Henrietta Thomas a century before Rothko's painting. Their work is similarly composed of blocks of color, and like Rothko, they produced their visual effect by arranging these flat chromatic shapes carefully and regularly on a rectangular field. But this quilt was not meant to hang on the wall of an art museum. It is the social product of a friendship, intended as an intimate gift, presented to a loved one for use in her home. An inscription on the quilt itself makes this clear—"From M. A. Knowles to her Sweet Sister Emma, 1843." Thousands of such friendship quilts

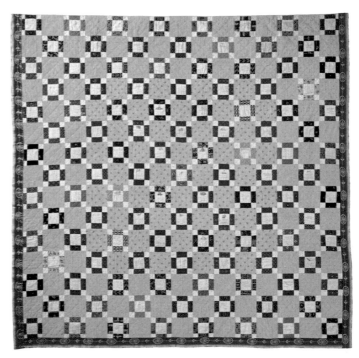

INTRO–2 • Martha Knowles and Henrietta Thomas
MY SWEET SISTER EMMA
1843. Cotton quilt, 8'11" × 9'1" (2.72 × 2.77 m). Courtesy of the International Quilt Study Center, University of Nebraska-Lincoln.

Art and Architecture

This book contains much more than paintings and textiles. Within these pages you will also encounter sculpture, vessels, books, jewelry, tombs, chairs, photographs, architecture, and more. But as with Rothko's *Magenta, Black, and Green on Orange* (SEE FIG. INTRO–1) and Knowles and Thomas's *My Sweet Sister Emma* (SEE FIG. INTRO–2), criteria have been used to determine which works are selected for inclusion in a book titled *Art History*. Architecture presents an interesting case.

Buildings meet functional human needs by enclosing human habitation or activity. Many works of architecture, however, are considered "exceptional" because they transcend functional demands by manifesting distinguished architectural design or because they embody in important ways the values and goals of the culture that built them. Such buildings are usually produced by architects influenced, like painters, by great works and traditions from the past. In some cases they harmonize with, or react to, their natural or urban surroundings. For such reasons, they are discussed in books on the history of art.

Typical of such buildings is the church of Nôtre-Dame-du-Haut in Ronchamp, France, designed and constructed between 1950 and 1955 by Swiss architect Charles-Edouard Jeanneret, better known by his pseudonym, Le Corbusier. This building is the product of a significant historical moment, rich in global cultural meaning. A pilgrimage church on this site had been destroyed during World War II, and the creation here of a new church symbolized the end of a devastating war, embodying hopes for a brighter global future. Le Corbusier's design—drawing on sources that ranged from Algerian mosques to imperial Roman villas, from crab shells to airplane wings—is sculptural as well as architectural. It soars at the crest of a hill toward the sky but at the same time seems solidly anchored in the earth. And its coordination with the curves of the natural landscape complement the creation of an outdoor setting for religious ceremonies (to the right in the figure) to supplement the church interior that Le Corbusier characterized as a "container for intense concentration." In fact, this building is so renowned today as a monument of modern architecture, that the bus-loads of pilgrims who arrive at the site are mainly architects and devotees of architectural history.

Le Corbusier **NÔTRE-DAME-DU-HAUT** 1950–1955. Ronchamp, France.

were made by women during the middle years of the nineteenth century for use on beds, either to provide warmth or as a covering spread. Whereas quilts were sometimes displayed to a broad and enthusiastic audience of producers and admirers at competitions held at state and county fairs, they were not collected by art museums or revered by artists until relatively recently.

In 1971, at the Whitney Museum in New York—an establishment bastion of the art world in which Rothko moved and worked—art historians Jonathan Holstein and Gail van der Hoof mounted an exhibition entitled "Abstract Design in American Quilts," demonstrating the artistic affiliation we have already noted in comparing the way Knowles and Thomas, like Rothko, create abstract patterns with fields of color. Quilts were later accepted—or should the word be "appropriated?"—as works of art and hung on the walls of a New York art museum because of their visual similarities with the avant-garde, abstract works of art created by establishment, New York artists.

Art historian Patricia Mainardi took the case for quilts one significant step further in a pioneering article of 1973 published in *The Feminist Art Journal*. Entitled, "Quilts: The Great American Art," her argument was rooted not only in the aesthetic affinity of quilts with the esteemed work of contemporary abstract painters, but also in a political conviction that the definition of art had to be broadened. What was at stake here was historical veracity. Mainardi began, "Women have always made art. But for most women, the arts highest valued by male society have been closed to them for just that reason. They have put their creativity instead into the needlework arts, which exist in fantastic variety wherever there are women, and which in fact are a universal female art, transcending race, class, and national borders." She argued for the inclusion of quilts within the history of art to give deserved attention to the work of women artists who had been excluded from discussion because they created textiles and because they worked outside the male-dominated professional structures of the art world—because they were women. Quilts now hang as works of art on the walls of museums and appear with regularity in books that survey the history of art.

As these two examples demonstrate, definitions of art are rooted in cultural systems of value that are subject to change. And as they change, the list of works considered by art historians is periodically revised. Determining what to study is a persistent part of the art historian's task.

WHAT IS ART HISTORY?

There are many ways to study or appreciate works of art. Art history represents one specific approach, with its own goals and its own methods of assessment and interpretation. Simply put, art historians seek to understand the meaning of art from the past within its original cultural contexts, both from the point of view of its producers—artists, architects, and patrons—as well as from the point of view of its consumers—those who formed its original audience. Coming to an understanding of the cultural meaning of a work of art requires detailed and patient investigation on many levels, especially with art that was produced long ago and in societies distinct from our own. This is a scholarly rather than an intuitive exercise. In art history, the work of art is seen as an embodiment of the values, goals, and aspirations of its time and place of origin. It is a part of culture.

Art historians use a variety of theoretical perspectives and a host of interpretive strategies to come to an understanding of works of art within their cultural contexts. But as a place to begin, the work of art historians can be divided into four types of investigation:

1. assessment of physical properties,
2. analysis of visual or formal structure,
3. identification of subject matter or conventional symbolism, and
4. integration within cultural context.

ASSESSING PHYSICAL PROPERTIES

Of the methods used by art historians to study works of art, this is the most objective, but it requires close access to the work itself. Physical properties include shape, size, materials, and technique. For instance, many pictures are rectangular (e.g., SEE FIG. INTRO–1), but some are round (see page xxxi, FIG. C). Paintings as large as Rothko's require us to stand back if we want to take in the whole image, whereas some paintings (see page xxx, FIG. A) are so small that we are drawn up close to examine their detail. Rothko's painting and Knowles and Thomas's quilt are both rectangles of similar size, but they are distinguished by the materials from which they are made—oil paint on canvas versus cotton fabric joined by stitching. In art history books, most physical properties can only be understood from descriptions in captions, but when we are in the presence of the work of art itself, size and shape may be the first thing we notice. To fully understand medium and technique, however, it may be necessary to employ methods of scientific analysis or documentary research to elucidate the practices of artists at the time when and place where the work was created.

ANALYZING FORMAL STRUCTURE

Art historians explore the visual character that artists bring to their works—using the materials and the techniques chosen to create them—in a process called **formal analysis**. On the most basic level, it is divided into two parts:

- assessing the individual visual elements or formal vocabulary that constitute pictorial or sculptural communication, and
- discovering the overall arrangement, organization, or structure of an image, a design system that art historians often refer to as **composition**.

THE ELEMENTS OF VISUAL EXPRESSION.   Artists control and vary the visual character of works of art to give their subjects and ideas meaning and expression, vibrancy and persuasion, challenge or delight (see "A Closer Look," pages xxx–xxxi). For example, the motifs, objects, figures, and environments within paintings can be sharply defined by line (SEE FIGS. INTRO–2 and INTRO–3), or they can be suggested by a sketchier definition (SEE FIGS. **INTRO**–1 and INTRO–4). Painters can simulate the appearance of three-dimensional form through **modeling** or shading (SEE FIG. INTRO–3 and page xxxi, FIG. C), that is by describing the way light from a single source will highlight one side of a solid while leaving the other side in shadow. Alternatively, artists can avoid any strong sense of three-dimensionality by emphasizing patterns on a surface rather than forms in space (SEE FIG. INTRO–1 and page xxx, FIG. A). In addition to revealing the solid substance of forms through modeling, dramatic lighting can guide viewers to specific areas of a

A CLOSER LOOK

Visual Elements of Pictorial Expression > Line, Light, Form, and Color.

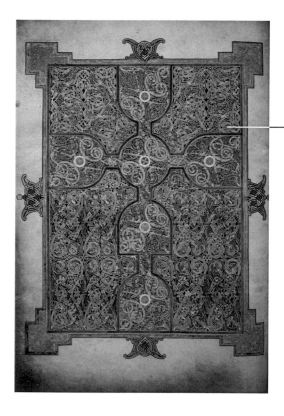

LINE

A. *Carpet Page* from the Lindisfarne Gospels
From Lindisfarne, England.
c. 715–720. Ink and tempera on vellum, 13⅜ × 9⁷⁄₁₆″ (34 × 24 cm). Courtesy of the British Library Board
Cotton MS Nero D.IV fol. 26v

Every element in this complicated painting is sharply outlined by abrupt barriers between light and dark or between one color and another; there are no gradual or shaded transitions. Since the picture was created in part with pen and ink, the linearity is a logical feature of medium and technique. And although line itself is a "flattening" or two-dimensionalizing element in pictures, a complex and consistent system of overlapping gives the linear animal forms a sense of shallow but carefully worked-out three-dimensional relationships to one another.

LIGHT

B. Georges de la Tour *The Education of the Virgin*
c. 1650. Oil on canvas, 33 × 39½″ (83.8 × 100.4 cm).
The Frick Collection, New York.

The source of illumination is a candle depicted within the painting. The young girl's upraised right hand shields its flame, allowing the artist to demonstrate his virtuosity in painting the translucency of human flesh.

Since the candle's flame is partially concealed, its luminous intensity is not allowed to distract from those aspects of the painting most brilliantly illuminated by it—the face of the girl and the book she is reading.

FORM

C. Michelangelo *The Holy Family* (*Doni Tondo*)
c. 1503. Oil and tempera on panel, diameter 3′11¼″ (1.2 m). Courtesy of Antonio Quattrone.

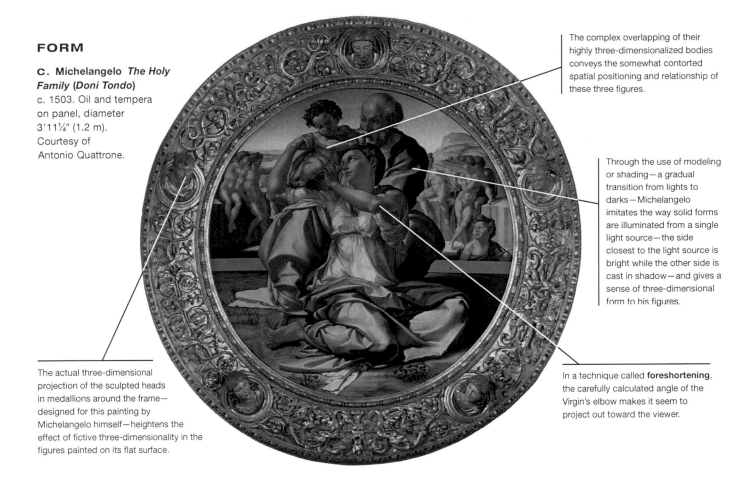

The complex overlapping of their highly three-dimensionalized bodies conveys the somewhat contorted spatial positioning and relationship of these three figures.

Through the use of modeling or shading—a gradual transition from lights to darks—Michelangelo imitates the way solid forms are illuminated from a single light source—the side closest to the light source is bright while the other side is cast in shadow—and gives a sense of three-dimensional form to his figures.

The actual three-dimensional projection of the sculpted heads in medallions around the frame—designed for this painting by Michelangelo himself—heightens the effect of fictive three-dimensionality in the figures painted on its flat surface.

In a technique called **foreshortening**, the carefully calculated angle of the Virgin's elbow makes it seem to project out toward the viewer.

Junayd chose to flood every aspect of his painting with light, as if everything in it were illuminated from all sides at once. As a result, the emphasis here is on jewel-like color. The vibrant tonalities and dazzling detail of the dreamy landscape are not only more important than the simulation of three-dimensional forms distributed within a consistently described space; they actually upstage the human drama taking place against a patterned, tipped-up ground in the lower third of the picture.

COLOR

D. Junayd *Humay and Humayun*, from a manuscript of the *Divan* of Kwaju Kirmani
Made in Baghdad, Iraq. 1396. Color, ink, and gold on paper, 12⅝ × 9⁷⁄₁₆″ (32 × 24 cm). Courtesy of the British Library Board. MS Add. 18113, fol. 31r

picture (see page xxx, FIG. B), or it can be lavished on every aspect of a picture to reveal all its detail and highlight the vibrancy of its color (see page xxxi, FIG. D). Color itself can be muted or intensified, depending on the mood artists want to create or the tastes and expectations of their audiences.

Thus artists communicate with their viewers by making choices in the way they use and emphasize the elements of visual expression, and art historical analysis seeks to reveal how artists' decisions bring meaning to a work of art. For example in two paintings of women with children (SEE FIGS. INTRO–3 and INTRO–4), Raphael and Renoir work with the same visual elements of line, form, light, and color in the creation of their images, but they employ these shared elements to differing expressive ends. Raphael concentrates on line to clearly differentiate each element of his picture as a separate form. Careful modeling describes these outlined forms as substantial solids surrounded by space. This gives his subjects a sense of clarity, stability, and grandeur. Renoir, on the other hand, foregrounds the flickering of light and the play of color as he downplays the sense of three-dimensionality in individual forms. This gives his image a more ephemeral, casual sense. Art historians pay close attention to such variations in the use of visual elements—the building blocks of artistic expression—and use visual analysis to characterize the expressive effect of a particular work, a particular artist, or a general period defined by place and date.

COMPOSITION. When art historians analyze composition, they focus not on the individual elements of visual expression but on the overall arrangement and organizing design or structure of a work of art. In Raphael's **MADONNA OF THE GOLDFINCH (FIG. INTRO–3)**, for example, the group of figures has been arranged in a triangular shape and placed at the center of the picture. Raphael emphasized this central weighting by opening the clouds to reveal a patch of blue in the middle of the sky, and by flanking the figural group with lace-like trees. Since the Madonna is

at the center and since the two boys are divided between the two sides of the triangular shape, roughly—though not precisely—equidistant from the center of the painting, this is a bilaterally symmetrical composition: on either side of an implied vertical line at the center of the picture, there are equivalent forms on left and right, matched and balanced in a mirrored correspondence. Art historians refer to such an implied line—around which the elements of a picture are organized—as an **axis**. Raphael's painting has not only a vertical, but also a horizontal axis, indicated by a line of demarcation between light and dark—as well as between degrees of color saturation—in the terrain of the landscape. The belt of the Madonna's dress is aligned with this horizontal axis, and this correspondence, taken with the coordination of her head with the blue patch in the sky, relates her to the order of the natural world in which she sits, lending a sense of stability, order, and balance to the picture as a whole.

INTRO–3 • Raphael **MADONNA OF THE GOLDFINCH (MADONNA DEL CARDELLINO)**
1506. Oil on panel, 42 × 29½″ (106.7 × 74.9 cm). Courtesy of Galleria degli Uffizi.

The vibrant colors of this important work were revealed in the course of a careful, ten-year restoration, completed only in 2008.

INTRO-4 •
Auguste Renoir
**MME. CHARPENTIER
AND HER CHILDREN**
1878. Oil on canvas,
60½ × 74⅞″ (153.7 ×
190.2 cm). Image copyright
(c) The Metropolitan Museum of Art,
Image Source: Art Resource, NY.

The main axis in Renoir's painting of **MME. CHARPENTIER AND HER CHILDREN (FIG. INTRO–4)** is neither vertical, nor horizontal, but diagonal, running from the upper right to the lower left corner of the painting. All major elements of the composition are aligned along this axis—dog, children, mother, and the table and chair that represent the most complex and detailed aspect of the setting. The upper left and lower right corners of the painting balance each other on either side of the diagonal axis as relatively simple fields of neutral tone, setting off and framing the main subjects between them. The resulting arrangement is not bilaterally symmetrical, but blatantly asymmetrical, with the large figural mass pushed into the left side of the picture. And unlike Raphael's composition, where the spatial relationship of the figures and their environment is mapped by the measured placement of elements that become increasingly smaller in scale and fuzzier in definition as they recede into the background, the relationship of Renoir's figures to their spatial environment is less clearly defined as they recede into the background along the dramatic diagonal axis. Nothing distracts us from the bold informality of this family gathering.

Both Raphael and Renoir arrange their figures carefully and purposefully, but they follow distinctive compositional systems that communicate different notions of the way these figures interact with each other and the world around them. Art historians pay special attention to how pictures are arranged because composition is one of the principal ways artists charge their paintings with expressive meaning.

IDENTIFYING SUBJECT MATTER

Art historians have traditionally sought subject matter and meaning in works of art with a system of analysis that was outlined by Irwin Panofsky (1892–1968), an influential German scholar who was expelled from his academic position by the Nazis in 1933 and spent the rest of his career of research and teaching in the United States. Panofsky proposed that when we seek to understand the subject of a work of art, we derive meaning initially in two ways:

- First we perceive what he called "natural subject matter" by recognizing forms and situations that we know from our own experience.
- Then we use what he called "**iconography**" to identify the conventional meanings associated with forms and figures as bearers of narrative or symbolic content, often specific to a particular time and place.

Some paintings, like Rothko's abstractions, do not contain subjects drawn from the world around us, from stories, or from conventional symbolism, but Panofsky's scheme remains a standard method of investigating meaning in works of art that present narrative subjects, portray specific people or places, or embody cultural values with iconic imagery or allegory.

Iconography ➤ The study and identification of conventional themes, motifs, and symbols to elucidate the subject matter of works of art.

These grapes sit on an imported, Italian silver *tazza*, a luxury object that may commemorate Northern European prosperity and trade. This particular object recurs in several of Peeters's other still lifes.

An image of the artist herself appears on the reflective surface of this pewter tankard, one of the ways that she signed her paintings and promoted her career.

Luscious fruits and flowers celebrate the abundance of nature, but because these fruits of the earth will eventually fade, even rot, they could be moralizing references to the transience of earthly existence.

These coins, including one minted in 1608–1609, help focus the dating of this painting. The highlighting of money within a still life could reference the wealth of the owner—or it could subtly allude to the value the artist has crafted here in paint.

Detailed renderings of insects showcased Peeters's virtuosity as a painter, but they also may have symbolized the vulnerability of the worldly beauty of flowers and fruit to destruction and decay.

This knife—which appears in several of Peeters's still lifes—is of a type that is associated with wedding gifts.

A. Clara Peeters *Still Life with Fruit and Flowers*
c. 1612. Oil on copper, 25⅕ × 35″ (64 × 89 cm). Ashmolean Museum, Oxford.

Quince is an unusual subject in Chinese painting, but the fruit seems to have carried personal significance for Zhu Da. One of his friends was known as the Daoist of Quince Mountain, a site in Hunan province that was also the subject of a work by one of his favorite authors, Tang poet Li Bai.

The artist's signature reads "Bada Shanren painted this," using a familiar pseudonym in a formula and calligraphic style that the artist ceased using in 1695.

This red block is a seal with an inscription drawn from a Confucian text: "teaching is half of learning." This was imprinted on the work by the artist as an aspect of his signature, a symbol of his identity within the picture, just as the reflection and inscribed knife identify Clara Peeters as the painter of her still life.

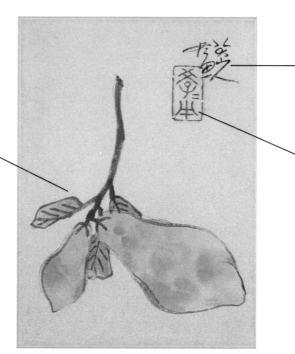

B. Zhu Da (Bada Shanren) *Quince (Mugua)*
1690. Album leaf mounted as a hanging scroll; ink and colors on paper, 7⅞ × 5¾″ (20 × 14.6 cm). Princeton University Art Museum.

NATURAL SUBJECT MATTER.   We recognize some things in works of visual art simply by virtue of living in a world similar to that represented by the artist. For example, in the two paintings by Raphael and Renoir just examined (SEE FIGS. INTRO–3 and INTRO–4), we immediately recognize the principal human figures in both as a woman and two children, boys in the case of Raphael's painting, girls in Renoir's. We can also make a general identification of the animals: a bird in the hand of Raphael's boys, and a pet dog under one of Renoir's girls. And natural subject matter can extend from an identification of figures to an understanding of the expressive significance of their postures and facial features. We might see in the boy who snuggles between the knees of the woman in Raphael's painting, placing his own foot on top of hers, an anxious child seeking the security of physical contact with a trusted caretaker—perhaps his mother—in response to fear of the bird he reaches out to touch. Many of us have seen insecure children take this very pose in response to potentially unsettling encounters.

The closer the work of art is in both time and place to our own situation temporally and geographically, the easier it sometimes is to identify what is represented. But although Renoir painted his picture over 125 years ago in France, the furniture in the background still looks familiar, as does the book in the hand of Raphael's Madonna, painted five centuries before our time. But the object hanging from the belt of the scantily clad boy at the left in this painting will require identification for most of us. Iconographic investigation is necessary to understand the function of this form.

ICONOGRAPHY.   Some subjects are associated with conventional meanings established at a specific time or place; some of the human figures portrayed in works of art have specific identities; and some of the objects or forms have symbolic or allegorical meanings in addition to their natural subject matter. Discovering these conventional meanings of art's subject matter is called iconography. (See "A Closer Look," opposite.)

For example, the woman accompanied in the outdoors by two boys in Raphael's *Madonna of the Goldfinch* (SEE FIG. INTRO–3) would have been immediately recognized by members of its intended sixteenth-century Florentine audience as the Virgin Mary. Viewers would have identified the naked boy standing between her knees as her son Jesus, and the boy holding the bird as Jesus' cousin John the Baptist, sheathed in the animal skin garment that he would wear in the wilderness and equipped with a shallow cup attached to his belt, ready to be used in baptisms. Such attributes of clothing and equipment are often critical in making iconographic identifications. The goldfinch in the Baptist's hand was at this time and place a symbol of Christ's death on the cross, an allegorical implication that makes the Christ Child's retreat into secure contact with his mother—already noted on the level of natural subject matter— understandable in relation to a specific story. The comprehension of conventional meanings in this painting would have been almost automatic among those for whom it was painted, but for us,

separated by time and place, some research is necessary to recover associations that are no longer part of our everyday world.

Although it may not initially seem as unfamiliar, the subject matter of Renoir's 1878 portrait of *Mme. Charpentier and her Children* (SEE FIG. INTRO–4) is in fact even more obscure. Although there are those in twenty-first-century American culture for whom the figures and symbols in Raphael's painting are still recognizable and meaningful, Marguérite-Louise Charpentier died in 1904, and no one living today would be able to identify her based on the likeness Renoir presumably gave to her face in this family portrait commissioned by her husband, wealthy and influential publisher George Charpentier. We need the painting's title to make that identification. And Mme. Charpentier is outfitted here in a gown created by English designer Charles Frederick Worth, the dominant figure in late nineteenth-century Parisian high fashion. Her clothing was a clear attribute of her wealth for those who recognized its source; most of us need to investigate to uncover its meaning. But a greater surprise awaits the student who pursues further research on her children. Although they clearly seem to our eyes to represent two daughters, the child closest to Mme. Charpentier is actually her son Paul, who at age three, following standard Parisian bourgeois practice, has not yet had his first hair cut and still wears clothing comparable to that of his older sister Georgette, perched on the family dog. It is not unusual in art history to encounter situations where our initial conclusions on the level of natural subject matter will need to be revised after some iconographic research.

INTEGRATION WITHIN CULTURAL CONTEXT

Natural subject matter and iconography were only two of three steps proposed by Panofsky for coming to an understanding of the meaning of works of art. The third step he labeled "**iconology**," and its aim is to interpret the work of art as an embodiment of its cultural situation, to place it within broad social, political, religious, and intellectual contexts. Such integration into history requires more than identifying subject matter or conventional symbols; it requires a deep understanding of the beliefs and principles or goals and values that underlie a work of art's cultural situation as well as the position of an artist and patron within it.

In "A Closer Look" (opposite), the subject matter of two **still life** paintings (pictures of inanimate objects and fruits or flowers taken out of their natural contexts) is identified and elucidated, but to truly understand these two works as bearers of cultural meaning, more knowledge of the broader context and specific goals of artists and audiences is required. For example, the fact that Zhu Da (1626–1705) became a painter was rooted more in the political than the artistic history of China at the middle of the seventeenth century. As a member of the imperial family of the Ming dynasty, his life of privilege was disrupted when the Ming were overthrown during the Manchu conquest of China in 1644. Fleeing for his life, he sought refuge in a Buddhist monastery, where he wrote poetry and painted. Almost 40 years later, in the aftermath of a nervous breakdown (that could have been staged to avoid retribution for his family background), Zhu Da abandoned his monastic life and developed a career as a professional painter, adopting a series of descriptive pseudonyms—most notably Bada Shanren ("mountain man of eight greatnesses") by which he is most often known today. His paintings are at times saturated with veiled political commentary; at times they seek to accommodate the expectations of collectors to assure their marketability; and in paintings like the one illustrated here (see page xxxiv, FIG. B), the artist seems to hark back to the contemplative, abstract, and spontaneous paintings associated with great Zen masters such as Muqi (c. 1201–after 1269), whose calligraphic pictures of isolated fruits seem almost like acts of devotion or detached contemplations on natural forms, rather than the works of a professional painter.

Clara Peeters's still life (see page xxxiv, FIG. A), on the other hand, fits into a developing Northern European painting tradition within which she was an established and successful professional, specializing in portrayals of food and flowers, fruit and reflective objects. Still-life paintings in this tradition could be jubilant celebrations of the abundance of the natural world and the wealth of luxury objects available in the prosperous mercantile society of the Netherlands. Or they could be moralizing "*vanitas*" paintings, warning of the ephemeral meaning of those worldly possessions, even of life itself. But this painting has also been interpreted in a more personal way. Because the type of knife that sits in the foreground near the edge of the table was a popular wedding gift, and since it is inscribed with the artist's own name, some have suggested that this still life could have celebrated Peeters's marriage. Or it could simply be a witty way to sign her picture. It certainly could be both personal and participate in the broader cultural meaning of still-life paintings at the same time. Mixtures of private and public meanings have been proposed for Zhu Da's paintings as well. The picture of quince illustrated here (see page xxxiv, FIG. B) has been seen as one in a series of allegorical "self-portraits" that extend across his career as a painter. Art historians frequently reveal multiple meanings when interpreting single works of art. They usually represent complex cultural and personal situations.

A CASE STUDY: ROGIER VAN DER WEYDEN'S PHILADELPHIA CRUCIFIXION

The basic, four-part method of art historical investigation and interpretation just outlined and explored, becomes clearer when its extended use is traced in relation to one specific work of art. A particularly revealing subject for such a case study is a seminal and somewhat perplexing painting now in the Philadelphia Museum of Art—the **CRUCIFIXION WITH THE VIRGIN AND ST. JOHN THE EVANGELIST (FIG. INTRO–5)** by Rogier van der Weyden (c. 1400–1464), a Flemish artist who will be featured in Chapter 18. Each of the four levels of art historical inquiry reveals important information about this painting, information that has been used by

art historians to reconstruct its relationship to its artist, its audience, and its broader cultural setting. The resulting interpretation is rich, but also complex. An investigation this extensive will not be possible for all the works of art in the following chapters, where the text will focus only on one or two facets of more expansive research. Because of the amount and complexity of information involved in a thorough art-historical interpretation, it is sometimes only in a second reading that we can follow the subtleties of its argument, after the first reading has provided a basic familiarity with the work of art, its conventional subjects, and its general context.

PHYSICAL PROPERTIES

Perhaps the most striking aspect of this painting's physical appearance is its division into two separate tall rectangular panels, joined by a frame to form a coherent, almost square composition. These are oak panels, prepared with chalk to form a smooth surface on which to paint with mineral pigments suspended in oil. A technical investigation of the painting in 1981 used infra-red reflectography to reveal a very sketchy underdrawing beneath the surface of the paint, proving to the investigators that this painting is almost entirely the work of Rogier van der Weyden himself. Famous and prosperous artists of this time and place employed many assistants to work in large production workshops, and they would render detailed underdrawings to assure that assistants replicated the style of the master. But in cases where the masters themselves intended to execute the work, only summary compositional outlines were needed. This modern technical investigation of Rogier's painting also used **dendrochronology** (the dating of wood based on the patterns of the growth rings) to date the oak panels and consequently the painting itself, now securely situated near the end of the artist's career, c. 1460.

The most recent restoration of the painting—during the early 1990s by Mark Tucker, Senior Conservator at the Philadelphia Museum of Art—returned it, as close as possible, to current views of its original fifteenth-century appearance (see "Recovering the Past," page xxxviii). This project included extensive technical analysis of almost every aspect of the picture, during which a critical clue emerged, one that may lead to a sharper understanding of its original use. X-rays revealed dowel holes and plugs running in a horizontal line about one-fourth of the way up from the bottom across the entire expanse of the two-panel painting. Tucker's convincing research suggests that the dowels would have attached these two panels to the backs of wooden boxes that contained sculptures in a complex work of art that hung over the altar in a fifteenth-century church.

FORMAL STRUCTURE

The visual organization of this two-part painting emphasizes both connection and separation. It is at the same time one painting and two. Continuing across both panels is the strip of midnight blue sky and the stone wall that constricts space within the picture to a shallow corridor, pushing the figures into the foreground and close

INTRO-5 • Rogier van der Weyden **CRUCIFIXION WITH THE VIRGIN AND ST. JOHN THE EVANGELIST**
c. 1460. Oil on oak panels, 71 × 73″ (1.8 × 1.85 m). The Philadelphia Museum of Art/Art Resource, NY.

to the viewer. The platform of mossy ground under the two-figure group in the left panel continues its sloping descent into the right panel, as does the hem of the Virgin's ice-blue garment. We look into this scene as if through a window with a mullion down the middle and assume that the world on the left continues behind this central strip of frame into the right side.

On the other hand, strong visual forces isolate the figures within their respective panels, setting up a system of "compare and contrast" that seems to be at the heart of the painting's design. The striking red cloths that hang over the wall are centered directly behind the figures on each side, forming internal frames that

highlight them as separate groups and focus our attention back and forth between them rather than on the pictorial elements that unite their environments. As we begin to compare the two sides, it becomes increasingly clear that the relationship between figures and environment is quite distinct on each side of the divide.

The dead figure of Christ on the cross, elevated to the very top of the picture, is strictly centered within his panel, as well as against the cloth that hangs directly behind him. The grid of masonry blocks and creases in the cloth emphasizes his rectilinear integration into a system of balanced, rigid regularity. His head is aligned with the cap of the wall, his flesh largely contained within

Ever since Rogier van der Weyden's strikingly asymmetrical, two-panel rendering of the *Crucifixion* (SEE FIG. INTRO–5) was purchased by Philadelphia lawyer John G. Johnson in 1906 for his spectacular collection of European paintings, it has been recognized not only as one of the greatest works by this master of fifteenth-century Flemish painting, but as one of the most important European paintings in North America. Soon after the Johnson Collection became part of the Philadelphia Museum of Art in 1933, however, this painting's visual character was significantly transformed. In 1941 the museum employed freelance restorer David Rosen to work on the painting. Deciding that Rogier's work was seriously marred by later overpainting and disfigured by the discoloration of old varnish, he subjected the painting to a thorough cleaning. He also removed the strip of dark blue paint forming the sky above the wall at the top—identifying it as an 18th-century restoration—and replaced it with gold leaf to conform with remnants of gold in this area that he assessed as surviving fragments of the original background. Rosen's restoration of Rogier's painting was uncritically accepted for almost half a century, and the gold background became a major factor in the interpretations of art historians as distinguished as Irwin Panofsky and Meyer Schapiro.

In 1990, in preparation for a new installation of the work, Rogier's painting received a thorough technical analysis by Mark Tucker, the museum's Senior Conservator. There were two startling discoveries:

- The dark blue strip that had run across the top of the picture before Rosen's intervention was actually original to the painting. Remnants of paint left behind in 1941 proved to be the same azurite blue that also appears in the clothing of the Virgin, and in no instance did the traces of gold discovered in 1941 run under aspects of the original paint surface. Rosen had removed Rogier's original midnight blue sky.

- What Rosen had interpreted as disfiguring varnish streaking the wall and darkening the brilliant cloths of honor hanging over it were actually Rogier's careful painting of lichens and water stains on the stone and his overpainting on the fabric that had originally transformed a vermillion undercoat into deep crimson cloth.

In meticulous work during 1992–1993, Tucker cautiously restored the painting based on the evidence he had uncovered. Neither the lost lichens and water stains nor the toning crimson overpainting of the hangings were replaced, but a coat of blue-black paint was laid over Rosen's gold leaf at the top of the panels, taking care to apply the new layer in such a way that should a later generation decide to return to the gold leaf sky, the midnight tonalities could be easily removed. That seems an unlikely prospect. The painting as exhibited today comes as close as possible to the original appearance of Rogier's *Crucifixion*. At least we think so.

---

the area defined by the cloth. His elbows mark the juncture of the wall with the edge of the hanging, and his feet extend just to the end of the cloth, where his toes substitute for the border of fringe they overlap. The environment is almost as balanced. The strip of dark sky at the top is equivalent in size to the strip of mossy earth at the bottom of the picture, and both are visually bisected by centered horizontals—the cross bar at the top and the alignment of bone and skull at the bottom. A few disruptions to this stable, rectilinear, symmetrical order draw the viewers' attention to the panel at the left: the downward fall of the head of Christ, the visual weight of the skull, the downturn of the fluttering loin cloth, and the tip of the Virgin's gown that transgresses over the barrier to move in from the other side.

John and Mary merge on the left into a single figural mass that could be inscribed into a half-circle. Although set against a rectilinear grid background comparable to that behind Jesus, they contrast with, rather than conform to, the regular sense of order. Their curving outlines offer unsettling unsteadiness, as if they are toppling to the ground, jutting into the other side of the frame. This instability is reinforced by their postures. The projection of Mary's knee in relation to the angle of her torso reveals that she is collapsing into a curve, and the crumpled mass of drapery circling underneath her only underlines her lack of support. John reaches out to catch her, but he has not yet made contact with her body. He strikes a stance of strident instability without even touching the ground, and he looks blankly out into space with an unfocused expression, distracted from, rather than concentrating on, the task at hand. Perhaps he will come to his senses and grab her. But will he be able to catch her in time, and even then support her given his unstable posture? The moment is tense; the outcome is unclear. But we are moving into the realm of natural subject matter. The poignancy of this concentrated portrayal seems to demand it.

ICONOGRAPHY

The subject of this painting is among the most familiar themes in the history of European art. The dead Jesus has been crucified on the cross, and two of his closest associates—his mother and John, one of his disciples—mourn his loss. Although easily recognizable, the austere and asymmetrical presentation is unexpected. More usual is an earlier painting of this subject by the same artist, **CRUCIFIXION TRIPTYCH WITH DONORS AND SAINTS (FIG. INTRO–6)**, where he situates the crucified Christ at the center of a symmetrical arrangement, the undisputed axial focus of the composition. The scene unfolds here within an expansive landscape, populated with a wider cast of participants, each of whom takes a place with symmetrical decorum on either side of the cross. Because most crucifixions follow some variation on this pattern, Rogier's two-panel portrayal (SEE FIG. INTRO-5) in which the cross is asymmetrically displaced to one side, with a spare cast of attendants relegated to a separately framed space, severely restricted by a stark stone wall, requires some explanation. As does the mysterious dark world beyond the wall, and the artificial backdrop of the textile hangings.

INTRO-6 • Rogier van der Weyden CRUCIFIXION TRIPTYCH WITH DONORS AND SAINTS
c. 1440. Oil on wooden panels, 39¾ × 55″ (101 × 140 cm). Kunsthistorisches Museum, Vienna.

This scene is not only austere and subdued; it is sharply focused, and the focus relates it to the specific moment in the story that Rogier decided to represent. The Christian Bible contains four accounts of Jesus' crucifixion, one in each of the four Gospels. Rogier took two verses in John's account as his painting's text (John 19:26–27), cited here in the Douay-Rheims literal English translation of the Latin Vulgate Bible used by Western European Christians during the fifteenth century:

> When Jesus therefore had seen his mother and the disciple standing whom he loved, he saith to his mother: Woman, behold thy son. After that, he saith to the disciple: Behold thy mother. And from that hour, the disciple took her to his own.

Even the textual source uses conventions that need explanation, specifically the way the disciple John is consistently referred to in this Gospel as "the disciple whom Jesus loved." Rogier's painting, therefore, seems to focus on Jesus' call for a newly expanded relationship between his mother and a beloved follower. More specifically, he has projected us slightly forward in time to the moment when John needs to respond to that call—Jesus has died; John is now in charge.

There are, however, other conventional iconographic associations with the crucifixion that Rogier has folded into this spare portrayal. Fifteenth-century viewers would have understood the skull and femur that lie on the mound at the base of the cross as

the bones of Adam—the first man in the Hebrew Bible account of creation—on whose grave Jesus' crucifixion was believed to have taken place. This juxtaposition embodied the Christian belief that Christ's sacrifice on the cross redeemed believers from the death that Adam's original sin had brought to human existence.

Mary's swoon and presumed loss of consciousness would have evoked another theological idea, the *co-passio*, in which Mary's anguish while witnessing Jesus' suffering and death was seen as a parallel passion of mother with son, both critical for human salvation. Their connection in this painting is underlined visually by the similar bending of their knees, inclination of their heads, and closing of their eyes. They even seem to resemble each other in facial likeness, especially when compared to John.

CULTURAL CONTEXT

In 1981 art historian Penny Howell Jolly published an interpretation of Rogier's Philadelphia *Crucifixion* as a product of a broad personal and cultural context. In addition to building on the work of earlier art historians, she pursued two productive lines of investigation to explain the rationale for this unusually austere presentation:

- the prospect that Rogier was influenced by the work of another artist, and
- the possibility that the painting was produced for an institutional context that called for a special mode of visual presentation and a particular iconographic focus.

INTRO-7 • VIEW OF A MONK'S CELL IN THE MONASTERY OF SAN MARCO, FLORENCE
Courtesy of Antonio Quattrone.

FRA ANGELICO AT SAN MARCO. We know very little about the life of Rogier van der Weyden, but we do know that in 1450, when he was already established as one of the principal painters in northern Europe, he made a pilgrimage to Rome. Either on his way to Rome, or during his return journey home, he stopped off in Florence and saw the altarpiece, and presumably also the frescos, that Fra Angelico (c. 1400–1455) and his workshop had painted during the 1440s at the monastery of San Marco. The evidence of Rogier's contact with Fra Angelico's work is found in a work Rogier painted after he returned home, based on a panel of the San Marco altarpiece. For the Philadelphia *Crucifixion*, however, it was Fra Angelico's devotional frescos on the walls of the monks' individual rooms (or cells) that seem to have had the greatest impact (FIG. INTRO–7). Jolly compared the Philadelphia *Crucifixion* with a scene of

the Man of Sorrows at San Marco to demonstrate the connection (FIG. INTRO–8). Fra Angelico presented the sacred figures with a quiet austerity that recalls Rogier's unusual composition. More specific parallels are the use of an expansive stone wall to restrict narrative space to a shallow foreground corridor, the description of the world beyond that wall as a dark sky that contrasts with the brilliantly illuminated foreground, and the use of a draped cloth of honor to draw attention to a narrative vignette from the life of Jesus, to separate it out as an object of devotion.

THE CARTHUSIANS. Having established a possible connection between Rogier's unusual late painting of the crucifixion and frescos by Fra Angelico that he likely saw during his pilgrimage to Rome in 1450, Jolly reconstructed a specific context of patronage and meaning within Rogier's own world in Flanders that could explain why the paintings of Fra Angelico would have had such an impact on him at this particular moment in his career.

During the years around 1450, Rogier developed a personal and profession relationship with the monastic order of the Carthusians, and especially with the Belgian Charterhouse (or Carthusian monastery) of Hérrines, where his only son was invested as a monk in 1450. Rogier gave money to Hérrines, and

INTRO-8 • Fra Angelico MAN OF SORROWS FRESCO IN CELL 7
Courtesy of Antonio Quattrone.

a poignant moment in the life of St. John (**FIG INTRO-9**) could have been especially meaningful to the artist himself at the time this work was painted?

A CONTINUING PROJECT. The final word has not been spoken in the interpretation of this painting. Mark Tucker's recent work on the physical evidence revealed by x-ray analysis points toward seeing these two panels as part of a large sculptured altarpiece. Even if this did preclude the prospect that it is the panel painting Rogier donated to the chapel of St. Catherine at Hérinnes, it does not negate the relationship Jolly drew with Fra Angelico, nor the Carthusian context she outlined for the work's original situation. It simply reminds us that our historical understanding of works such as this will evolve when new evidence about them emerges.

As the history of art unfolds in the ensuing chapters of this book, it will be important to keep two things in mind as you read the characterizations of individual works of art and the larger story of their integration into the broader cultural contexts of those who made them and those for whom they were initially made. Art-historical interpretations are built on extended research comparable to that we have just summarily surveyed for Rogier van der Weyden's Philadelphia *Crucifixion*. But the work of interpretation is never complete. Art history is a continuing project, a work perpetually in progress.

texts document his donation of a painting to its chapel of Saint Catherine. Jolly suggested that the Philadelphia *Crucifixion* could be that painting. Its subdued colors and narrative austerity are consistent with Carthusian aesthetic attitudes, and the walled setting of the scene recalls the enclosed gardens that were attached to the individual dormitory rooms of Carthusian monks. The reference in this painting to the *co-passio* of the Virgin provides supporting evidence since this theological idea was central to Carthusian thought and devotion. The *co-passio* was even reflected in the monks' own initiation rites, during which they reenacted and sought identification with both Christ's sacrifice on the cross and the Virgin's parallel suffering.

In Jolly's interpretation, the religious framework of a Carthusian setting for the painting emerges as a personal framework for the artist himself, since this *Crucifixion* seems to be associated with important moments in his own life—his religious pilgrimage to Rome in 1450 and the initiation of his only son as a Carthusian monk at about the same time. Is it possible that the sense of loss and separation that Rogier evoked in his portrayal of

THINK ABOUT IT

I.1   How would you define a work of art?

I.2   What are the four separate steps proposed here for characterizing the methods used by art historians to interpret works of art?

I.3   Choose a painting illustrated in this chapter and analyze its composition.

I.4   Characterize the difference between natural subject matter and iconography, focusing your discussion on one work discussed in this chapter.

I.5   What aspect of the case study of Rogier van der Weyden's Philadelphia *Crucifixion* was especially interesting to you? Explain why. How did it broaden your understanding of what you will learn in this course?

PRACTICE MORE: Compose answers to these questions, get flashcards for images and terms, and review chapter material with quizzes **www.myartslab.com**

ART OF SOUTH AND SOUTHEAST ASIA BEFORE 1200

According to legend, the ruler Ashoka (r. 273–232 BCE) was stunned by grief and remorse as he looked across the battlefield. As was the custom of his dynasty, he had gone to war, expanding his empire until he had conquered many of the kingdoms that had comprised the Indian subcontinent. Now, about 265 BCE, after the final battle in his conquest of the northern kingdoms, he was suddenly—unexpectedly—shocked by the horror of the suffering he had caused. In the traditional account, it is said that only one form on the battlefield moved: The stooped figure of a Buddhist monk slowly making his way through the carnage. Watching this spectral figure, Ashoka abruptly turned the moment of triumph into one of renunciation. Decrying violence and warfare, he vowed to become a *chakravartin* ("world-conquering ruler"), not through the force of arms but through spreading the teachings of the Buddha and establishing Buddhism as the major religion of his realm.

Although there is no proof that Ashoka himself converted to Buddhism, he erected and dedicated monuments to the Buddha throughout his empire—shrines, monasteries, and the columns commonly called **Ashokan pillars (FIG. 9–1)**. With missionary ardor, he dispatched delegates throughout the Indian subcontinent and to countries as distant as Syria, Egypt, and Greece. In his impassioned propagation of Buddhism, perhaps as a means of securing his enormous empire, Ashoka stimulated an intensely rich period of art.

Despite the emissaries he sent and his widespread placement of inscriptions on the face of large rocks, his pillars are few in number and quite concentrated in location. Only eight can be attributed to Ashoka's time by the inscriptions they bear, although several other pillars are commonly assigned to this period. Most were placed at the site of Buddhist monasteries along a route leading from Punjab in the northwest to Ashoka's capital, Pataliputra, in the northeast. One pillar some distance from this route, at Sanchi, suggests that others, perhaps not yet discovered, may have been placed along a more southerly path.

Not only are the pillars the first sculptural remains in India after a hiatus of some 1,600 years, but their inscriptions are the first preserved Indian writing that we can read and interpret. The script, known as Brahmi, was deciphered in 1837 by James Prinsep, a brilliant amateur scholar who served the East India Company as assay master of the Calcutta mint. He discovered that the inscriptions were written in Prakrit, a language closely related to classical Sanskrit, and that they set down laws of righteous behavior for the monks and nuns resident in the monasteries where the pillars were erected, as well as for passing travelers. Like so many aspects of Indian art, these pillars raise intriguing questions that have yet to be answered, most notably: How could such pillars be made in the absence of any known precedent?

LEARN ABOUT IT

9.1 Recognize the characteristic differences between a Hindu temple and a Buddhist stupa.

9.2 Appreciate the diffusion of religion in Southeast Asia.

9.3 Understand the correlation between religious worldviews and architectural form.

9.4 Assess the variety of ways in which storytelling can be accomplished in pictorial art.

9.5 Identify the distinguishing features of a Buddha image.

HEAR MORE: Listen to an audio file of your chapter **www.myartslab.com**

THE INDIAN SUBCONTINENT

The South Asian subcontinent, or Indian subcontinent, as it is commonly called, is a peninsular region that includes the present-day countries of India, Afghanistan, Pakistan, Nepal, Bhutan, Bangladesh, and Sri Lanka (MAP 9–1). From the beginning, these areas have been home to societies whose cultures are closely linked and which have maintained remarkable continuity over time. (South Asia is distinct from Southeast Asia, which includes Brunei, Myanmar, Cambodia, East Timor, Indonesia, Laos, Malaysia, the Philippines, Singapore, Thailand, and Vietnam.) Although the modern Republic of India is about a third the size of the United States, South Asia as a whole is about two-thirds its size. A low mountain range, the Vindhya Hills, acts as a natural division that separates north India from south India. On the northern border rises the protective barrier of the Himalayas, the world's highest mountains. To the northwest are other mountains through whose passes came invasions and immigrations that profoundly affected the civilization of the subcontinent. Over these passes, too, wound the major trade routes that linked the Indian subcontinent by land to the rest of Asia and to Europe. Surrounded on its remaining sides by oceans since ancient times, the subcontinent has also been connected to the world by maritime trade, and during much of the period under discussion here it formed part of a coastal trading network that extended from eastern Africa to China.

Differences in language, climate, and terrain within India have fostered distinct regional and cultural characteristics and artistic traditions. However, despite such diversity, several overarching traits tend to unite Indian art. Most evident is a distinctive sense of beauty, with voluptuous forms and a profusion of ornament, texture, and color. Visual abundance is considered auspicious, and it reflects a belief in the generosity and favor of the gods. Another characteristic is the pervasive symbolism that enriches all Indian arts with intellectual and emotional layers. Third, and perhaps most important, is an emphasis on capturing the vibrant quality of a world seen as infused with the dynamics of the divine. Gods and humans, ideas and abstractions, are given tactile, sensuous forms, radiant with inner spirit.

INDUS CIVILIZATION

The earliest civilization of South Asia was nurtured in the lower reaches of the Indus River, in present-day Pakistan and in north-western India. Known as the Indus or Harappan civilization (after Harappa, the first-discovered site), it flourished from approximately 2600 to 1900 BCE, or during roughly the same time as the Old Kingdom period of Egypt, the Minoan civilization of the Aegean, and the dynasties of Ur and Babylon in Mesopotamia. Indeed, it is considered, along with Egypt and Mesopotamia, to be one of the world's earliest urban river-valley civilizations.

It was the chance discovery in the late nineteenth century of some small seals, such as those in FIGURE 9–2, that provided the

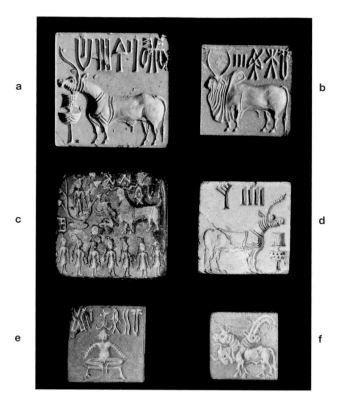

9-2 • SEAL IMPRESSIONS
a., d. horned animal; b. buffalo; c. sacrificial rite to a goddess (?); e. yogi; f. three-headed animal. Indus Valley civilization, c. 2500–1500 BCE. Steatite, each seal approx. 1¼ × 1¼" (3.2 × 3.2 cm).

The more than 2,000 small seals and impressions that have been found offer an intriguing window on the Indus Valley civilization. Usually carved from steatite stone, the seals were coated with alkali and then fired to produce a lustrous, white surface. A perforated knob on the back of each may have been for suspending them. The most popular subjects are animals, most commonly a one-horned bovine standing before an altarlike object (a, d). Animals on Indus Valley seals are often portrayed with remarkable naturalism, their taut, well-modeled surfaces implying their underlying skeletons. The function of the seals remains enigmatic, and the script that is so prominent in the impressions has yet to be deciphered.

first clue that an ancient civilization had existed in this region. The seals appeared to be related to, but not the same as, seals known from ancient Mesopotamia (SEE FIG. 2–5). Excavations begun in the 1920s and continuing into the present subsequently uncovered a number of major urban areas at points along the lower Indus River, including Harappa, Mohenjo-Daro, and Chanhu-Daro.

MOHENJO-DARO. The ancient cities of the Indus Valley resemble each other in design and construction, suggesting a coherent culture. At Mohenjo-Daro, the best preserved of the sites, archaeologists discovered an elevated citadel area about 50 feet high, presumably containing important government structures, surrounded by a wall. Among the buildings is a remarkable water tank, a large watertight pool that may have been a public bath but could also have had a ritual use (FIG. 9–3). Stretching out below the elevated area was the city, arranged in a gridlike plan with wide avenues and narrow side streets. Its houses, often two stories high, were generally built

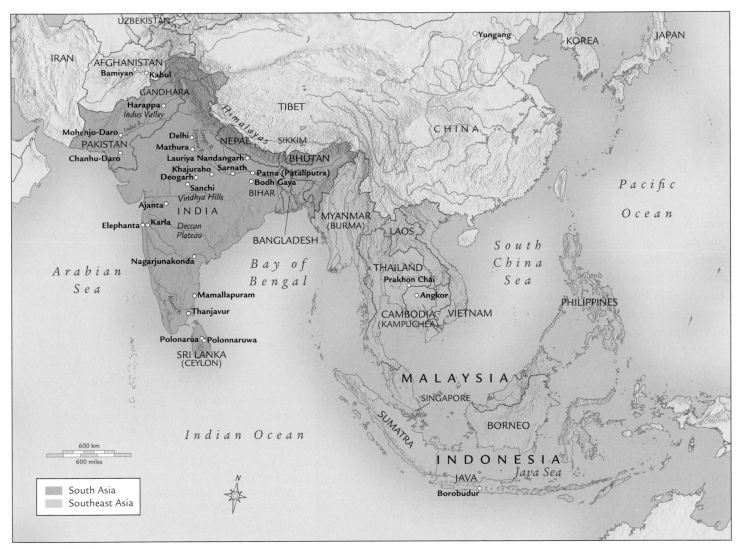

MAP 9-1 • SOUTH AND SOUTHEAST ASIA

The borders of India are created by natural features, with the Himalayas to the north and the Indian Ocean on the remaining borders. Nearly all the rivers in the region flow east–west and are an important conduit for trade and new ideas.

9-3 • LARGE WATER TANK, MOHENJO-DARO
Indus Valley civilization (Harappan), c. 2600–1900 BCE.

Possibly a public or ritual bathing area.

around a central courtyard. Like other Indus Valley cities, Mohenjo-Daro was constructed of fired brick, in contrast to the less durable sun-dried brick used in other cultures of the time. The city included a network of covered drainage systems that channeled away waste and rainwater. Clearly the technical and engineering skills of this civilization were highly advanced. At its peak, about 2500 to 2000 BCE, Mohenjo-Daro was approximately 6–7 square miles in size and had a population of about 20,000–50,000.

INDUS VALLEY SEALS.   Although our knowledge of the Indus civilization is limited by the fact that we cannot read its writing, motifs on seals as well as the few artworks that have been discovered strongly suggest continuities with later South Asian cultures. The seal in FIGURE 9–2e, for example, depicts a man in the meditative posture associated in Indian culture with a yogi, one who seeks mental and physical purification and self-control, usually for spiritual purposes. In FIGURE 9–2c, the persons with elaborate headgear in a row or procession observe a figure standing in a tree—possibly a goddess—and a kneeling worshiper. This scene may offer some insight into the religious or ritual customs of Indus people, whose deities may have been ancient prototypes of later Indian gods and goddesses.

Numerous terra-cotta figurines and a few stone and bronze statuettes have been found at Indus sites. They reveal a confident maturity of artistic conception and technique. The terra cottas resemble Mesopotamian art in their motifs and rather abstract rendering. On the other hand, the stone figures foreshadow the later Indian artistic tradition in their sensuous naturalism.

9-4 • TORSO OF A "PRIEST-KING"
From Mohenjo-Daro. Indus Valley civilization, c. 2600–1900 BCE. Steatite, height 6⅞″ (17.5 cm). National Museum of Pakistan, Karachi.

"PRIEST-KING" FROM MOHENJO-DARO.   The identity of the male torso in FIGURE 9–4, sometimes called the "priest-king," is uncertain, suggesting a structure of society—where priests functioned as kings—for which we have no evidence at all. Several features of this figure, including a low forehead, a broad nose, thick lips, and long slit eyes, are seen on other works from Mohenjo-Daro. The man's garment is patterned with a **trefoil** (three-lobed) motif. The depressions of the trefoil pattern were originally filled with red paint, and the eyes were inlaid with colored shell or stone. A narrow band with a circular ornament encircles the upper arm and the head. It falls in back into two long strands and may be an indication of rank. Certainly, with its formal pose and simplified, geometric form, the statue conveys a commanding human presence.

NUDE TORSO FROM HARAPPA.   Although its date is disputed by some, a nude male torso found at Harappa is an example of a contrasting naturalistic style (FIG. 9–5) of ancient Indus origins. Less than 4 inches tall, it is one of the most extraordinary portrayals of the human form to survive from any early civilization. In contrast to the more athletic male ideal developed much later in ancient Greece, this sculpture emphasizes the soft texture of the human body and the subtle nuances of muscular form. The abdomen is relaxed in the manner of a yogi able to control his breath. With these characteristics the Harappa torso forecasts the essential aesthetic attributes of later Indian sculpture.

The reasons for the demise of this flourishing civilization are not yet understood. All we know is

9-5 • TORSO
From Harappa. Indus Valley civilization, c. 2600–1900 BCE. Red sandstone, height 3¾" (9.5 cm). National Museum, New Delhi.

that between 2000 and 1750—possibly because of climate change, a series of natural disasters, and invasions—the cities of the Indus civilization declined, and predominantly rural societies evolved.

THE VEDIC PERIOD

About 2000 BCE nomadic shepherds, the Aryans, entered India from central Asia and the Russian steppes. Gradually they supplanted the indigenous populations and introduced the horse and chariot, the Sanskrit language, a hierarchical social order, and religious practices that centered on the propitiation of gods through fire sacrifice. Their sacred writings known as the Vedas, gave the period its name. The earliest Veda consists of hymns to various Aryan gods including the divine king Indra. The importance of the fire sacrifice, overseen by a powerful priesthood—the Brahmins—and religiously sanctioned social classes, persisted through the Vedic period. At some point, the class structure became hereditary and immutable, with lasting consequences for Indian society.

During the latter part of this period, from about 800 BCE, the Upanishads were composed. These metaphysical texts examine the meanings of the earlier, more cryptic Vedic hymns. They focus on the relationship between the individual soul, or *atman*, and the universal soul, or Brahman, as well as on other concepts central to subsequent Indian philosophy. One is the assertion that the material world is illusory and that only Brahman is real and eternal. Another holds that our existence is cyclical and that beings are caught in *samsara*, a relentless cycle of birth, life, death, and rebirth. Believers aspire to attain liberation from *samsara* and to unite the individual *atman* with the eternal, universal Brahman.

The latter portion of the Vedic period also saw the flowering of India's epic literature, written in the melodious and complex Sanskrit language. By around 400 BCE, the 18-volume *Mahabharata*, the longest epic in world literature, and the *Ramayana*, the most popular and enduring religious epic in India and Southeast Asia, were taking shape. These texts, the cornerstones of Indian literature, relate histories of gods and humans that bring the philosophical ideas of the Vedas to a more accessible and popular level.

In this stimulating religious, philosophical, and literary climate numerous religious communities arose. The most influential teachers of these times were Shakyamuni Buddha and Mahavira. The Buddha, or "enlightened one," lived and taught in India around 500 BCE; his teachings form the basis of the Buddhist religion (see "Buddhism," page 297). Mahavira (c. 599–527 BCE), regarded as the last of 24 highly purified superbeings called pathfinders (*tirthankaras*), was the founder of the Jain religion. Both Shakyamuni Buddha and Mahavira espoused some basic Upanishadic tenets, such as the cyclical nature of existence and the need for liberation from the material world. However, they rejected the authority of the Vedas, and with it the legitimacy of the fire sacrifice and the hereditary class structure of Vedic society, with its powerful, exclusive priesthood. In contrast, Buddhism and Jainism were open to all, regardless of social position.

Buddhism became a vigorous force in South Asia and provided the impetus for much of the major surviving art created between the third century BCE and the fifth century CE. The Vedic tradition, meanwhile, continued to evolve, emerging later as Hinduism, a loose term that encompasses the many religious forms that resulted from the mingling of Vedic culture with indigenous beliefs (see "Hinduism," page 298).

THE MAURYA PERIOD

After about 700 BCE, cities again began to reappear on the subcontinent, especially in the north, where numerous kingdoms arose. For most of its subsequent history, India was a shifting mosaic of regional kingdoms. From time to time, however, a particularly powerful dynasty formed an empire. The first of these was the Maurya dynasty (c. 322–185 BCE), which extended its rule over all but the southernmost portion of the subcontinent.

FEMALE FIGURE FROM DIDARGANJ. The art of the Maurya period reflects an age of heroes. At this time emerged the ideal of upholding *dharma*, the divinely ordained moral law believed to keep the universe from falling into chaos. This heroic ideal seems fully embodied in a life-size statue found at Didarganj, near the Maurya capital of Pataliputra **(FIG. 9–6)**. The statue, dated by most scholars to the Maurya period, probably represents a **yakshi**, a spirit associated with the productive forces of nature. With its large breasts and pelvis, the figure embodies the association of female beauty with procreative abundance, bounty, and auspiciousness—qualities that in turn reflect the generosity of the gods and the workings of *dharma* in the world.

Sculpted from fine-grained sandstone, the statue conveys the *yakshi*'s authority through the frontal rigor of her pose, the massive volumes of her form, and the strong, linear patterning of her

9-6 • FEMALE FIGURE HOLDING A FLY-WHISK
From Didarganj, Patna, Bihar, India. Probably Maurya period, c. 250 BCE. Polished sandstone, height 5′4¼″ (1.63 m). Patna Museum, Patna.

Commonly identified as a *yakshi*, this sculpture has become one of the most famous works of Indian art. Holding a fly-whisk in her raised right hand, the figure wears only a long shawl and a skirtlike cloth. The cloth rests low on her hips, held in place by a girdle. Subtly sculpted parallel creases indicate that it is gathered closely about her legs. The ends, drawn back up over the girdle, cascade down to her feet in a broad, central loop of flowing folds ending in a zigzag of hems. Draped low over her back, the shawl passes through the crook of her arm and then flows to the ground. (The missing left side of the shawl probably mirrored this motion.) The figure's jewelry is prominent. A double strand of pearls hangs between her breasts, its shape echoing and emphasizing the voluptuous curves of her body. Another strand of pearls encircles her neck. She wears a simple tiara, plug earrings, and rows of bangles. The nubbled tubes about her ankles probably represent anklets made of beaten gold. Her hair is bound behind in a large bun, and a small bun sits on her forehead. This hairstyle appears again in Indian sculpture of the later Kushan period (c. second century CE).

9-7 • LION CAPITAL
From Ashokan pillar at Sarnath, Uttar Pradesh, India. Maurya period, c. 250 BCE. Polished sandstone, height 7′ (2.13 m). Archaeological Museum, Sarnath.

Buddhism

The Buddhist religion developed from the teachings of Shakyamuni Buddha, who lived from about 563 to 483 BCE in the present-day regions of Nepal and northern India. At his birth, it is believed, seers foretold that the infant prince, named Siddhartha Gautama, would become either a *chakravartin* ("world-conquering ruler") or a *buddha* ("fully enlightened being"). Hoping for a ruler like himself, Siddhartha's father tried to surround his son with pleasure and shield him from pain. Yet the prince was eventually exposed to the sufferings of old age, sickness, and death—the inevitable fate of all mortal beings. Deeply troubled by the human condition, Siddhartha at age 29 left the palace, his family, and his inheritance to live as an ascetic in the wilderness. After six years of meditation, he attained complete enlightenment at a site in India now called Bodh Gaya.

Following his enlightenment, the Buddha ("Enlightened One") gave his first teaching in the Deer Park at Sarnath. Here he expounded the Four Noble Truths that are the foundation of Buddhism: (1) life is suffering; (2) this suffering has a cause, which is ignorance; (3) this ignorance can be overcome and extinguished; (4) the way to overcome this ignorance is by following the eightfold path of right view, right resolve, right speech, right action, right livelihood, right effort, right mindfulness, and right concentration. After the Buddha's death at age 80, his many disciples developed his teachings and established the world's oldest monastic institutions.

A buddha is not a god but rather one who sees the ultimate nature of the world and is therefore no longer subject to *samsara*, the cycle of birth, death, and rebirth that otherwise holds us in its grip, whether we are born into the world of the gods, humans, animals, demons, tortured spirits, or hellish beings.

The early form of Buddhism, known as Theravada or Hinayana, stresses self-cultivation for the purpose of attaining *nirvana*, which is the extinction of *samsara* for oneself. Theravada Buddhism has continued mainly in Sri Lanka and Southeast Asia. Within 500 years of the Buddha's death, another form of Buddhism, known as Mahayana, became popular mainly in northern India; it eventually flourished in China, Korea, Japan, and in Tibet (as Vajrayana). Compassion for all beings is the foundation of Mahayana Buddhism, whose goal is not *nirvana* for oneself but buddhahood (enlightenment) for every being throughout the universe. Mahayana Buddhism recognizes buddhas other than Shakyamuni from the past, present, and future. One such is Maitreya, the next buddha to appear on earth. Another is Amitabha Buddha, the Buddha of Infinite Light and Infinite Life (that is, incorporating all space and time), who dwells in a paradise known as the Western Pure Land. Amitabha Buddha became particularly popular in east Asia. Mahayana Buddhism also developed the category of **bodhisattvas** ("those whose essence is wisdom"), saintly beings who are on the brink of achieving buddhahood but have vowed to help others achieve buddhahood before crossing over themselves. In art, bodhisattvas and buddhas are most clearly distinguished by their clothing and adornments: bodhisattvas wear the princely garb of India, while buddhas wear monks' robes.

EXPLORE MORE: Gain insight from a primary source of words spoken by the Buddha **www.myartslab.com**

ornaments and dress. Alleviating and counterbalancing this hierarchical formality are her soft, youthful face, the precise definition of prominent features such as the stomach muscles, and the polished sheen of her exposed flesh. This lustrous polish is a special feature of Maurya sculpture.

THE RISE OF BUDDHISM. During the reign of the third Maurya emperor Ashoka (ruled c. 273–232 BCE), Buddhism was expanded from a religion largely localized in the Maurya heartland, a region known as Magadha, to one extending across the entire empire. Among the monuments he erected were monolithic pillars set up primarily at the sites of Buddhist monasteries.

Pillars may have been used as flag-bearing standards in India since earliest times. Thus the creators of the pillars erected during Ashoka's reign may have adapted this already ancient form to the symbolism of Indian creation myths and the new religion of Buddhism. The fully developed Ashokan pillar—a slightly tapered sandstone shaft that usually rested on a stone foundation slab sunk more than 10 feet into the ground—rose to a height of around 50 feet (SEE FIG. 9–1). On it were carved inscriptions relating to rules of *dharma* that ideal kings were enjoined to uphold, and that many later Buddhists interpreted as also referring to Buddhist teachings or exhorting the Buddhist community to unity. At the top, carved from a separate block of sandstone, an elaborate capital bore animal sculpture. Both shaft and capital were given the characteristic Maurya polish. Scholars believe that the pillars symbolized the **axis mundi** ("axis of the world"), joining earth with the cosmos. It represented the vital link between the human and celestial realms, and through it the cosmic order was impressed onto the terrestrial.

LION CAPITAL FROM SARNATH. The capital in FIGURE 9–7 originally crowned the pillar erected at Sarnath in north central India, the site of the Buddha's first sermon. The lowest portion represents the down-turned petals of a lotus blossom. Because the lotus flower emerges from murky waters without any mud sticking to its petals, it symbolizes the presence of divine purity in the imperfect world. Above the lotus is an **abacus** (the slab forming the top of a capital) embellished with low-relief carvings

Hinduism

Hinduism is not one religion but many related beliefs and innumerable sects. It results from the mingling of Vedic beliefs with indigenous, local beliefs and practices. All three major Hindu sects draw upon the texts of the Vedas, which are believed to be sacred revelations set down about 1200–800 BCE. The gods lie outside the finite world, but they can appear in visible form to believers. Each Hindu sect takes its particular deity as supreme. By worshiping gods with rituals, meditation, and intense love, individuals may be reborn into increasingly higher positions until they escape the cycle of life, death, and rebirth, which is called *samsara*. The most popular deities are Vishnu, Shiva, and the Great Goddess, Devi. Deities are revealed and depicted in multiple aspects.

Vishnu: Vishnu is a benevolent god who works for the order and well-being of the world. He is often represented lying in a trance or asleep on the Cosmic Waters, where he dreams the world into existence. His symbols are the wheel and a conch shell, the mace and lotus. He usually has four arms and wears a crown and lavish jewelry. He rides a man-bird, Garuda. Vishnu appears in ten different incarnations, including Rama and Krishna, who have their own sects. Rama embodies virtue, and, assisted by the monkey king, he fights the demon Ravana. As Krishna, Vishnu is a supremely beautiful, blue-skinned youth who lives with the cowherds, loves the maiden Radha, and battles the demon Kansa.

Shiva: Shiva is both creative and destructive, light and dark, male and female. His symbol is the *linga*, an upright phallus, which is represented as a low pillar. As an expression of his power and creative energy, he is often represented as Lord of the Dance, dancing the Cosmic Dance, the endless cycle of death and rebirth,

destruction and creation (see "Shiva Nataraja of the Chola Dynasty," page 314). He dances within a ring of fire, his four hands holding fire, a drum, and gesturing to the worshipers. Shiva's animal vehicle is the bull. His consort is Parvati; their sons are the elephant-headed Ganesha, the overcomer of obstacles, and Karttikeya, often associated with war.

Devi: Devi, the Great Goddess, controls material riches and fertility. She has forms indicative of beauty, wealth, and auspiciousness, but also forms of wrath, pestilence, and power. As the embodiment of cosmic energy, she provides the vital force to all the male gods. Her symbol is an abstract depiction of female genitals, often associated with the *linga* of Shiva. When armed and riding a lion (as the goddess Durga), she personifies righteous fury. As the goddess Lakshmi, she is the goddess of wealth and beauty. She is often represented by the basic geometric forms: squares, circles, triangles.

Brahma: Brahma, who once had his own cult, embodies spiritual wisdom. His four heads symbolize the four cosmic cycles, four earthly directions, and four classes of society: priests (brahmins), warriors, merchants, and laborers.

There are countless other deities, but central to Hindu practice are *puja* (forms of worship) and *darshan* (beholding a deity), generally performed to obtain a deity's favor and in the hope that this favor will lead to liberation from *samsara*. Because desire for the fruits of our actions traps us, the ideal is to consider all earthly endeavors as sacrificial offerings to a god. Pleased with our devotion, he or she may grant us an eternal state of pure being, pure consciousness, and pure bliss.

---

of wheels, called in Sanskrit *chakra*s, alternating with four different animals: lion, horse, bull, and elephant. The animals may symbolize the four great rivers of the world, which are mentioned in Indian creation myths. Standing on this abacus are four back-to-back lions. Facing the four cardinal directions, the lions may be emblematic of the universal nature of Buddhism and the universal currency of Ashoka's law inscribed on the pillar. Their roar might be compared with the speech of the Buddha that spreads far and wide. The lions may also refer to the Buddha himself, who is known as "the lion of the Shakya clan" (the clan into which the Buddha was born as prince). The lions originally supported a great wheel, now lost. A universal Buddhist symbol, the wheel refers to Buddhist teaching, for with his sermon at Sarnath the Buddha "set the wheel of the law [*dharma*] in motion." The wheel is also a symbol of the *chakravartin*, the ideal universal monarch, and so refers to Ashoka as well as the Buddha.

Their formal, heraldic pose imbues the lions with something of the monumental quality evident in the statue of the *yakshi* of the same period. We also find the same strong patterning of realistic

elements: Veins and tendons stand out on the legs; the claws are large and powerful; the mane is richly textured; and the jaws have a loose and fluttering edge.

THE PERIOD OF THE SHUNGAS AND EARLY ANDHRAS

With the demise of the Maurya Empire, India returned to rule by regional dynasties. Between the second century BCE and the early first century CE, two of the most important of these dynasties were the Shunga dynasty (185–72 BCE) in central India and the Andhra dynasty (72 BCE–third century CE) who initially ruled in central India and after the first century in the south. During this period, some of the most magnificent early Buddhist structures were created.

STUPAS

Religious monuments called **stupas**, solid mounds enclosing a reliquary, are fundamental to Buddhism (see "Stupas and Temples," page 301). A stupa may be small and plain or large and elaborate. Its

9-8 • GREAT STUPA, SANCHI
Madhya Pradesh, India. Founded 3rd century BCE, enlarged c. 150–50 BCE.

SEE MORE: View a video about the Great Stupa, Sanchi **www.myartslab.com**

form may vary from region to region, but its symbolic meaning remains virtually the same, and its plan is a carefully calculated **mandala**, or diagram of the cosmos as it is envisioned in Buddhism. Stupas are open to all for private worship.

The first stupas were constructed to house the Buddha's remains after his cremation. According to tradition, the relics were divided into eight portions and placed in eight **reliquaries**. Each reliquary was then encased in its own burial mound, called a stupa. Since the early stupas held actual remains of the Buddha, they were venerated as his body and, by extension, his enlightenment and attainment of *nirvana* (liberation from rebirth). The method of veneration was, and still is, to circumambulate, or walk around, the stupa in a clockwise direction. In the mid third century BCE, King Ashoka is said to have opened the original eight stupas and divided their relics among many more stupas, probably including the Great Stupa at Sanchi.

THE GREAT STUPA AT SANCHI. Probably no early Buddhist structure is more famous than the **GREAT STUPA** at Sanchi in central India **(FIG. 9–8)**. In its original form probably dating to the

time of Ashoka, the Great Stupa was part of a large monastery complex crowning a hill. During the mid second century BCE, it was enlarged to its present size, and the surrounding stone railing was constructed. About 100 years later, elaborately carved stone gateways were added to the railing.

The Great Stupa at Sanchi is a representative of the early central Indian type. Its solid, hemispherical dome was built up from rubble and dirt, faced with dressed stone, then covered with a shining white plaster made from lime and powdered seashells. The dome—echoing the arc of the sky—sits on a raised base. Around the perimeter is a walkway enclosed by a railing; an elevated walkway is approached by a staircase on the south side. As is often true in religious architecture, the railing provides a physical and symbolic boundary between an inner, sacred area and the outer, profane world. On top of the dome, another stone railing, square in shape, defines the abode of the gods atop the cosmic mountain. It encloses the top of a mast bearing three stone disks, or "umbrellas," of decreasing size. These disks have been interpreted in various ways. They may correspond to the "Three Jewels of Buddhism"—the Buddha, the Law, and the Monastic

inscription, also on the south gateway, specifies a gift during the reign of King Satakarni of the Andhra dynasty, providing the first-century BCE date for the gateways. The only elements of the Great Stupa at Sanchi to be ornamented with sculpture, the gateways rise to a height of 35 feet. Their square posts and horizontal members are carved with symbols and scenes drawn mostly from the Buddha's life and the **jataka tales**, stories of the Buddha's past lives. A relief from the east gateway is illustrated in **FIGURE 9–9**. Typical of Indian narrative relief of the second and first centuries BCE, the scenes are organized not in a time sequence, but according to where they take place. Thus, at the top of this relief is a scene of Queen Maya's dream anticipating the birth of the Buddha, while below is a scene showing the Buddha's father in a chariot, riding out to greet his return, and at the bottom the Buddha, symbolized by a plank, levitates above the crowd gathered to witness the gift of a garden for the Buddha and his followers. All three of these scenes take place at Kapilavastu, the city of his birth.

9-9 • RELIEF FROM EAST GATEWAY OF THE GREAT STUPA, SANCHI
Early Andhra period, mid 1st century BCE. Stone.

This relief illustrates the birth of the Buddha at the top and the return of the Buddha to the city of his birth in the panels below.

Order—and they may also refer to the Buddhist concept of the three realms of existence: desire, form, and formlessness. The mast itself symbolizes an *axis mundi*, connecting the Cosmic Waters below the earth with the celestial realm above it and anchoring everything in its proper place.

A 10-foot-tall stone railing demarcates a circumambulatory path at ground level. Carved with octagonal uprights and lens-shaped crossbars, it probably simulates the wooden railings of the time. This design pervaded early Indian art, appearing in relief sculpture and as architectural ornament. Four stone gateways, or **toranas**, punctuate the railing. Aligned with the four cardinal directions, the gateways symbolize the Buddhist cosmos. An inscription on the south gateway indicates that it was provided by ivory carvers from the nearby town of Vidisha, while another

9-10 • *YAKSHI* BRACKET FIGURE
East *torana* of the Great Stupa at Sanchi. Stone, height approx. 60″ (152.4 cm).

Buddhist architecture in South Asia consists mainly of stupas and temples, often at monastic complexes containing **viharas** (monks' cells and common areas). These monuments may be either structural—built up from the ground—or rock-cut—hewn out of a mountainside. Stupas derive from burial mounds and contain relics beneath a solid, dome-shaped core. A major stupa is surrounded by a railing that creates a sacred path for ritual circumambulation at ground level. This railing is punctuated by gateways, called **toranas** in Sanskrit, aligned with the cardinal points. The stupa sits on a round or square terrace; stairs lead to an upper circumambulatory path around the platform's edge. On top of the stupa's dome a railing defines a square, from the center of which rises a mast supporting tiers of disk-shaped "umbrellas."

Hindu architecture in South Asia consists mainly of temples, either structural or rock-cut, executed in a number of styles and dedicated to diverse deities. The two general Hindu temple types are the northern and southern styles prevalent in northern India and southern India respectively. Within these broad categories is great stylistic diversity, though all are raised on plinths and dominated by their superstructures. In north India, the term **shikhara** is used to refer to the entire superstructure, while in the south it refers only to the finial, that is, the uppermost member of the superstructure. North Indian *shikhara*s are crowned by **amalakas**. Inside, a series of **mandapas** (halls) leads to an inner sanctuary, the **garbhagriha**, which contains a sacred image. An *axis mundi* is imagined to run vertically up from the Cosmic Waters below the earth, through the *garbhagriha*'s image, and out through the top of the tower.

Jain architecture consists mainly of structural and rock-cut monasteries and temples that have much in common with their Buddhist and Hindu counterparts. Buddhist, Hindu, and Jain temples may share a site, as may the structures of still other religions.

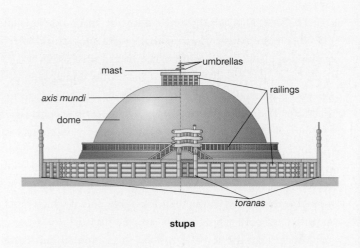

stupa

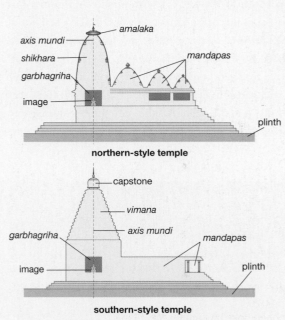

northern-style temple

southern-style temple

SEE MORE: View a simulation of stupas and temples www.myartslab.com

The capitals above the posts consist of four back-to-back elephants on the north and east gates, dwarfs on the west gate, and lions on the south gate. The capitals in turn support a three-tiered superstructure in which posts and crossbars are elaborately carved with still more symbols and scenes, and studded with free-standing sculptures depicting such subjects as *yakshi*s and *yaksha*s, riders on real and mythical animals, and the Buddhist wheel. As in other early Buddhist art before the late first century BCE, the Buddha himself is not shown in human form. Instead, he is represented by symbols such as his footprints, an empty "enlightenment" seat, or a plank.

Forming a bracket between each capital and the lowest cross-bar is a sculpture of a *yakshi* (**FIG. 9–10**). These *yakshi*s are some of the finest female figures in Indian art, and they make an instructive comparison with the *yakshi* of the Maurya period (SEE FIG. 9–6).

The earlier figure was distinguished by a formal, somewhat rigid pose, an emphasis on realistic details, and a clear distinction between clothed and nude parts of the body. In contrast, the Sanchi *yakshi* leans daringly into space with casual abandon, supported by one leg as the other charmingly crosses behind. Her thin, diaphanous garment is noticeable only by its hems, and so she appears almost nude, which emphasizes her form. The band pulling gently at her abdomen accentuates the suppleness of her flesh. The swelling, arching curves of her body evoke this deity's procreative and bountiful essence. As the personification of the waters, she is the source of life. Here she symbolizes the sap of the tree, which flowers at her touch.

The profusion of designs, symbols, scenes, and figures carved on all sides of the gateways to the Great Stupa not only relates the history and lore of Buddhism, but also represents the teeming life of the world and the gods.

BUDDHIST ROCK-CUT HALLS

From ancient times, caves have been considered hallowed places in India, for they were frequently the abode of holy men and ascetics. Around the second century BCE, cavelike sanctuaries were hewn out of the stone plateaus in the region of south central India known as the Deccan. Made for the use of Buddhist monks, the sanctuaries were carved from top to bottom like great pieces of sculpture, with all details completely finished in stone. To enter one of these remarkable halls is to feel transported to an otherworldly, sacred space. The atmosphere created by the dark recess and the echo that magnifies the smallest sound combine to promote a state of heightened awareness.

THE CHAITYA HALL AT KARLE.   The monastic community made two types of rock-cut halls. One was the **vihara**, used for the monks' living quarters, and the other was the **chaitya** ("sanctuary"), which usually enshrined a stupa. A *chaitya* hall at Karle, dating from the first century BCE to the first century CE, is one of the largest and most fully developed examples of these early Buddhist works (**FIG. 9–11**). At the entrance, columns once supported a balcony, in front of which a pair of Ashokan-type

9-11 • *CHAITYA* HALL, KARLE
Maharashtra, India. 1st century BCE–1st century CE.

pillars stood. The walls of the vestibule are carved in relief with rows of small balcony railings and arched windows, simulating the façade of a great multi-storied palace. At the base of the side walls, enormous statues of elephants seem to be supporting the entire structure on their backs. Dominating the upper portion of the main façade is a large horseshoe-shaped opening, which provides the hall's main source of light. The window was originally fitted with a carved wood screen, some of which remains, that filtered the light streaming inside.

Three entrances pierce the main façade. Flanking the entrances are sculpted panels of **mithuna** couples, amorous male and female figures that evoke the harmony and fertility of life and suggest the devotion with which the worshiper should confront the Buddha represented by the stupa inside. The interior hall, 123 feet long, has a 46-foot-high ceiling carved in the form of a barrel vault ornamented with arching wooden ribs. Both the interior and exterior of the hall were once brightly painted. Pillars demarcate a pathway for circumambulation around the stupa in the apse at the far end.

The side aisles are separated from the main aisle by closely spaced columns whose bases resemble a large pot set on a stepped pyramid of planks. From this potlike form rises a massive octagonal shaft. Crowning the shaft, a bell-shaped lotus capital supports an inverted pyramid of planks, which serves in turn as a platform for sculpture. The statues depict pairs of kneeling elephants, each bearing a *mithuna* couple. These figures, the only sculpture within this austere hall, may represent the nobility coming to pay homage at the temple. The pillars around the apse are plain, and the stupa is simple. A railing motif ornaments the base; the dome was once topped with wooden "umbrella" disks, only one of which remains. As with nearly everything in the cave, the stupa is carved from the cliff's rock. Like the stupa at Sanchi, the sculptural decoration is restricted to the entranceway. This stupa, however, could not contain the Buddha's relics because it is solid rock; likely it was worshiped as if it did.

THE KUSHAN AND LATER ANDHRA PERIODS

Around the first century CE, the regions of present-day Afghanistan, Pakistan, and north India came under the control of the Kushans, originally a nomadic people forced out of northwest China by the Han. Exact dates are uncertain, but they ruled from the first to the third century CE. The beginning of the long reign of their most illustrious king, Kanishka, is variously dated from 78 to 143 CE.

Buddhism during this period underwent a profound evolution that resulted in the form known as Mahayana, or Great Vehicle (see "Buddhism," page 297). This vital new movement, which was to sweep most of northern India and eastern Asia, probably inspired the first depictions of the Buddha himself in art. (Previously, as in the Great Stupa at Sanchi, the Buddha had been indicated solely by symbols.) Distinctive styles arose in the Gandhara region in the northwest (present-day Pakistan and Afghanistan) and in the famous religious center of Mathura in central India. Both of these areas were ruled by the Kushans. About the same time, a third style evolved in southeast India under the Andhra dynasty, whose rule continued in this region through the third century CE.

9–12 • STANDING BUDDHA
From Gandhara, Pakistan. Kushan period, c. 2nd–3rd century CE. Schist, height 7′6″ (2.28 m). Lahore Museum, Lahore.

While all three styles are quite distinct, they shared a basic visual language, or iconography, in which the Buddha is readily recognized by certain characteristics. He wears a monk's robe, a long length of cloth draped over the left shoulder and around the body. The Buddha is said to have had 32 major distinguishing marks, called **lakshanas**, some of which are reflected in the iconography (see "Buddhist Symbols," page 362). These include a golden-colored body, long arms that reached to his knees, the impression of a wheel (chakra) on the palms of his hands and the soles of his feet, and the **urna**—a tuft of white hair between his eyebrows. Because he had been a prince in his youth and had worn the customary heavy earrings, his earlobes are usually shown elongated. The top of his head is said to have had a protuberance called an **ushnisha**, which in images often resembles a bun or top-knot and symbolizes his enlightenment.

THE GANDHARA STYLE

Gandhara art combines elements of Hellenistic, Persian, and Indian styles. A typical image from Gandhara portrays the Buddha as a superhuman figure, more powerful and heroic than an ordinary human (**FIG. 9–12**). Although it is difficult to determine the dates of Gandhara images, this over-life-size Buddha may date to the fully developed stage of the Gandhara style, possibly around the third century CE. It is carved from schist, a fine-grained dark stone. The Buddha's body, revealed through the folds of the garment, is broad and massive, with heavy shoulders and limbs and a well-defined torso. His left knee bends gently, suggesting a slightly relaxed posture.

The treatment of the robe is especially characteristic of the Gandhara manner. Tight, riblike folds alternate with delicate creases, setting up a clear, rhythmic pattern of heavy and shallow lines. On the upper part of the figure, the folds break asymmetrically along the left arm; on the lower part, they drape in a symmetric U shape. The strong tension of the folds suggests life and power within the image. This complex fold pattern resembles the treatment of togas on certain Roman statues (SEE PAGE 177, FIG. A), and it exerted a strong influence on portrayals of the Buddha in central and east Asia. The Gandhara region's relations with the Hellenistic world may have led to this strongly Western style in its art. Pockets of Hellenistic culture had thrived in neighboring Bactria (present-day northern Afghanistan and southern Uzbekistan) since the fourth century BCE, when the Greeks under Alexander the Great reached the borders of India. Also, Gandhara's position near the east–west trade routes appears to have stimulated contact with Roman culture in the Near East during the early centuries of the first millennium CE.

THE MATHURA STYLE

The second major style of Buddhist art in the Kushan period—that found at Mathura—was not allied with the Hellenistic-Roman tradition. Instead, the Mathura style evolved from representations of yakshas, the indigenous male nature deities. Images produced at

Mudras

*Mudra*s (the Sanskrit word for "signs") are ancient symbolic hand gestures that are regarded as physical expressions of different states of being. In Buddhist art, they function iconographically. *Mudra*s are also used during meditation to release these energies. The following are the most common *mudra*s in Asian art.

Dharmachakra Mudra
The gesture of teaching, setting the *chakra* (wheel) of the *dharma* (law or doctrine) in motion. Hands are at chest level.

Dhyana Mudra
A gesture of meditation and balance, symbolizing the path toward enlightenment. Hands are in the lap, the lower representing *maya*, the physical world of illusion, the upper representing *nirvana*, enlightenment and release from the world.

Vitarka Mudra
This variant of *dharmachakra mudra* stands for intellectual debate. The right and/or left hand is held at shoulder level with thumb and forefinger touching.

Abhaya Mudra
The gesture of reassurance, blessing, and protection, this *mudra* means "have no fear." The right hand is at shoulder level, palm outward.

Bhumisparsha Mudra
This gesture calls upon the earth to witness Shakyamuni Buddha's enlightenment at Bodh Gaya. A seated figure's right hand reaches toward the ground, palm inward.

Varada Mudra
The gesture of charity, symbolizing the fulfillment of all wishes. Alone, this *mudra* is made with the right hand; but when combined with *abhaya mudra* in standing Buddha figures (as is most common), the left hand is shown in *varada mudra*.

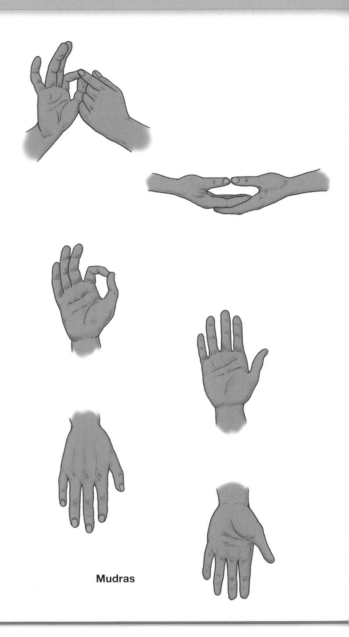

Mudras

Mathura during the early days of the Kushan period may be the first representations of the Buddha to appear in art.

The stele in **FIGURE 9–13** is one of the finest of the early Mathura images. The sculptors worked in a distinctive red sandstone flecked with cream-colored spots. Carved in **high relief** (forms projecting strongly from the background), it depicts a seated Buddha with two attendants. The Buddha sits in a yogic posture on a pedestal supported by lions. His right hand is raised in a symbolic gesture meaning "have no fear." Images of the Buddha rely on a repertoire of such gestures, called **mudras**, to communicate certain ideas, such as teaching, meditation, or the attaining of enlightenment (see "Mudras," above). The Buddha's *urna*, his *ushnisha*, and the impressions of wheels on his palms and soles are all clearly visible in this figure. Behind his head is a large, circular halo; the scallop points of its border represent radiating light. Behind the halo are branches of the pipal tree, the tree under which the Buddha was seated when he achieved enlightenment. Two celestial beings hover above.

As in Gandhara sculptures, the Mathura work gives a powerful impression of the Buddha. Yet this Buddha's riveting outward gaze and alert posture impart a more intense, concentrated energy. The robe is pulled tightly over the body, allowing the fleshy form to be seen as almost nude. Where the pleats of the robe appear, such as over the left arm and fanning out between the legs, they are depicted abstractly through compact parallel formations of ridges with an incised line in the center of each ridge. This characteristic

9-13 • BUDDHA AND ATTENDANTS
From Katra Keshavdev, Mathura, Madhya Pradesh, India. Kushan period, c. late 1st–early 2nd century CE. Red sandstone, height 27¼″ (69.2 cm). Government Museum, Mathura.

Mathura tendency to abstraction also appears in the face, whose features take on geometric shapes, as in the rounded forms of the widely opened eyes. Nevertheless, the torso with its subtle and soft modeling is strongly naturalistic.

THE SOUTHEAST INDIAN STYLE

Events from the Buddha's life were popular subjects in the reliefs decorating stupas and Buddhist temples. One example from Nagarjunakonda depicts a scene when he was Prince Siddhartha, before his renunciation of his princely status and his subsequent quest for enlightenment (**FIG. 9–14**). Carved in low relief, the panel reveals a scene of pleasure around a pool of water. Gathered around Siddhartha, the largest figure and the only male, are some of the palace women. One holds his foot, entreating him to come into the water; another sits with legs drawn up on the nearby rock; others lean over his shoulder or fix their hair; one comes into the scene with a box of jewels on her head. The panel is framed by decorated columns, crouching lions, and amorous *mithuna* couples. (One of these couples is visible at the right of the illustration.) The scene is skillfully orchestrated to revolve around the prince as the main focus of all eyes. Typical of the southeast Indian style, the figures are slighter than those of Gandhara and Mathura. They are sinuous and mobile, even while at rest. The rhythmic nuances of the limbs and varied postures not only create interest in the activity of each individual but also engender a light and joyous effect.

During the first to third century CE, each of the three major styles of Buddhist art developed its own distinct idiom for expressing the complex imagery of Buddhism and depicting the image of the Buddha. The production of art in Gandhara and the region around Nagarjunakonda declined over the ensuing centuries. However, the artists of central India continued to work productively, and from them came the next major development in Indian Buddhist art.

9-14 • SIDDHARTHA IN THE PALACE
Detail of a relief from Nagarjunakonda, Andhra Pradesh, India. Later Andhra period, c. 3rd century CE. Limestone. National Museum, New Delhi.

EXPLORE MORE: Gain insight from a primary source about the life of the Buddha
www.myartslab.com

THE FOURTH THROUGH SEVENTH CENTURIES

The Guptas, who founded a dynasty in the eastern region of central India known as Magadha, expanded their territories during the fourth century CE to form an empire that encompassed northern and much of central India. Although Gupta power ended in 550, the influence of Gupta culture was felt long after that.

The period of the Guptas and their contemporaries is renowned for the flourishing artistic and literary culture that brought forth some of India's most widely admired sculpture and painting. While Buddhism continued to be a major religion, the earliest surviving Hindu temples also date from this time.

BUDDHIST SCULPTURE

Two distinctive styles of Gupta Buddhist sculpture prevailed during the second and third quarters of the fifth century and dominated in northern India: one was based at Mathura, the major center of north Indian sculpture during the Kushan period, and the other at Sarnath, whose style is reflected in Buddhist sculpture over much of northern India.

The **STANDING BUDDHA** in **FIGURE 9–15** embodies the fully developed Sarnath Gupta style. Carved from fine-grained sandstone, the figure stands in a mildly relaxed pose, the body clearly visible through a clinging robe. This plain robe, portrayed with none of the creases and folds so prominent in the Kushan period images, is distinctive of the Sarnath style. Its effect is to concentrate attention on the form of the body, which emerges in high relief. The body is graceful and slight, with broad shoulders and a well-proportioned torso. Only a few lines of the garment at the neck, waist, and hems interrupt the purity of its subtly shaped surfaces; the face, smooth and ovoid, has the same refined elegance. The downcast eyes suggest otherworldly introspection, yet the gentle, open posture maintains a human link. Behind the head are the remains of a large, circular halo. Carved in concentric circles of pearls and foliage, the ornate halo contrasted with the plain surfaces of the figure. Details also may have been indicated by paint.

At the site of Bamiyan, about 155 miles northwest of Kabul, Afghanistan, were two enormous Buddhas carved from the rock of a cliff, one some 115 feet in height **(FIG. 9–16)**, the other about 165 feet. They were seen by a Chinese pilgrim who came to Bamiyan in the fifth century, so they clearly date before his visit, probably to the early fifth century. Pilgrims could walk within the cliff up a staircase on the right side of the smaller figure that ended at the Buddha's shoulder. There they could look into the vault of the niche and see a painted image of the sun god, suggesting a metaphoric pilgrimage to the heavens. They then could circumambulate the figure at the level of the head and return to ground level on a staircase on the figure's left side. These huge figures likely served as the model for those at rock-cut sanctuaries in China, for example, at Yungang. Despite the historical and religious importance of these figures, and

9-15 • STANDING BUDDHA
From Sarnath, Uttar Pradesh, India. Gupta period, 474 CE. Chunar sandstone, height 6′4″ (1.93 m). Archaeological Museum, Sarnath.

ignoring the pleas of world leaders, the Taliban demolished the Bamiyan Buddhas in 2001.

PAINTING

The Gupta aesthetic also found expression in painting, though in a region of India just beyond the Gupta realm. Some of the finest surviving works are murals from the Buddhist rock-cut halls of Ajanta, in the western Deccan region of India **(FIG. 9–17)**. Under a ruling house known as the Vakataka dynasty, many caves were carved around 475 CE, including Cave I, a large *vihara* hall with monks' chambers around the sides and a Buddha shrine chamber in the back. The walls of the central court were covered with murals painted in mineral pigments on a prepared plaster surface. Some of these paintings depict episodes from the Buddha's past lives. Flanking the entrance to the shrine chamber are two large **bodhisattvas**, one of which is seen in FIGURE 9–17.

9-16 • STANDING BUDDHA
Bamiyan, Afghanistan. c. 5th century CE.

Bodhisattvas are enlightened beings who postpone *nirvana* and buddhahood to help others achieve enlightenment. They are distinguished from Buddhas in art by their princely garments. The bodhisattva here is lavishly adorned with delicate ornaments. He wears a bejeweled crown, large earrings, a pearl necklace, armbands, and bracelets. A striped cloth covers his lower body. The graceful bending posture and serene gaze impart a sympathetic attitude. His spiritual power is suggested by his large size in comparison to the surrounding figures, and his identity as the compassionate bodhisattva Avalokiteshvara is indicated by the lotus flower he holds in his right hand.

The naturalistic style balances outline and softly graded color tones. Outline drawing, always a major ingredient of Indian painting, clearly defines shapes; tonal gradations impart the illusion of three-dimensional form, with lighter tones used for protruding parts such as the nose, brows, shoulders, and chest muscles. Together with the details of the jewels, these highlighted areas resonate against the subdued tonality of the figure. Sophisticated, realistic detail is balanced by the languorous human form. In no other known examples of Indian painting do bodhisattvas appear so graciously divine yet, so palpably human. This particular synthesis is evident also in the Sarnath statue (SEE FIG. 9–15), which shares much in common as well with the sculpture of Ajanta.

Although Buddhism had flourished in India during the fifth century, some of the most important Buddhist monasteries, attracting pilgrims from as far away as China, prospered especially after the Gupta period. Hindu temples, generally small and relatively simple structures during the fifth century, subsequently became increasingly complex and elaborately adorned with sculptured images.

9-17 • BODHISATTVA
Detail of a wall painting in Cave I, Ajanta, Maharashtra, India. Vakataka dynasty, c. 475 CE.

9-18 • VISHNU TEMPLE, DEOGARH
Uttar Pradesh, India. Gupta dynasty, c. 530 CE.

THE EARLY NORTHERN TEMPLE

The Hindu temple developed many different forms throughout India, but it can be classified broadly into two types: northern and southern. The northern type is chiefly distinguished by a superstructure called a **shikhara** (see "Stupas and Temples," page 301). The *shikhara* rises as a solid mass above the flat stone ceiling and windowless walls of the sanctum, or **garbhagriha**, which houses an image of the temple's deity. As it rises, it curves inward in a mathematically determined ratio. (In geometric terms, the *shikhara* is a paraboloid.) Crowning the top is a circular, cushion-like element called an **amalaka**, a fruit. From the *amalaka*, a **finial** (a knoblike decoration at the top point of a spire) takes the eye to a point where the earthly world is thought to join the cosmic world. An imaginary *axis mundi* penetrates the entire temple, running from the point of the finial, through the exact center of the *amalaka* and *shikhara*, down through the center of the *garbhagriha* and its image, finally passing through the base of the temple and into the earth below. In this way the temple becomes a conduit between the celestial realms and the earth. This theme, familiar from Ashokan pillars and Buddhist stupas, is carried out with elaborate exactitude in Hindu temples, and it is one of the most important elements underlying their form and function (see "Meaning and Ritual in Hindu Temples and Images," page 310).

TEMPLE OF VISHNU AT DEOGARH.   One of the earliest northern-style temples is the temple of Vishnu at Deogarh in north central India, which dates from around 530 CE (**FIG. 9–18**). Much of the *shikhara* has crumbled away, so we cannot determine its original shape with precision. Nevertheless, it was clearly a massive, solid structure built of large cut stones. It would have given the impression of a mountain, which is one of several metaphoric meanings of a Hindu temple. This early temple has only one chamber, the *garbhagriha*, which corresponds to the center of a sacred diagram called a *mandala* on which the entire temple site is patterned. As the deity's residence, the *garbhagriha* is likened to a sacred cavern within the "cosmic mountain" of the temple.

Large panels sculpted in relief with images of Vishnu appear as "windows" on the temple's exterior. These elaborately framed panels do not function literally to let light *into* the temple; they function symbolically to let the light of the deity *out* of the temple to be seen by those outside.

One panel depicts Vishnu lying on the Cosmic Waters at the beginning of creation (**FIG. 9–19**). He sleeps on the serpent of infinity, Ananta, whose body coils endlessly into space. Stirred by his female aspect (*shakti*, or female energy), personified here by the goddess Lakshmi, seen holding his foot, Vishnu dreams the universe into existence. From his navel springs a lotus (shown in this relief behind Vishnu), and the unfolding of space-time begins.

9-19 • VISHNU ON THE COSMIC WATERS
Relief panel in the Vishnu Temple, Deogarh. c. 530 CE. Stone, height approx. 5' (1.5 m).

SEE MORE: View a video about the process of sculpting in relief
www.myartslab.com

frieze below personify Vishnu's four attributes. They stand ready to fight the appearance of evil, represented at the left of the frieze by two demons who threaten to kill Brahma and jeopardize all creation.

The birth of the universe and the appearance of evil are thus portrayed here in three clearly organized registers. Typical of Indian religious and artistic expression, these momentous events are set before our eyes not in terms of abstract symbols, but as a drama acted out by gods in super-human form.

MONUMENTAL NARRATIVE RELIEFS

The Hindu god Shiva exhibits a wide range of aspects or forms, both gentle and wild: He is the Great Yogi who dwells for vast periods of time in meditation in the Himalayas; he is also the husband par excellence who makes love to the goddess Parvati for eons at a time; he is the Slayer of Demons; and he is the Cosmic Dancer who dances the destruction and re-creation of the world.

TEMPLE OF SHIVA AT ELEPHANTA.
Many of these forms of Shiva appear in the monumental relief panels adorning the cave-temple of Shiva carved in the mid sixth century on the island of Elephanta off the coast of Mumbai in western India. The cave-temple is complex in layout and conception, perhaps to reflect the nature of Shiva. While most temples have one entrance, this temple offers three—one facing north, one east, and one west. The interior, impressive in its size and grandeur, is designed along two main axes, one running north–south, the other

The first being to be created is Brahma (not to be confused with Brahman), who appears here as the central, four-headed figure in the row of gods portrayed above the reclining Vishnu. Brahma turns himself into the universe of space and time by thinking, "May I become Many."

The sculptor has depicted Vishnu as a large, resplendent figure with four arms. His size and his multiple arms denote his omnipotence. He is lightly garbed but richly ornamented. The ideal of the Gupta style is evident in the smooth, perfected shape of the body and in the lavishly detailed jewelry, including Vishnu's characteristic cylindrical crown. The four figures on the right in the

east–west. The three entrances provide the only source of light, and the resulting cross and backlighting effects add to the sense of the cave as a place of mysterious, almost confusing complexity.

Along the east–west axis, large pillars cut from the rock appear to support the low ceiling and its beams, although, as with all architectural elements in a cave-temple, they are not structural **(FIG. 9–20)**. The pillars form orderly rows, but the rows are hard to discern within the framework of the cave shape, which is neither square nor longitudinal, but formed of overlapping *mandalas* that create a symmetric yet irregular space. The pillars are an important aesthetic component of the cave. Each has an

Meaning and Ritual in Hindu Temples and Images

The Hindu temple is one of the most complex and meaningful architectural forms in Asian art. Age-old symbols and ritual functions are embedded not only in a structure's many parts, but also in the process of construction itself. Patron, priest, and architect worked as a team to ensure the sanctity of the structure from start to finish. No artist or artisan was more highly revered in ancient Indian society than the architect, who could oversee the construction of an abode in which a deity would dwell.

For a god to take up residence, however, everything had to be done properly in exacting detail. By the end of the first millennium, the necessary procedures had been recorded in texts called the *Silpa Shastra*. First, an auspicious site was chosen; a site near water was especially favored, for water makes the earth fruitful. Next, the ground was prepared in an elaborate process that took several years: Spirits already inhabiting the site were invited to leave; the ground was planted and harvested through two seasons; then cows—sacred beasts since the Indus civilization—were pastured there to lend their potency to the site. When construction began, each phase was accompanied by ritual to ensure its purity and sanctity.

All Hindu temples are built on a plan known as a ***mandala***, a schematic design of a sacred realm or space—specifically, Vastupurusha *mandala*, the *mandala* of the Cosmic Man, the primordial progenitor of the human species. His body, fallen on earth, is imagined as superimposed on the *mandala* design; together, they form the base on which the temple rises. The Vastupurusha *mandala* always takes the form of a square subdivided into a number of equal squares (usually 64) surrounding a central square. The central square represents Brahman, the primordial, unmanifest Formless One. This square corresponds to the temple's sanctum, the windowless *garbhagriha* ("womb chamber"). The nature of Brahman is clear, pure light; that we perceive the *garbhagriha* as dark is considered a testament to our deluded nature. The surrounding squares belong to lesser deities, while the outermost compartments hold protector gods. These compartments are usually represented by the enclosing wall of a temple compound.

The *garbhagriha* houses the temple's main image—most commonly a stone, bronze, or wood statue of Vishnu, Shiva, or Devi. In the case of Shiva, the image is often symbolic rather than anthropomorphic. To ensure perfection, the proportions of the image follow a set canon, and rituals surround its making. When the image is completed, a priest recites *mantras* (mystic syllables), that bring the deity into the image. The belief that a deity is literally present is not taken lightly. Even in India today, any image "under worship"—whether it be in a temple or a field, an ancient work or a modern piece—will be respected and not taken from the people who worship it.

A Hindu temple is a place for individual devotion, not congregational worship. It is the place where a devotee can make offerings to one or more deities and be in the presence of the god who is embodied in the image in the *garbhagriha*. Worship generally consists of prayers and offerings such as food and flowers or water and oil for the image, but it can also be much more elaborate, including dancing and ritual sacrifices.

---

unadorned, square base rising to nearly half its total height. Above is a circular column, which has a curved contour and a billowing "cushion" capital. Both column and capital are delicately fluted, adding a surprising refinement to these otherwise sturdy forms. The focus of the east–west axis is a square **linga shrine**, shown here at the center of illustration 9–20. Each of its four entrances is flanked by a pair of colossal standing guardian figures. In the center of the shrine is the *linga*, the phallic symbol of Shiva. The *linga* represents the presence of Shiva as the unmanifest Formless One, or Brahman. It symbolizes both his erotic nature and his aspect as the Great Yogi who controls his seed. The *linga* is synonymous with Shiva and is seen in nearly every Shiva temple and shrine.

The focus of the north–south axis, in contrast, is a relief on the south wall with a huge bust of Shiva representing his Sadashiva, or **ETERNAL SHIVA**, aspect **(FIG. 9–21)**. Three heads are shown resting upon the broad shoulders of the upper body, but five heads are implied: the fourth behind and the fifth, never depicted, on top. The heads summarize Shiva's fivefold nature as creator (back),

protector (left), destroyer (right), obscurer (front), and releaser (top). The head in the front depicts Shiva deep in introspection. The massiveness of the broad head, the large eyes barely delineated, and the mouth with its heavy lower lip suggest the god's serious depths. Lordly and majestic, he easily supports his huge crown, intricately carved with designs and jewels, and the matted, piled-up hair of a yogi. On his left shoulder, his protector nature is depicted as female, with curled hair and a pearl-festooned crown. On his right shoulder, his wrathful, destroyer nature wears a fierce expression, and snakes encircle his neck.

Like the relief panels at the temple to Vishnu in Deogarh (SEE FIG. 9–19), the reliefs at Elephanta are early examples of the Hindu monumental narrative tradition. Measuring 11 feet in height, they are set in recessed niches. The panels portray the range of Shiva's powers and some of his different aspects, presented in the context of narratives that help devotees understand his nature. Taken as a whole, the reliefs represent the manifestation of Shiva in our world. Indian artists often convey the many aspects or essential nature of a deity through multiple heads or arms—which they

9-20 • CAVE-TEMPLE OF SHIVA, ELEPHANTA
Maharashtra, India. Post-Gupta period, mid 6th century CE. View along the east–west axis to the *linga* shrine.

do with such convincing naturalism that we readily accept the additions. Here, for example, the artist has united three heads onto a single body so skillfully that we still relate to the statue as an essentially human presence.

"DESCENT OF THE GANGES" RELIEF AT MAMALLAPURAM. An enormous relief at Mamallapuram, near Chennai, in southeastern India, depicts the penance of a king, Bhagiratha, who sought to save his people from drought by subjecting himself to terrible austerities. In response, the god Shiva sent the Ganges River, represented by the natural cleft in the rock, to earth, thereby ending the drought (see "A Closer Look," page 313). Bhagiratha is shown standing in frigid waters while staring directly at the sun through his parted fingers, standing for interminable periods on

9-21 • ETERNAL SHIVA
Rock-cut relief in the cave-temple of Shiva, Elephanta.
Mid 6th century CE. Height approx. 11′ (3.4 m).

one foot, and in deep prayer before a temple. In the upper left part of the relief, Shiva, shown four-armed, appears before Bhagiratha to grant his wish. Elsewhere in the relief, animal families are depicted, generally in mutually protective roles.

This richly carved relief was executed under the Pallava dynasty, which flourished in southeastern India from the seventh to ninth century CE. It very likely serves as a visual allegory for the benevolent king, who protects his people, perhaps specifically by providing canals to control water, a notion reinforced by the relief carved in a cave-temple on the same boulder, to the left of the Descent relief. It shows the god Krishna protecting his people from a deluge by raising a mountain to serve as a sort of natural umbrella. Themes relating to water are particularly appropriate to Mamallapuram, situated on the Bay of Bengal and possibly serving as a port for the Pallavas.

THE EARLY SOUTHERN TEMPLE

The coastal city of Mamallapuram was also a major temple site under the Pallavas. Along the shore are many large granite boulders and cliffs, and from these the Pallava-period stonecutters carved entire temples as well as reliefs such as the one discussed in "A Closer Look," opposite. Among the most interesting of these rock-cut temples is a group known as the Five Rathas, which preserve diverse early architectural styles that probably reflect the forms of contemporary wood or brick structures that have long since disappeared.

DHARMARAJA RATHA AT MAMALLAPURAM. One of this group, called today the Dharmaraja Ratha, epitomizes the early southern-style temple (FIG. 9–22). Although strikingly different in appearance from the northern style, it uses the same symbolism to link the heavens and earth and it, too, is based on a *mandala*. The temple, square in plan, remains unfinished, and the *garbhagriha* usually found inside was never hollowed out, suggesting that, like cave-temples, Dharmaraja Ratha was executed from the top downward. On the lower portion, only the columns and niches have been carved. The use of a single deity in each niche forecasts the main trend in temple sculpture in the centuries ahead: The tradition of narrative reliefs declined, and the stories they told became concentrated in statues of individual deities, which conjure up entire mythological episodes through characteristic poses and a few symbolic objects.

Southern- and northern-style temples are most clearly distinguished by their superstructures. The Dharmaraja Ratha does not culminate in the paraboloid of the northern *shikhara* but in a pyramidal tower. Each story of the superstructure is articulated by a cornice and carries a row of miniature shrines. Both shrines and cornices are decorated with a window motif from which faces peer. The shrines not only demarcate each story, but also provide loftiness for this palace intended to enshrine a god. Crowning the superstructure is a dome-shaped octagonal capstone quite different from the *amalaka* of the northern style.

During the centuries that followed, both northern- and southern-style temples developed into complex, monumental forms, but their basic structure and symbolism remained the same as those we have seen in these simple, early examples at Deogarh and Mamallapuram.

THE EIGHTH THROUGH THE FOURTEENTH CENTURIES

During the eighth through the fourteenth centuries, regional styles developed in the realms of the dynasties ruling kingdoms that were generally smaller than the Maurya and Kushan empires. Some dynasties were relatively long-lived, such as the Pallavas and Cholas in the south and the Palas in the northeast. Although Buddhism remained strong in a few areas—notably under the Palas—it generally declined, while the Hindu gods Vishnu, Shiva, and the Great Goddess (mainly Durga) grew increasingly popular. Monarchs rivaled each other in the building of temples to their favored deity, and many complicated and subtle variations of the Hindu temple emerged with astounding rapidity in different regions. By around 1000 the Hindu temple reached unparalleled heights of grandeur and engineering.

9-22 • DHARMARAJA RATHA, MAMALLAPURAM
Tamil Nadu, India. Pallava period, c. mid 7th century CE.

"Descent of the Ganges" Relief ›

Rock-cut relief, Mamallapuram, Tamil Nadu, India.
Pallava period, c. mid 7th century CE. Granite, height approx. 20′ (6 m).

Unfinished cave. Beyond it, on the same rock formation, is the Krishna Cave.

Unfinished portion of the relief suggesting work from the top downward, as at other Mamallapuram monuments.

Shiva offering boon to Bhagiratha.

Bhagiratha meditating in front of a temple.

Bhagiratha gazing directly at the sun.

A cat imitating the penance of Bhagiratha, a whimsical touch by the artist.

A family of elephants, the bull elephant in front protecting his young elephant, probably a metaphor for the king's protection of his people.

SEE MORE: View the Closer Look feature for the "Descent of the Ganges" relief at Mamallapuram
www.myartslab.com

THE MONUMENTAL NORTHERN TEMPLE

The Kandariya Mahadeva, a temple dedicated to Shiva at Khajuraho, in central India, was probably built by a ruler of the Chandella dynasty in the late tenth or early eleventh century **(FIG. 9–23)**. Khajuraho was the capital and main temple site for the Chandellas, who constructed more than 80 temples there, about 25 of which are well preserved. The Kandariya Mahadeva Temple is in the northern style, with a curvilinear *shikhara* rising over its *garbhagriha*. Larger, more extensively ornamented, and expanded through the addition of halls on the front and porches to the sides and back, the temple seems at first glance to have little in common with its precursor at Deogarh (SEE FIG. 9–18). Actually, however, the basic elements and their symbolism remain unchanged.

Shiva Nataraja of the Chola Dynasty

Perhaps no sculpture is more representative of Hinduism than the statues of Shiva Nataraja, or Dancing Shiva, a form perfected by sculptors under the royal patronage of the south Indian Chola dynasty in the late tenth to eleventh century. (For the architecture and painting of the period, SEE FIGS. 9–25, 9–26.) The dance of Shiva is a dance of cosmic proportions, signifying the universe's cycle of death and rebirth; it is also a dance for each individual, signifying the liberation of the believer through Shiva's compassion. In the iconography of the Nataraja, this sculpture shows Shiva with four arms dancing on the prostrate body of Apasmara, a dwarf figure who symbolizes "becoming" and whom Shiva controls. Shiva's extended left hand holds a ball of fire; a circle of fire rings the god. The fire is emblematic of the destruction of *samsara* and the physical universe as well as the destruction of *maya* (illusion) and our ego-centered perceptions. Shiva's back right hand holds a drum; its beat represents the irrevocable rhythms of creation and destruction, birth and death. His front right arm gestures the "have no fear" *mudra* (see "Mudras," page 304). The front left arm, gracefully stretched across his body with the hand pointing to his raised foot, signifies the promise of liberation.

The artist has rendered the complex pose with great clarity. The central axis, which aligns the nose, navel, and insole of the weight-bearing foot, maintains the figure's equilibrium while the remaining limbs asymmetrically extend far to each side. Shiva wears a short loincloth, a ribbon tied above his waist, and delicately tooled ornaments. The scant clothing reveals his perfected form with its broad shoulders tapering to a supple waist. The jewelry is restrained and the detail does not detract from the beauty of the body.

The deity does not appear self-absorbed and introspective as he did in the Eternal Shiva relief at Elephanta (SEE FIG. 9–21). He turns to face the viewer, appearing lordly and aloof yet fully aware of his benevolent role as he generously displays himself for the devotee. Like the Sarnath Gupta Buddha (SEE FIG. 9–15), the Chola Shiva Nataraja presents a characteristically Indian synthesis

of the godly and the human, this time expressing the *bhakti* belief in the importance of an intimate relationship with a lordly god through whose compassion one is saved. The earlier Hindu emphasis on ritual and the depiction of the heroic feats of the gods is subsumed into the all-encompassing, humanizing factor of grace.

The fervent religious devotion of the *bhakti* movement was fueled by the sublime writings of a series of poet-saints who lived in the south of India. One of them, Appar, who lived from the late sixth to mid seventh century CE, wrote this vision of the Shiva Nataraja. The ash the poem refers to is one of many symbols associated with the deity.

In penance for having lopped off one of the five heads of Brahma, the first created being, Shiva smeared his body with ashes and went about as a beggar.

> If you could see
> the arch of his brow,
> the budding smile
> on lips red as the kovvai fruit,
> cool matted hair,
> the milk-white ash on coral skin,
> and the sweet golden foot
> raised up in dance,
> then even human birth on this wide earth
> would become a thing worth having.

(Translated by Indira Vishvanathan Peterson)

SHIVA NATARAJA
From Thanjavur, Tamil Nadu. Chola dynasty, 12th century CE. Bronze, height 32″ (81.25 cm). National Museum of India, New Delhi.

9-23 • KANDARIYA MAHADEVA TEMPLE, KHAJURAHO
Madhya Pradesh, India. Chandella dynasty, c. 1000 CE.

As at Deogarh, the temple rests on a stone terrace that sets off a sacred space from the mundane world. A steep flight of stairs at the front (to the right in the illustration) leads to a series of three halls, called **mandapas** (distinguished on the outside by pyramidal roofs), preceding the *garbhagriha*. The *mandapas* serve as spaces for ritual, such as dances performed for the deity, and for the presentation of offerings. The temple is built of stone blocks using only post-and-lintel construction. Because vault and arch techniques are not used, the interior spaces are not large.

The exterior has a strong sculptural presence, its massiveness suggesting a "cosmic mountain" composed of ornately carved stone. The *shikhara* rises more than 100 feet over the *garbhagriha* and is crowned by a small *amalaka*. The *shikhara* is bolstered by the many smaller *shikhara* motifs bundled around it. This decorative scheme adds a complex richness to the surface, but it also obscures the shape of the main *shikhara*, which is slender, with a swift and impetuous upward movement. The roofs of the *mandapas* contribute to the impression of rapid ascent by growing progressively taller as they near the *shikhara*.

Despite its apparent complexity, the temple has a clear structure and unified composition. The towers of the superstructure are separated from the lower portion by strong horizontal moldings and by the open spaces over the *mandapas* and porches. The **moldings** (shaped or sculpted strips) and rows of sculpture adorning the lower part of the temple create a horizontal emphasis that stabilizes the vertical thrust of the superstructure. Three rows of sculpture—some 600 figures—are integrated into the exterior walls. Approximately 3 feet tall and carved in high relief, the sculptures depict gods and goddesses, as well as figures in erotic postures. They are thought to express Shiva's divine bliss, the manifestation of his presence within, and the transformation of one into many.

In addition to its horizontal emphasis, the lower portion of the temple is characterized by a verticality that is created by protruding and receding elements. Their visual impact is similar to that of engaged columns and buttresses, and they account for much of the rich texture of the exterior. The porches, two on each side and one in the back, contribute to the complexity by outwardly expanding the ground plan, yet their bases also

9-24 • EROTIC COUPLES ON WALL OF KANDARIYA MAHADEVA TEMPLE, KHAJURAHO
Height of sculptures approx. 3'3" (1 m).

reinforce the sweeping vertical movements that unify the entire structure.

The Khajuraho temples are especially well known for their numerous erotic sculptures such as those illustrated in **FIGURE 9–24**. These carvings are not placed haphazardly, but rather in a single vertical line at the juncture of the walls enclosing the *garbhagriha* and the last *mandapa*. Their significance is uncertain; perhaps they derive from the amorous couples that adorn temple doorways leading to the *garbhagriha*. Such couples are found on some early temples such as the Deogarh temple as well as on Buddhist rock-cut sanctuaries such as the one at Karle, serving as reminders that devotion to god resembles the passion of love.

THE MONUMENTAL SOUTHERN TEMPLE

The Cholas, who succeeded the Pallavas in the mid ninth century, founded a dynasty that governed most of the far south well into the late thirteenth century. The Chola dynasty reached its peak during the reign of Rajaraja I (r. 985–1014). As an expression of gratitude for his many victories in battle, Rajaraja built the Rajarajeshvara Temple to Shiva in his capital, Thanjavur (formerly known as Tanjore). The name Rajarajeshvara means the temple of Rajaraja's Lord, that is, Shiva. Commonly called the Brihadeshvara (the temple of the Great Lord), this temple is a remarkable achievement of the southern style of Hindu architecture (**FIG. 9–25**). It stands within a huge, walled compound near the banks of the Kaveri River. Although smaller shrines dot the compound, the Rajarajeshvara dominates the area.

Clarity of design, a formal balance of parts, and refined décor contribute to the Rajarajeshvara's majesty. Rising to an astonishing height of 216 feet, this temple was probably the tallest structure in India in its time. Like the contemporaneous Kandariya Mahadeva Temple at Khajuraho, the Rajarajeshvara has a longitudinal axis and greatly expanded dimensions, especially with regard to its superstructure. Typical of the southern style, the *mandapa* at the front of the Rajarajeshvara has a flat roof, as opposed to the pyramidal roofs of the northern style. The walls of the sanctum rise for two

9-25 • RAJARAJESHVARA TEMPLE OF SHIVA, THANJAVUR
Tamil Nadu, India. Chola Dynasty, 1003–1010 CE.

stories, with each story emphatically articulated by a large cornice. The exterior walls are ornamented with niches, each of which holds a single statue, usually depicting a form of Shiva. The clear, regular, and wide spacing of the niches imparts a calm balance and formality to the lower portion of the temple, in marked contrast to the irregular, concave-convex rhythms of the northern style.

The superstructure of the Rajarajeshvara is a four-sided, hollow pyramid that rises for 13 stories. Each story is decorated with miniature shrines, window motifs, and robust dwarf figures who seem to be holding up the next story. Because these sculptural elements are not large in the overall scale of the superstructure, they appear well integrated into the surface and do not obscure the thrusting shape. This is quite different from the effect of the small

shikhara motifs on the superstructure of the Kandariya Mahadeva Temple (SEE FIG. 9–23). Notice also that in the earlier southern style, as embodied in the Dharmaraja Ratha (SEE FIG. 9–22), the shrines on the temple superstructure were much larger in proportion to the whole and thus each appeared to be nearly as prominent as the superstructure's overall shape.

Because the Rajarajeshvara superstructure is not obscured by its decorative motifs, it forcefully ascends skyward. At the top is an octagonal dome-shaped capstone similar to the one that crowned the earlier southern-style temple. This huge capstone is exactly the same size as the *garbhagriha* housed 13 stories directly below. It thus evokes the shrine a final time before the eye ascends to the point separating the worldly from the cosmic sphere above.

THE BHAKTI MOVEMENT IN ART

Throughout this period, two major religious movements were developing that affected Hindu practice and its art: the Tantric, or Esoteric, and the *bhakti*, or devotional. Although both movements evolved throughout India, the influence of Tantric sects appeared during this period primarily in the art of the north (see Chapter 23 for a discussion of their continued development), while the *bhakti* movements found artistic expression in the south as well as the north.

The *bhakti* devotional movement was based on ideas expressed in ancient texts, especially the *Bhagavad-Gita*. *Bhakti* revolves around the ideal relationship between humans and deities. According to *bhakti*, it is the gods who create *maya* (illusion), in which we are all trapped. They also reveal truth to those who truly love them and whose minds are open to them. Rather than focusing on ritual and the performance of *dharma* according to the Vedas, *bhakti* stresses an intimate, personal, and loving relation with the god, and complete devotion and surrender to the deity. Inspired and influenced by *bhakti*, Indian artists produced some of South Asia's most interesting works, among them the few remaining mural paintings and the famous bronze works of sculpture (see "Shiva Nataraja of the Chola Dynasty," page 314).

WALLPAINTING AT RAJARAJESHVARA TEMPLE. Rajaraja's building of the Rajarajeshvara was in part a reflection of the fervent Shiva *bhakti* movement which had reached its peak by that time. The corridors of the circumambulatory passages around the *garbhagriha* were originally adorned with wall paintings. Overpainted later, they were only recently rediscovered. One painting apparently depicts the ruler Rajaraja himself, not as a warrior or majestic king on his throne, but as a simple mendicant humbly standing behind his religious teacher (FIG. 9–26). With his white beard and dark

9-26 • RAJARAJA I AND HIS TEACHER
Detail of a wall painting in the Rajarajeshvara Temple to Shiva. Chola dynasty, c. 1010 CE.

skin, the aged teacher contrasts with the youthful, bronze-skinned king. The position of the two suggests that the king treats the saintly teacher, who in the devotee's or *bhakta*'s view is equated with god, with intimacy and respect. Both figures allude to their devotion to Shiva by holding a small flower as an offering, and both emulate Shiva in their appearance by wearing their hair in the "ascetic locks" of Shiva in his Great Yogi aspect.

The portrayal does not represent individuals so much as a contrast of types: the old and the youthful, the teacher and the devotee, the saint and the king—the highest religious and worldly models, respectively—united as followers of Shiva. Line is the essence of the painting. With strength and grace, the even, skillfully executed line defines the boldly simple forms and features. With less shading and fewer details, these figures are flattened, more linear versions of those in the earlier paintings at Ajanta (SEE FIG. 9–17). A cool, sedate calm infuses the monumental figures, but the power of line also invigorates them with a sense of strength and inner life.

The *bhakti* movement spread during the ensuing centuries into northern India. However, during this period a new religious culture penetrated the subcontinent: Turkic peoples, Persians, and Afghans had been crossing the northwest passes into India since the tenth century, bringing with them Islam and its artistic tradition. New religious forms eventually evolved from Islam's long and complex interaction with the peoples of the subcontinent, and so too arose uniquely Indian forms of Islamic art, adding yet another dimension to India's artistic heritage.

ART OF SOUTHEAST ASIA

Trade and cultural exchange, notably by the sea routes linking China and India, brought Buddhism, Hinduism, and other aspects of India's civilization to the various regions of Southeast Asia and the Asian archipelago. Although Theravada Buddhism (see "Buddhism," page 297) had the most lasting impact in the region, other trends in Buddhism, including Mahayana and esoteric (tantric) traditions, also played a role. Elements of Hinduism, including its epic literature, were also adopted.

THAILAND—PRAKHON CHAI STYLE. Even the earliest major flowering of Buddhist art in eighth- and ninth-century Southeast Asia was characterized by distinctly local interpretations of the inheritance from India. For example, a strikingly beautiful style of Buddhist sculpture in Thailand, one with distinct iconographic elements, has been identified based on the 1964 discovery of a hoard of images in an underground burial chamber in the vicinity of Prakhon Chai, Buriram Province, near the present-day border with Cambodia. Distinguished by exquisite craftsmanship and a charming naturalism, enhanced by inlaid materials for the eyes, a standing figure of the bodhisattva Maitreya (FIG. 9–27) exemplifies the lithe and youthful proportions typical of the Prakhon Chai style. The iconography departs from the princely interpretation of

9-27 • BUDDHA MAITREYA
From Buriram Province, Thailand. 8th century CE. Copper alloy with inlaid black glass eyes, 38″ (96.5 cm). Asia Society, New York.
Mr. and Mrs. John D. Rockefeller 3rd Collection, 1979.063

the Buddha, presenting instead ascetic elements—abbreviated clothing and a loose arrangement of long hair. The esoteric (tantric) associations of these features are further emphasized by the multiple forearms, an element that was highly developed in Hindu sculpture and which came to be common in Esoteric Buddhist art.

9-28 • BUDDHA SHAKYAMUNI
From Thailand. Mon Dvaravati period, 9th century CE. Sandstone.
Norton Simon Museum, Los Angeles.

THAILAND—DVARAVATI STYLE. The Dvaravati kingdom, of Mon people, flourished in central Thailand from at least the sixth to the eleventh century. This kingdom embraced Theravada Buddhism and produced some of the earliest Buddhist images in Southeast Asia, perhaps based on Gupta-period Indian models. During the later centuries, Dvaravati sculptors restated elements of the Gupta style (SEE FIG. 9–15), and introduced Mon characteristics into classical forms inherited from India (FIG. 9–28).

9-29 • PLAN OF BOROBUDUR

JAVA—BOROBUDUR. The most monumental of Buddhist sites in Southeast Asia is **BOROBUDUR** (FIGS. 9–29, 9–30) in central Java, an island of Indonesia. Built about 800 CE and rising more than 100 feet from ground level, this stepped pyramid of volcanic-stone blocks is surmounted by a large stupa, itself ringed by 72 smaller openwork stupas. Probably commissioned to celebrate the Buddhist merit of the Shailendra dynasty rulers, the monument expresses a complex range of Mahayana symbolism, incorporating earthly and cosmic realms. Jataka tales and scenes from the Buddha's life are elaborately narrated in the reliefs of the lower galleries (FIG. 9–31), and more than 500 sculptures of transcendental buddhas on the balustrades and upper terraces complete the monument, conceived as a *mandala* in three dimensions.

CAMBODIA—ANGKOR VAT. In Cambodia, Khmer kings ruled at Angkor for more than 400 years, from the ninth to the thirteenth century. Among the state temples, Buddhist as well as Hindu, they built **ANGKOR VAT** (FIG. 9–32), the crowning achievement of Khmer architecture. Angkor had already been the site of royal capitals of the Khmer, who had for centuries vested temporal as well as spiritual authority in their kings, long before King Suryavarman II (r. 1113–1150) began to build the royal complex known today as Angkor Vat. Dedicated to the worship of Vishnu, the vast array of structures is both a temple and a symbolic cosmic mountain. The complex incorporates a stepped pyramid with five towers set within four enclosures of increasing perimeter. Suryavarman's predecessors had associated themselves with Hindu and Buddhist deities at Angkor by building sacred structures. His

9-34 • PARINIRVANA
OF THE BUDDHA
Gal Vihara, near
Polonnaruwa, Sri Lanka.
11th–12th century CE. Stone.

construction pairs him with Vishnu to affirm his royal status as well as his ultimate destiny of union with the Hindu god. Low-relief sculptures illustrate scenes from the *Ramayana*, the *Mahabharata*, and other Hindu texts (FIG. 9–33), and also depict Suryavarman with his armies.

SRI LANKA.   Often considered a link to Southeast Asia, the island of Sri Lanka is so close to India's southeastern coast that Ashoka's son is said to have brought Buddhism there within his father's lifetime. Sri Lanka played a major role in the strengthening of Theravada traditions, especially by preserving scriptures and relics, and it became a focal point for the Theravada Buddhist world. Sri Lankan sculptors further refined Indian styles and iconography in colossal Buddhist sculptures. The rock-cut Parinirvana of the Buddha at Gal Vihara (FIG. 9–34) is one of three colossal Buddhas at the site. This serene and dignified image restates one of the early themes of Buddhist art, that of the Buddha's final transcendence, with a sophistication of modeling and proportion that updates and localizes the classical Buddhist tradition.

THINK ABOUT IT

9.1   Describe the typical form of Indian temples. Contrast the stupa and the temple directly, paying attention to specific building features, such as the superstructure.

9.2   Angkor Vat in Cambodia draws both religious and architectural influence from the Indian subcontinent. Explain what the Khmer architects in Cambodia took from India, with reference to specific religious architectural forms borrowed.

9.3   How does architecture in India and Southeast Asia express a view of the world, even the cosmos?

9.4   Select one architectural work from the chapter, and explain how either Buddhist or Hindu stories are told through its decoration.

9.5   What are some distinguishing features of representations of Buddha?

PRACTICE MORE: Compose answers to these questions, get flashcards for images and terms, and review chapter material with quizzes
www.myartslab.com

10-1 • SOLDIERS   From the mausoleum of Emperor Shihuangdi, Lintong, Shaanxi.
Qin dynasty, c. 210 BCE. Earthenware, life-size.

CHINESE AND
KOREAN ART BEFORE 1279

As long as anyone could remember, the huge mound in China's Shaanxi Province in northern China had been part of the landscape. No one dreamed that an astonishing treasure lay beneath the surface until one day in 1974 peasants digging a well accidentally brought to light the first hint of riches. When archaeologists began to excavate, they were stunned by what they found: a vast underground army of some 8,000 life-size terra-cotta soldiers with 100 life-size ceramic horses standing in military formation, facing east, supplied with weapons, and ready for battle (FIG. 10–1). For more than 2,000 years, while the tumultuous history of China unfolded overhead, they had guarded the tomb of Emperor Shihuangdi, the ruthless ruler who first united the states of China into an empire, the Qin.

In ongoing excavations at the site, additional bronze carriages and horses were found, further evidence of the technology and naturalism achieved by artisans during Qin Shihuangdi's reign. The tomb mound itself has not been excavated.

China has had a long-standing fascination with antiquity, but archaeology is a relatively young discipline there. Only since the 1920s have scholars methodically dug into the layers of history at thousands of sites across the country, yet so much has been unearthed that ancient Chinese history has been rewritten many times.

The archaeological record shows that Chinese civilization arose several millennia ago, and was distinctive for its early advances in ceramics and metalwork, as well as for the elaborate working of jade. Early use of the potter's wheel, mastery of reduction firing, and the early invention of high-fired stoneware and porcelain distinguish the technological advancement of Chinese ceramics. Highly imaginative bronze castings and proficient techniques of mold making characterize early Chinese metalworking. Early attainments in jade reflect a technological competence with rotary tools and abrasive techniques, and a passion for the subtleties of shape, proportion, and surface texture.

Archaeology has supplemented our understanding of historically appreciated Chinese art forms. These explored human relationships and heroic ideals, exemplifying Confucian values and teaching the standards of conduct that underlie social order. Later, China also came to embrace the Buddhist tradition from India. In princely representations of Buddhist divinities and in sublime and powerful, but often meditative, figures of the Buddha, China's artists presented the divine potential of the human condition. Perhaps the most distinguished Chinese tradition is the presentation of philosophical ideals through the theme of landscape. Paintings simply in black ink, depictions of mountains and water, became the ultimate artistic medium for expressing the vastness, abundance, and endurance of the universe.

Chinese civilization radiated its influence throughout east Asia. Chinese learning repeatedly stimulated the growth of culture in Korea, which in turn transmitted influence to Japan.

LEARN ABOUT IT

10.1 Examine the interaction of art and ritual in early periods of Chinese and Korean history.

10.2 Discuss the development of Confucian philosophy and its impact on the pictorial art of China.

10.3 Analyze the Daoist elements in early landscape motifs of China.

10.4 Assess the introduction and spread of Buddhism, and its adherents as patrons (including the court) in both China and Korea.

10.5 Discuss the development of naturalistic depiction and the achievement of verisimilitude in both landscapes and figures in the painting and sculpture of China before 1279.

HEAR MORE: Listen to an audio file of your chapter **www.myartslab.com**

THE MIDDLE KINGDOM

Among the cultures of the world, China is distinguished by its long, uninterrupted development, now traced back some 8,000 years. From Qin, pronounced "chin," comes our name for the country that the Chinese call the Middle Kingdom, the country in the center of the world. Present-day China occupies a large landmass in the center of Asia, covering an area slightly larger than the continental United States. Within its borders lives one-fifth of the human race.

The historical and cultural heart of China is the land watered by its three great rivers, the Yellow, the Yangzi, and the Xi (**MAP 10–1**). The Qinling Mountains divide Inner China into north and south, regions with strikingly different climates, cultures, and historical fates. In the south, the Yangzi River flows through lush green hills to the fertile plains of the delta. Along the southern coastline, rich with natural harbors, arose China's port cities, the focus of a vast maritime trading network. The Yellow River, nicknamed "China's Sorrow" because of its disastrous floods, winds through the north. The north country is a dry land of steppe and desert, hot in the summer and lashed by cold winds in the winter. Over its vast and vulnerable frontier have come the nomadic invaders that are a recurring theme in Chinese history, but caravans and emissaries from Central Asia, India, Persia, and, eventually, Europe also crossed this border.

10-2 • BOWL

From Banpo, near Xi'an, Shaanxi. Neolithic period, Yangshao culture, 5000–4000 BCE. Painted pottery, height 7″ (17.8 cm). Banpo Museum.

NEOLITHIC CULTURES

Early archaeological evidence had led scholars to believe that agriculture, the cornerstone technology of the Neolithic period, made its way to China from the ancient Near East. More recent findings, however, suggest that agriculture based on rice and millet arose independently in east Asia before 5000 BCE and that knowledge of Near Eastern grains followed some 2,000 years later. One of the clearest archaeological signs of Neolithic culture in China is evidence of the vigorous emergence of towns and cities. At Jiangzhai, near modern Xi'an, for example, the foundations of more than 100 dwellings have been discovered surrounding the remains of a community center, a cemetery, and a kiln. Dated to about 4000 BCE, the ruins point to the existence of a highly developed early society. Elsewhere in China, the foundations of the earliest known palace have been uncovered and dated to about 2000 BCE.

PAINTED POTTERY CULTURES

In China, as in other places, distinctive forms of Neolithic pottery identify different cultures. One of the most interesting objects thus far recovered is a shallow red bowl with a turned-out rim (**FIG. 10–2**). Found in the village of Banpo near the Yellow River, it was crafted sometime between 5000 and 4000 BCE. The bowl is an artifact of the Yangshao culture, one of the most important of the so-called Painted Pottery cultures of Neolithic China. Although the potter's wheel had not yet been developed, the bowl is perfectly round and its surfaces are highly polished, bearing witness to a distinctly advanced technology. The decorations are especially intriguing. The marks on the rim may be evidence of the beginnings of writing in China, which was fully developed by the time the first definitive examples appear during the second millennium BCE, in the later Bronze Age.

Inside the bowl, a pair of stylized fish suggests that fishing was an important activity for the villagers. The image between the two fish represents a human face with four more fish, one on each side. Although there is no certain interpretation of the image, it may be a depiction of an ancestral figure who could assure an abundant catch, for the worship of ancestors and nature spirits was a fundamental element of later Chinese beliefs.

LIANGZHU CULTURE

Banpo lies near the great bend in the Yellow River, in the area traditionally regarded as the cradle of Chinese civilization, but archaeological finds have revealed that Neolithic cultures arose over a far broader area. Recent excavations in sites more than 800 miles away, near Hangzhou Bay, in the southeastern coastal region, have turned up human and animal images—often masks or faces—more than 5,000 years old (**FIG. 10–3**). Large, round eyes, a flat nose, and a rectangular mouth protrude slightly from the background pattern of wirelike lines. Above the forehead, a second, smaller face grimaces from under a huge headdress. The upper face may be human, perhaps riding the animal figure below. The image is one of eight that were carved in low relief on the outside of a large jade **cong**, an object resembling a cylindrical tube encased in

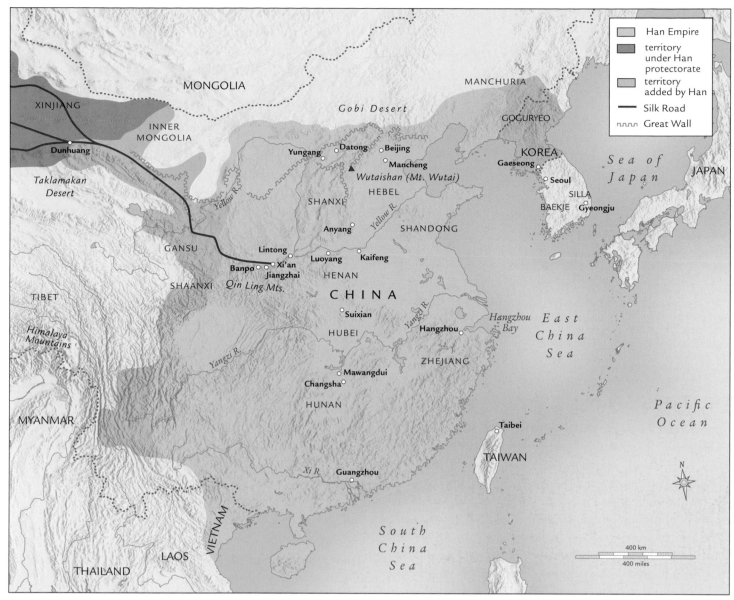

MAP 10-1 • CHINA AND KOREA

The map shows the borders of contemporary China and Korea. Bright-colored areas indicate the extent of China's Han dynasty (206 BCE–221 CE).

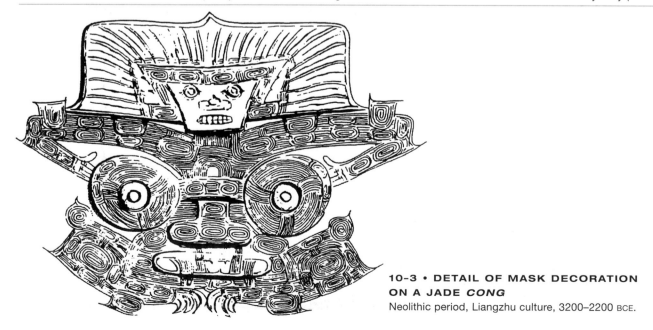

10-3 • DETAIL OF MASK DECORATION ON A JADE *CONG*

Neolithic period, Liangzhu culture, 3200–2200 BCE.

10-4 • *CONG*
Neolithic period, Liangzhu culture, 3200–2200 BCE. Jade, height 1⅞ × width 2⅝″ (5 × 6.6 cm). Shanghai Museum.

The *cong* is one of the most prevalent and mysterious of early Chinese jade shapes. Originating in the Neolithic period, it continued to play a prominent role in burials through the Shang and Zhou dynasties. Many experts believe the *cong* was connected with the practice of contacting the spirit world. They suggest that the circle symbolized heaven; the square, earth; and the hollow, the axis connecting these two realms.

a rectangular block. Another *cong* (FIG. 10–4) also from Liangzhu bears a beautiful finish and similar delineated mask motifs. These were found near the remains of persons buried with what appear to be sets of numerous jade objects.

The intricacy of the carving shows the technical sophistication of this jade-working culture, named the Liangzhu, which seems to have emerged around 3300 BCE. Jade, a stone cherished by the Chinese throughout their history, is extremely hard and is difficult to carve. Liangzhu artists must have used sand as an abrasive to slowly grind the stone down; modern artisans marvel at how they produced such fine work.

The meaning of the masklike image in FIGURE 10–3 is open to interpretation. Its combination of human and animal features seems to show how the ancient Chinese imagined supernatural beings, either deities or dead ancestors. Similar masks later formed the primary decorative motif of Bronze Age ritual objects. Still later, Chinese historians began referring to the ancient mask motif as **taotie**, but the motif's original meaning had already been lost. The jade carving here seems to be a forerunner of this most central and mysterious image.

BRONZE AGE CHINA

China entered its Bronze Age in the second millennium BCE. As with agriculture, scholars at first theorized that the technology had been imported from the Near East. Archaeological evidence now makes clear, however, that bronze casting using the **piece-mold casting** technique arose independently in China, where it attained an un-paralleled level of excellence (see "Piece-Mold Casting," opposite).

SHANG DYNASTY

Traditional Chinese histories tell of three Bronze Age dynasties: the Xia, the Shang, and the Zhou. Experts at one time tended to dismiss the Xia and Shang as legendary, but twentieth-century archaeological discoveries fully established the historical existence of the Shang (c. 1700–1100 BCE) and point strongly to the historical existence of the Xia as well.

Shang kings ruled from a succession of capitals in the Yellow River Valley, where archaeologists have found walled cities, palaces, and vast royal tombs. Their state was surrounded by numerous other states—some rivals, others clients—and their culture spread widely. Society seems to have been highly stratified, with a ruling group that had the bronze technology needed to make weapons. They maintained their authority in part by claiming power as intermediaries between the supernatural and human realms. The chief Shang deity, Shangdi, may have been a sort of "Great Ancestor." It is thought that nature and fertility spirits were also honored, and that regular sacrifices were thought necessary to keep the spirits of dead ancestors vital so that they might help the living.

Shang priests communicated with the supernatural world through oracle bones. An animal bone or piece of tortoiseshell was inscribed with a question and heated until it cracked, then the crack was interpreted as an answer. Oracle bones, many of which have been recovered and deciphered, contain the earliest known form of Chinese writing, a script fully recognizable as the ancestor of the system still in use today (see "Chinese Characters," page 331).

RITUAL BRONZES.   Shang tombs reveal a warrior culture of great splendor and violence. Many humans and animals were sacrificed to accompany the deceased. In one tomb, for example, chariots were found with the skeletons of their horses and drivers; in another, dozens of human skeletons lined the approaches to the central burial chamber. The tombs contain hundreds of jade, ivory, and lacquer objects, gold and silver ornaments, and bronze vessels. The enormous scale of Shang burials illustrates the great wealth of the civilization and the power of a ruling class able to consign such great quantities of treasure to the earth, and also suggests this culture's reverence for the dead.

Bronze vessels are the most admired and studied of Shang artifacts. Like oracle bones and jade objects, they were connected with ritual practices, serving as containers for offerings of food and wine. A basic repertoire of about 30 shapes evolved. Some shapes derive from earlier pottery forms, while others seem to reproduce wooden containers. Still others are highly sculptural and take the form of fantastic composite animals.

One functional shape, the **fang ding**, a rectangular vessel with four legs, was used for food offerings. Early examples (see "Piece-Mold Casting," oppposite) featured decoration of raised bosses and mask-like (*taotie*) motifs in horizontal registers on the sides and the legs. A late Shang example, one of hundreds of vesesels recovered from the royal tombs near the last of the Shang capitals, Yin

The early piece-mold technique for bronze casting is different from the lost-wax process developed in the ancient Mediterranean and Near East. Although we do not know the exact steps ancient Chinese artists followed, we can deduce the general procedure for casting a vessel.

First, a model of the bronze-to-be was made of clay and dried. Then, to create a mold, damp clay was pressed onto the model; after the clay mold dried, it was cut away in pieces, which were keyed for later reassembly and then fired. The original model itself was shaved down to serve as the core for the mold. After this, the pieces of the mold were reassembled around the core and held in place by bronze spacers, which locked the core in position and ensured an even casting space around the core. The reassembled mold was then covered with another layer of clay, and a sprue, or pouring duct, was cut into the clay to receive the molten metal. A riser duct may also have been cut to allow the hot gases to escape. Molten bronze was then poured into the mold. When the metal cooled, the mold was broken apart to reveal a bronze copy of the original clay model. Finely cast relief decoration could be worked into the model or carved into the sectional molds, or both. Finally, the vessel could be burnished—a long process that involved scouring the surface with increasingly fine abrasives.

The vessel shown here is a *fang ding*. A *ding* is a ceremonial cooking vessel used in Shang rituals and buried in Shang tombs. The Zhou people also made, used, and buried *ding* vessels.

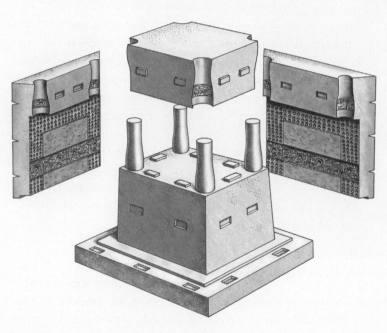

Sectional clay molds for casting bronze vessels. This sketch is based on a vessel in the Zhengzhou Institute of Cultural Relics and Archaeology.

(present-day Anyang), is extraordinary for its size. Weighing nearly 2,000 pounds, it is the largest Shang *ding* vessel thus far recovered. In typical Shang style, its surface is decorated with a complex array of images based on animal forms, including *taotie* masks, confronting horned animals (dragons?) and composite beaked animals (birds?). A ritual pouring vessel, called a *guang* (FIG. 10–5), shows a highly sculptural rendition of animal forms. The pouring spout and cover are modeled as the head and body of a tiger, while the rear portion of the vessel and cover is conceived as an owl. Overall geometric decoration combines with suggestive zoomorphic forms. Such images seem to be related to the hunting life of the Shang, but their deeper significance is unknown. Sometimes strange, sometimes fearsome, Shang creatures seem always to have a sense of mystery, evoking the Shang attitude toward the supernatural world.

ZHOU DYNASTY

Around 1100 BCE, the Shang were conquered by the Zhou from western China. During the Zhou dynasty (1100–221 BCE) a feudal society developed, with nobles related to the king ruling over numerous small states. (Zhou nobility are customarily ranked in English by such titles as duke and marquis.) The supreme deity became known as Tian, or Heaven, and the king ruled as the Son of Heaven. Later Chinese ruling dynasties continued to follow the belief that imperial rule emanated from a mandate from Heaven.

The first 300 years of this longest-lasting Chinese dynasty were generally stable and peaceful. In 771 BCE, however, the Zhou suffered defeat in the west at the hands of a nomadic tribe. Although they quickly established a new capital to the east, their authority had been crippled, and the later Eastern Zhou period was a troubled one. States grew increasingly independent, giving

10-5 • COVERED RITUAL WINE-POURING VESSEL (*GUANG*) WITH TIGER AND OWL DÉCOR

Shang dynasty, 13th century BCE. Cast bronze, height with cover 9¾" (25 cm), width including handle 12⅜" (31.5 cm). Arthur M. Sackler Museum, Harvard Art Museum, Cambridge, Massachusetts. Bequest of Grenville L. Winthrop 1943.52.103

the Zhou kings merely nominal allegiance. Smaller states were swallowed up by their larger neighbors. During the time historians call the Spring and Autumn period (722–481 BCE), 10 or 12 states, later reduced to seven, emerged as powers. During the ensuing Warring States period (481–221 BCE) intrigue, treachery, and increasingly ruthless warfare became routine.

Against this background of social turmoil, China's great philosophers arose—such thinkers as Confucius, Laozi, and Mozi. Traditional histories speak of China's "one hundred schools" of philosophy, indicating a shift of focus from the supernatural to the human world. Nevertheless, elaborate burials on an even larger scale than before reflected the continuation of traditional beliefs.

BRONZE BELLS. Ritual bronze objects continued to play an important role during the Zhou dynasty, and new forms developed. One of the most spectacular recent discoveries is a carillon of 65 bronze components, mostly bells arranged in a formation 25 feet long (FIG. 10–6), found in the tomb of Marquis Yi of the state of Zeng. Each bell is precisely calibrated to sound two tones—one when struck at the center, another when struck at a corner. The bells are arranged in scale patterns in a variety of registers, and several musicians would have moved around the carillon, striking the bells in the appointed order.

Music may well have played a part in rituals for communicating with the supernatural, for the *taotie* typically appears on the front and back of each bell. The image is now much more intricate and stylized, partly in response to the refinement available with the lost-wax casting process (see "Lost-Wax Casting," page 413), which had replaced the older piece-mold technique. On the coffin of the marquis are painted guardian warriors with half-human, half-animal attributes. The marquis, who died in 433 BCE, must have considered music important, for among the more than 15,000 objects recovered from his tomb were many musical instruments. Zeng was one of the smallest and shortest-lived states of the Eastern Zhou, but the contents of this tomb, in quantity and quality, attest to the high level of its culture.

Chinese Characters

Each word in Chinese is represented by its own unique symbol, called a character. Some characters originated as **pictographs**, images that mean what they depict. Writing reforms over the centuries have often disguised the resemblance, but if we place modern characters next to their ancestors, the picture comes back into focus:

	water	horse	moon	child	tree	mountain
Ancient	水	馬	月	子	木	山
Modern	水	馬	月	子	木	山

Other characters are **ideographs**, pictures that represent abstract concepts or ideas:

sun	+	moon	=	bright
日		月		明

woman	+	child	=	good
女		子		好

Most characters were formed by combining a radical, which gives the field of meaning, with a phonetic, which originally hinted at pronunciation. For example, words that have to do with water have the character for "water" 水 abbreviated to three strokes 氵 as their radical. Thus "to bathe," 沐 pronounced *mu*, consists of the water radical and the phonetic 木 , which by itself means "tree" and is also pronounced *mu*. Here are other "water" characters. Notice that the connection to water is not always literal.

river	sea	weep	pure, clear	extinguish, destroy
河	海	泣	清	滅

These phonetic borrowings took place centuries ago. Many words have shifted in pronunciation, and for this and other reasons there is no way to tell how a character is pronounced or what it means just by looking at it. While at first this may seem like a disadvantage, in the case of Chinese it is advantageous. Spoken Chinese has many dialects. Some are so far apart in sound as to be virtually different languages. But while speakers of different dialects cannot understand each other, they can still communicate through writing, for no matter how they say a word, they write it with the same character. Writing has thus played an important role in maintaining the unity of Chinese civilization through the centuries.

10-6 • SET OF BELLS
From the tomb of Marquis Yi of Zeng, Suixian, Hubei. Zhou dynasty, 433 BCE. Bronze, with bronze and timber frame, frame height 9′ (2.74 m), length 25′ (7.62 m). Hubei Provincial Museum, Wuhan.

THE CHINESE EMPIRE: QIN DYNASTY

Toward the middle of the third century BCE, the state of Qin launched military campaigns that led to its triumph over the other states by 221 BCE. For the first time in its history, China was united under a single ruler. This first emperor of Qin, Shihuangdi, a man of exceptional ability, power, and ruthlessness, was fearful of both assassination and rebellion. Throughout his life, he sought ways to attain immortality. Even before uniting China, he began his own mausoleum at Lintong, in Shaanxi Province. This project continued throughout his life and after his death, until rebellion abruptly ended the dynasty in 206 BCE. Since that time, the mound over the mausoleum has always been visible, but not until an accidental discovery in 1974 was its army of terra-cotta soldiers and horses even imagined (SEE FIG. 10–1). Modeled from clay and then fired, the figures claim a prominent place in the great tradition of Chinese ceramic art. Individualized faces and meticulously rendered uniforms and armor demonstrate the sculptors' skill. Literary sources suggest that the tomb itself, which has not yet been opened, reproduces the world as it was known to the Qin, with stars overhead and rivers and mountains below. Thus did the tomb's architects try literally to ensure that the underworld—the world of souls and spirits—would match the human world.

Qin rule was harsh and repressive. Laws were based on a totalitarian philosophy called legalism, and all other philosophies were banned, their scholars executed, and their books burned. Yet the Qin also established the mechanisms of centralized bureaucracy that molded China both politically and culturally into a single entity. Under the Qin, the country was divided into provinces and prefectures, the writing system and coinage were standardized, roads were built to link different parts of the country with the capital, and battlements on the northern frontier were connected to form the Great Wall. To the present day, China's rulers have followed the administrative framework first laid down by the Qin.

HAN DYNASTY

The commander who overthrew the Qin became the next emperor and founded the Han dynasty (206 BCE–220 CE). During this period the Chinese enjoyed peace, prosperity, and stability. Borders were extended and secured, and Chinese control over strategic stretches of Central Asia led to the opening of the Silk Road, a land route that linked China by trade all the way to Rome. One of the precious goods traded, along with spices, was silk, which had been cultivated and woven in China since at least the third millennium BCE. From as early as the third century BCE, Chinese silk cloth was treasured in Greece and Rome (for more on this topic, see "The Silk Road during the Tang Period," page 342).

PAINTED BANNER FROM CHANGSHA. The early Han dynasty marks the twilight of China's so-called mythocentric age, when people believed in a close relationship between the human and supernatural

10-7 • PAINTED BANNER
From the tomb of the Marquess of Dai, Mawangdui, Changsha, Hunan. Han dynasty, c. 160 BCE. Colors on silk, height 6′8½″ (2.05 m). Hunan Provincial Museum.

worlds. The most elaborate and most intact painting that survives from this time is a T-shaped silk banner, which summarizes this early worldview (FIG. 10–7). Found in the tomb of a noblewoman on the outskirts of present-day Changsha, the banner dates from the second century BCE and is painted with scenes representing three levels of the universe: heaven, earth, and underworld. The pictorial motifs include a portrait of the deceased.

The heavenly realm is shown at the top, in the crossbar of the T. In the upper-right corner is the sun, inhabited by a mythical crow; in the upper left, a mythical toad stands on a crescent moon. Between them is a primordial deity shown as a man with a long serpent's tail—a Han image of the Great Ancestor. Dragons and other celestial creatures swarm below.

A gate guarded by two seated figures stands where the horizontal of heaven meets the banner's long, vertical stem. Two intertwined dragons loop through a circular jade piece known as a **bi**, itself usually a symbol of heaven, dividing this vertical segment into two areas. The portion above the *bi* represents the earthly realm. Here, the deceased woman and three attendants stand on a platform while two kneeling figures offer gifts. The portion beneath the *bi* represents the underworld. Silk draperies and a stone chime hanging from the *bi* form a canopy for the platform below. Like the bronze bells we saw earlier, stone chimes were ceremonial instruments dating from Zhou times. On the platform, ritual bronze vessels contain food and wine for the deceased, just as they did in Shang tombs. The squat, muscular man holding up the platform stands in turn on a pair of fish whose bodies form another *bi*. The fish and the other strange creatures in this section are inhabitants of the underworld.

PHILOSOPHY AND ART

The Han dynasty marked the beginning of a new age. During this dynasty, the philosophical ideals of Daoism and Confucianism, formulated during the troubled times of the Eastern Zhou, became central to Chinese thought. Their influence since then has been continuous and fundamental.

DAOISM AND NATURE.   Daoism emphasizes the close relationship between humans and nature. It is concerned with bringing the individual life into harmony with the Dao, or the Way, of the universe (see "Daoism," page 334). For some a secular, philosophical path, Daoism on a popular level developed into an organized religion, absorbing many traditional folk practices and the search for immortality.

Immortality was as intriguing to Han rulers as it had been to the first emperor of Qin. Daoist adepts experimented with diet, physical exercise, and other techniques in the belief that immortal life could be achieved on earth. Popular Daoist legend told of the Land of Immortals in the Eastern Sea, depicted on a bronze **INCENSE BURNER** from the tomb of Prince Liu Sheng, who died in 113 BCE **(FIG. 10–8)**. Around the bowl, gold inlay outlines the stylized waves of the sea. Above them rises the mountainous island, busy with birds, animals, and the immortals themselves, all cast in bronze with highlights of inlaid gold. Technically, this exquisite piece represents the ultimate development of the long tradition of bronze casting in China.

10-8 • INCENSE BURNER
From the tomb of Prince Liu Sheng, Mancheng, Hebei. Han dynasty, 113 BCE. Bronze with gold inlay, height 10½″ (26 cm). Hebei Provincial Museum, Shijiazhuang.

CONFUCIANISM AND THE STATE.   In contrast to the metaphysical focus of Daoism, Confucianism is concerned with the human world, and its goal is the attainment of equity. To this end, it proposes a system of ethics based on reverence for ancestors and the correct relationships among people. Beginning with self-discipline in the individual, Confucianism teaches how to rectify relationships within the family, and then, in ever-widening circles, with friends and others, all the way up to the level of the emperor and the state (see "Confucius and Confucianism," page 337).

Emphasis on social order and respect for authority made Confucianism especially attractive to Han rulers, who were eager to distance themselves from the disastrous legalism of the Qin. The Han emperor Wudi (r. 141–87 BCE) made Confucianism the official imperial philosophy, and it remained the state ideology of China for more than 2,000 years, until the end of imperial rule in the twentieth century. Once institutionalized, Confucianism took on so many rituals that it too eventually assumed the form and force of a religion. Han philosophers contributed to this process by

Daoism

Daoism is an outlook on life that brings together many ancient ideas regarding humankind and the universe. Its primary text, a slim volume called the *Daodejing* (*The Way and Its Power*), is ascribed to the Chinese philosopher Laozi, who is said to have been a contemporary of Confucius (551–479 BCE). Later, a philosopher named Zhuangzi (369–286 BCE) took up many of the same ideas in a book that is known simply by his name: *Zhuangzi*. Together the two texts formed a body of ideas that crystallized into a school of thought during the Han period.

A *dao* is a way or path. The Dao is the Ultimate Way, the Way of the universe. The Way cannot be named or described, but it can be hinted at. It is like water. Nothing is more flexible and yielding, yet water can wear down the hardest stone. Water flows downward, seeking the lowest ground. Similarly, a Daoist sage seeks a quiet life, humble and hidden, unconcerned with worldly success. The Way is great precisely because it is small. The Way may be nothing, yet nothing turns out to be essential.

To recover the Way, we must unlearn. We must return to a state of nature. To follow the Way, we must practice *wu wei* (nondoing). "Strive for nonstriving," advises the *Daodejing*.

All our attempts at asserting ourselves, at making things happen, are like swimming against a current and are thus ultimately futile, even harmful. If we let the current carry us, however, we will travel far. Similarly, a life that follows the Way will be a life of pure effectiveness, accomplishing much with little effort.

It is often said that the Chinese are Confucians in public and Daoists in private, and the two approaches do seem to balance each other. Confucianism is a rational political philosophy that emphasizes propriety, deference, duty, and self-discipline. Daoism is an intuitive philosophy that emphasizes individualism, nonconformity, and a return to nature. If a Confucian education molded scholars outwardly into responsible, ethical officials, Daoism provided some breathing room for the artist and poet inside.

infusing Confucianism with traditional Chinese cosmology. They emphasized the Zhou idea, taken up by Confucius, that the emperor ruled by the mandate of Heaven. Heaven itself was reconceived more abstractly as the moral force underlying the universe. Thus the moral system of Confucian society became a reflection of universal order (see "Confucius and Confucianism," page 337).

Confucian subjects turn up frequently in Han art. Among the most famous examples are the reliefs from the Wu family shrines built in 151 CE in Jiaxiang. Carved and engraved in low relief on stone slabs, the scenes were meant to teach Confucian themes such as respect for the emperor, filial piety, and wifely devotion. Daoist motifs also appear, as do figures from traditional myths and legends. Such mixed iconography is characteristic of Han art (see "A Closer Look," opposite).

When compared with the Han-dynasty banner (SEE FIG. 10–7), this late Han relief clearly shows the change that took place in the Chinese worldview in the span of 300 years. The banner places equal emphasis on heaven, earth, and the underworld; human beings are dwarfed by a great swarming of supernatural creatures and divine beings. In the relief in the Wu shrine, the focus is clearly on the human realm. The composition conveys the importance of the emperor as the holder of the

10-9 • TOMB MODEL OF A HOUSE
Eastern Han dynasty, 1st–mid 2nd century CE. Painted earthenware, 52 × 33½ × 27″ (132.1 × 85.1 × 68.6 cm). The Nelson-Atkins Museum of Art, Kansas City, Missouri. Purchase, Nelson Trust (33-521)

Rubbing of a Stone Relief ›

Detail from a rubbing of a stone relief in the Wu family shrine (Wuliangci). Jiaxiang, Shandong. Han dynasty, 151 CE. 27½ × 66½" (70 × 169 cm).

Birds and small figures, possibly alluding to mythical creatures or immortals.

Women—and an empress?—receiving visitors on the upper floor.

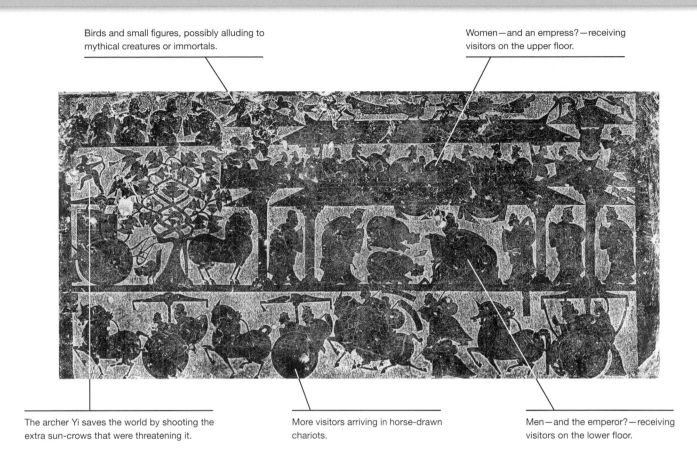

The archer Yi saves the world by shooting the extra sun-crows that were threatening it.

More visitors arriving in horse-drawn chariots.

Men—and the emperor?—receiving visitors on the lower floor.

mandate of Heaven and illustrates fundamental Confucian themes of social order and decorum.

ARCHITECTURE

Contemporary literary sources are eloquent on the wonders of the Han capital. Unfortunately, nothing of Han architecture remains except ceramic models. One model of a house found in a tomb, where it was provided for the dead to use in the afterlife, represents a Han dwelling (**FIG. 10–9**). Its four stories are crowned with a watchtower and face a small walled courtyard. Pigs and oxen probably occupied the ground floor, while the family lived in the upper stories.

Aside from the multi-level construction, the most interesting feature of the house is the **bracketing** system (architectural elements projecting from the wall) that supports the rather broad eaves of its tiled roofs. Bracketing became a standard element of east Asian

architecture, not only in private homes but more typically in palaces and temples (SEE, FOR EXAMPLE, FIG. 10–15). Another interesting aspect of the model is the elaborate painting on the exterior walls. Much of the painting is purely decorative, though some of it illustrates structural features such as posts and lintels. Still other images evoke the world outdoors, for example, the trees flanking the gateway with crows perched in their branches. Literary sources describe the walls of Han palaces as decorated with paint and lacquer, and also inlaid with precious metals and stones.

SIX DYNASTIES

With the fall of the Han in 220 CE, China splintered into three warring kingdoms. In 280 CE the empire was briefly reunited, but invasions by nomadic peoples from central Asia, a source of disruption throughout Chinese history, soon forced the court to flee south. For the next three centuries, northern and southern China developed separately. In the north, 16 kingdoms carved out by invaders rose and fell before giving way to a succession of largely foreign dynasties. Warfare was commonplace. Tens of thousands of Chinese fled south, where six short-lived dynasties succeeded each other in an age of almost constant turmoil broadly known as the Six Dynasties period or the period of the Southern and Northern dynasties (265–589 CE).

In such chaos, the Confucian system lost influence. In the south especially, many intellectuals—the creators and custodians of China's high culture—turned to Daoism, which contained a strong escapist element. Educated to serve the government, they increasingly withdrew from public life. They wandered the landscape, drank, wrote poems, practiced calligraphy, and expressed their disdain for the world through willfully eccentric behavior.

The rarefied intellectual escape route of Daoism was available only to the educated elite. Far more people sought answers in the magic and superstitions of Daoism in its religious form. Though weak and disorganized, the southern courts continued to patronize traditional Chinese culture, and Confucianism remained the official doctrine. Yet ultimately it was a newly arrived religion, Buddhism, that flourished in the troubled China of the Six Dynasties.

PAINTING

Although few paintings survive from the Six Dynasties, abundant descriptions in literary sources make clear that the period was an important one for painting. Landscape, later a major theme of Chinese art, first appeared as a subject during this era. For Daoists, wandering through China's countryside was a source of spiritual refreshment. Painters and scholars of the Six Dynasties found that wandering in the mind's eye through a painted landscape could serve the same purpose. This new emphasis on the spiritual value

of painting contrasted with the Confucian view, which had emphasized art's moral and didactic uses.

Reflections on the tradition of painting also inspired the first works on theory and aesthetics. Some of the earliest and most succinct formulations of the ideals of Chinese painting are the six principles set out by the scholar Xie He (fl. c. 500–535 CE). The first two principles in particular offer valuable insight into the spirit in which China's painters worked.

The first principle announces that "spirit consonance" imbues a painting with "life's movement." This "spirit" is the Daoist *qi*, the breath that animates all creation, the energy that flows through all things. When a painting has *qi*, it will be alive with inner essence, not merely outward resemblance. Artists must cultivate their own spirit so that this universal energy flows through them and infuses their work. The second principle recognizes that brushstrokes are the "bones" of a picture, its primary structural element. Traditional Chinese judge a painting above all by the quality of its brushwork. Each brushstroke is a vehicle of expression; it is through the vitality of a painter's brushwork that "spirit consonance" makes itself felt. We can sense this attitude already in the rapid, confident brushstrokes that outline the figures of the Han banner (SEE FIG. 10–7) and again in the more controlled, rhythmical lines of one of the most important works associated with this period, a painted scroll known as *Admonitions of the Imperial Instructress to Court Ladies*. Attributed to the painter Gu Kaizhi (344–407 CE), it alternates illustrations and text to relate seven Confucian stories of wifely virtue from Chinese history.

The first illustration depicts the courage of Lady Feng (FIG. 10–10). An escaped circus bear rushes toward her husband, a Han emperor, who is filled with fear. Behind his throne, two female servants have turned to run away. Before him, two male attendants, themselves on the verge of panic, try to fend off the bear with

10–10 • After Gu Kaizhi DETAIL OF ADMONITIONS OF THE IMPERIAL INSTRUCTRESS TO COURT LADIES
Six Dynasties period. Handscroll, ink and colors on silk, 9¾″ × 11′6″ (24.8 × 348.2 cm). British Museum, London.

Confucius and Confucianism

Confucius was born in 551 BCE in the state of Lu, roughly present-day Shandong Province, into a declining aristocratic family. While still in his teens he set his heart on becoming a scholar; by his early twenties he had begun to teach.

By this time, wars for supremacy had begun among the various states of China, and the traditional social fabric seemed to be breaking down. Looking back to the early Zhou dynasty as a sort of golden age, Confucius thought about how a just and harmonious society could again emerge. For many years he sought a ruler who would put his ideas into effect, but to no avail. Frustrated, he spent his final years teaching. After his death in 479 BCE, his conversations with his students were collected by his disciples and their followers into a book known in English as the *Analects*, which is the only record of his words.

At the heart of Confucian thought is the concept of *ren* (human-heartedness). *Ren* emphasizes morality and empathy as the basic standards for all human interaction. The virtue of *ren* is most fully realized in the Confucian ideal of the *junzi* (gentleman). Originally indicating noble birth, the term was redefined to mean one who through education and self-cultivation had become a superior person, right-thinking and right-acting in all situations. A *junzi* is the opposite of a petty or small-minded person. His characteristics include moderation, integrity, self-control, loyalty, reciprocity, and altruism. His primary concern is justice.

Together with human-heartedness and justice, Confucius emphasized *li* (etiquette). *Li* includes everyday manners as well as ritual, ceremony, and protocol—the formalities of all social conduct and interaction. Such forms, Confucius felt, choreographed life so that an entire society moved in harmony. *Ren* and *li* operate in the realm of the Five Constant Relationships that define Confucian society: parent and child, husband and wife, elder sibling and younger sibling, elder friend and younger friend, ruler and subject. Deference to age is clearly built into this view, as is the deference to authority that made Confucianism attractive to emperors. Yet responsibilities flow the other way as well: The duty of a ruler is to earn the loyalty of subjects, of a husband to earn the respect of his wife, of age to guide youth wisely.

During the early years of the People's Republic of China, and especially during the Great Proletarian Cultural Revolution (1966–1976), Confucius and Confucian thought were denigrated. Recently, however, Confucian temples in Beijing and elsewhere have been restored. Notably, the Chinese government has used the philosopher's name officially in establishing hundreds of Confucius Institutes in more than 80 countries, to promote the learning of the Chinese language abroad.

---

spears. Only Lady Feng is calm as she rushes forward to place herself between the beast and the emperor.

The figures are drawn with a brush in a thin, even-width line, and a few outlined areas are filled with color. Facial features, especially those of the men, are quite well depicted. Movement and emotion are shown through conventions such as the scarves flowing from Lady Feng's dress, indicating that she is rushing forward, and the upturned strings on both sides of the emperor's head, suggesting his fear. There is no hint of a setting; instead, the artist relies on careful placement of the figures to create a sense of depth.

The painting is on silk, which was typically woven in bands about 12 inches wide and up to 20 or 30 feet long. Early Chinese painters thus developed the format used here, the **handscroll**—a long, narrow, horizontal composition, compact enough to be held in the hand when rolled up. Handscrolls are intimate works, meant to be viewed by only two or three people at a time. They were not displayed completely unrolled as we commonly see them today in museums. Rather, viewers would open a scroll and savor it slowly from right to left, displaying only an arm's length at a time.

CALLIGRAPHY

The emphasis on the expressive quality and structural importance of brushstrokes finds its purest embodiment in calligraphy. The same brushes are used for both painting and calligraphy, and a relationship between them was recognized as early as Han times. In his teachings, Confucius had extolled the importance of the pursuit of knowledge and the arts. Among the visual arts, painting was felt to reflect moral concerns, while calligraphy was believed to reveal the character of the writer.

Calligraphy is regarded as one of the highest forms of expression in China. For more than 2,000 years, China's **literati**, Confucian scholars and literary men who also served the government as officials, have enjoyed being connoisseurs and practitioners of this abstract art. During the fourth century CE, calligraphy came to full maturity. The most important practitioner of the day was Wang Xizhi (c. 307–365), whose works have served as models of excellence for all subsequent generations. The example here comes from a letter, now somewhat damaged and mounted as part of an album, known as *Feng Ju* (**FIG. 10–11**).

Feng Ju is an example of "walking" or semicursive style, which is neither too formal nor too free but is done in a relaxed, easy-going manner. Brushstrokes vary in width and length, creating rhythmic vitality. Individual characters remain distinct, yet within each character the strokes are run together and simplified as the brush moves from one to the other without lifting off the page. The effect is fluid and graceful, yet still strong and dynamic. The

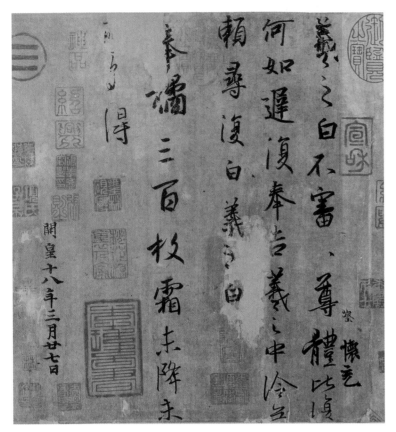

10-11 • Wang Xizhi PORTION OF A LETTER FROM THE FENG JU ALBUM

Six Dynasties period, mid-4th century CE. Ink on paper, 9¾ × 18½″ (24.7 × 46.8 cm). National Palace Museum, Taibei, Taiwan, Republic of China.

The stamped characters that appear on Chinese artworks are **seals**—personal emblems. The use of seals dates from the Zhou dynasty, and to this day seals traditionally employ the archaic characters, known appropriately as "seal script," of the Zhou or Qin. Cut in stone, a seal may state a formal, given name, or it may state any of the numerous personal names that China's painters and writers adopted throughout their lives. A treasured work of art often bears not only the seal of its maker, but also those of collectors and admirers through the centuries. In the Chinese view, these do not disfigure the work but add another layer of interest. This sample of Wang Xizhi's calligraphy, for example, bears the seals of two Song-dynasty emperors, a Song official, a famous collector of the sixteenth century, and two Qing-dynasty emperors of the eighteenth and nineteenth centuries.

walking style as developed by Wang Xizhi came to be officially accepted and learned along with other script styles.

BUDDHIST ART AND ARCHITECTURE

Buddhism originated in India during the fifth century BCE (see Chapter 9), then gradually spread north into central Asia. With the opening of the Silk Road during the Han dynasty, its influence reached China. To the Chinese of the Six Dynasties, beset by constant warfare and social devastation, Buddhism offered consolation in life and the promise of salvation after death. The faith spread throughout the country to all social levels, first in the north, where many of the invaders promoted it as the official religion, then

slightly later in the south, where it found its first great patron in the emperor Liang Wu Di (r. 502–549 CE). Thousands of temples and monasteries were built, and many people became monks and nuns.

Almost nothing remains in China of the Buddhist architecture of the Six Dynasties, but we can see what it must have looked like in the Japanese temple Horyuji (SEE FIG. 11–4), which was based on Chinese models of this period. The slender forms and linear grace of Horyuji might be compared to the figures in Gu Kaizhi's handscroll (SEE FIG. 10–10), and they indicate the delicate, almost weightless style cultivated in southern China.

ROCK-CUT CAVES OF THE SILK ROAD. The most impressive works of Buddhist art surviving from the Six Dynasties are the hundreds of northern rock-cut caves along the trade routes between Xinjiang in central Asia and the Yellow River Valley. Both the caves and the sculptures that fill them were carved from the solid rock of the cliffs. Small caves high above the ground were retreats for monks and pilgrims, while larger caves at the base of the cliffs were wayside shrines and temples.

The caves at Yungang, in Shanxi Province in central China, contain many examples of the earliest phase of Buddhist sculpture in China, including the monumental seated Buddha in Cave 20 (FIG. 10–12). The figure was carved in the latter part of the fifth century by the imperial decree of a ruler of the Northern Wei dynasty (386–534 CE), the longest-lived and most stable of the northern kingdoms. Most Wei rulers were avid patrons of Buddhism, and under their rule the religion made its greatest advances in the north.

The front part of the cave has crumbled away, and the 45-foot statue, now exposed to the open air, is clearly visible from a distance. The elongated ears, protuberance on the head (*ushnisha*), and monk's robe are traditional attributes of the Buddha. The masklike face, full torso, massive shoulders, and shallow, stylized drapery indicate strong central Asian influence. The overall effect of this colossus is remote and austere, less human than the more sensuous expression of the early Buddhist traditions in India.

SUI AND TANG DYNASTIES

In 581 CE, a general from the last of the northern dynasties replaced a child emperor and established a dynasty of his own, the Sui. Defeating all opposition, he molded China into a centralized empire as it had been in Han times. The short-lived Sui dynasty fell in 618, but, in reunifying the empire, paved the way for one of the greatest dynasties in Chinese history: the Tang (618–907). Even today many Chinese living abroad still call themselves "Tang people." To them, Tang implies that part of the Chinese character that is strong and vigorous (especially in military power), noble and idealistic, but also realistic and pragmatic.

10-12 • SEATED BUDDHA, CAVE 20, YUNGANG
Datong, Shanxi. Northern Wei dynasty, c. 460. Stone, height 45′ (13.7 m).

BUDDHIST ART AND ARCHITECTURE

The new Sui emperor was a devout Buddhist, and his reunification of China coincided with a fusion of the several styles of Buddhist sculpture that had developed. This new style is seen in a bronze altar to Amitabha Buddha **(FIG. 10–13)**, one of the many Buddhas of Mahayana Buddhism. Amitabha dwelled in the Western Pure Land, a paradise into which his faithful followers were promised rebirth. With its comparatively simple message of salvation, the Pure Land sect eventually became the most popular form of Buddhism in China and one of the most popular in Japan (see Chapter 11).

The altar depicts Amitabha in his paradise, seated on a lotus throne beneath a canopy of trees. Each leaf cluster is set with jewels. Seven celestial figures sit on the topmost clusters, and ropes of "pearls" hang from the tree trunks. Behind Amitabha's head is a halo of flames. To his left, the bodhisattva Guanyin holds a pomegranate; to his right, another bodhisattva clasps his hands in prayer. Behind are four disciples who first preached the teachings of the Buddha. On the lower level, an incense burner is flanked by

10-13 • ALTAR TO AMITABHA BUDDHA
Sui dynasty, 593. Bronze, height 30⅛″ (76.5 cm). Museum of Fine Arts, Boston. Gift of Mrs. W. Scott Fitz (22.407) and Gift of Edward Holmes Jackson in memory of his mother, Mrs. W. Scott Fitz (47.1407–1412)

10-14 • THE WESTERN PARADISE OF AMITABHA BUDDHA
Detail of a wall painting in Cave 217, Dunhuang, Gansu. Tang dynasty, c. 750. 10′2″ × 16′ (3.1 × 4.86 m).

seated lions and two smaller bodhisattvas. Focusing on Amitabha's benign expression and filled with objects symbolizing his power, the altar combines the sensuality of Indian styles, the schematic abstraction of central Asian art, and the Chinese emphasis on linear grace and rhythm into a harmonious new style.

Buddhism reached its greatest development in China during the subsequent Tang Dynasty, which for nearly three centuries ruled China and controlled much of Central Asia. From emperors and empresses to common peasants, virtually the entire country adopted the Buddhist faith. A Tang vision of the most popular sect, Pure Land, was expressed in a wall painting from a cave in Dunhuang **(FIG. 10–14)**. A major stop along the Silk Road, Dunhuang has nearly 500 caves carved out of its sandy cliffs, all filled with painted clay sculpture and decorated with wall paintings from floor to ceiling. The site was worked on continuously from the fourth to the fourteenth century, a period of almost 1,000 years. In the detail shown here, Amitabha Buddha is seated in the center, surrounded by four bodhisattvas, who serve as his messengers to the

world. Two other groups of bodhisattvas are clustered at the right and left. In the foreground, musicians and dancers create a heavenly atmosphere. In the background, great halls and towers rise. The artist has imagined the Western Paradise in terms of the grandeur of Tang palaces. Indeed, the lavish entertainment depicted could just as easily be taking place at the imperial court. This worldly vision of paradise, recorded with great attention to naturalism in the architectural setting, gives us our best visualization of the splendor of Tang civilization at a time when Chang'an (present-day Xi'an) was probably the greatest city in the world.

The early Tang emperors proclaimed a policy of religious tolerance, but during the ninth century a conservative reaction set in. Confucianism was reasserted and Buddhism was briefly persecuted as a "foreign" religion. Thousands of temples, shrines, and monasteries were destroyed and innumerable bronze statues melted down. Nevertheless, several Buddhist structures survive from the Tang dynasty. One of them, the Nanchan Temple, is the earliest important example of surviving Chinese architecture.

NANCHAN TEMPLE. Of the few structures earlier than 1400 CE to have survived, the Nanchan Temple is the most significant, for it shows characteristics of both temples and palaces of the Tang Dynasty **(FIG. 10–15)**. Located on Mount Wutai (Wutaishan) in the eastern part of Shanxi Province, this small hall was constructed in 782. The tiled roof, seen earlier in the Han tomb model (SEE FIG. 10–9), has taken on a curved silhouette. Quite subtle here, this curve became increasingly pronounced in later centuries. The very broad overhanging eaves are supported by a correspondingly elaborate bracketing system.

Also typical is the bay system of construction, in which a cubic unit of space, a bay, is formed by four posts and their lintels. The bay functioned in Chinese architecture as a **module**, a basic unit of construction. To create larger structures, an architect multiplied the number of bays. Thus the Nanchan Temple—modest in scope with three bays—gives an idea of the vast, multi-storied palaces of the Tang depicted in such paintings as FIGURE 10–14.

GREAT WILD GOOSE PAGODA. Another important monument of Tang architecture is the Great Wild Goose Pagoda at the Ci'en Temple in Chang'an, the Tang capital **(FIG. 10–16)**. The temple was constructed in 645 for the famous monk Xuanzang (600–664) on his return from a 16-year pilgrimage to India. At the Ci'en Temple, Xuanzang taught and translated the materials he had brought back with him.

The **pagoda**, a typical east Asian Buddhist structure, originated in the Indian Buddhist stupa, the elaborate burial mound that housed relics of the Buddha (see "Pagodas," page 345). In India the stupa had developed a multi-storied form in the Gandhara region under the Kushan dynasty (c. 50–250 CE). In China this form blended with a traditional Han watchtower to produce the pagoda. Built entirely in masonry, the Great Wild Goose Pagoda nevertheless imitates the wooden architecture of the time. The walls are decorated in low relief to resemble bays,

and bracket systems are reproduced under the projecting roofs of each story. Although modified and repaired in later times (its seven stories were originally five, and a new finial has been added), the pagoda still preserves the essence of Tang architecture in its simplicity, symmetry, proportions, and grace.

10-16 • GREAT WILD GOOSE PAGODA AT CI'EN TEMPLE, CHANG'AN
Shanxi. Tang dynasty, first erected 645; rebuilt mid 8th century CE.

The Silk Road during the Tang Period

Under a series of ambitious and forceful Tang emperors, Chinese control once again extended over central Asia. Goods, ideas, and influence flowed along the Silk Road. In the South China Sea, Arab and Persian ships carried on a lively trade with coastal cities. Chinese cultural influence in east Asia was so important that Japan and Korea sent thousands of students to study Chinese civilization.

Cosmopolitan and tolerant, Tang China was confident and curious about the world. Many foreigners came to the splendid new capital Chang'an (present-day Xi'an), and they are often depicted in the art of the period. A ceramic statue of a camel carrying a troupe of musicians reflects the Tang fascination with the "exotic" Turkic cultures of central Asia. The three bearded musicians (one with his back to us) are central Asian, while the two smooth-shaven ones are Han Chinese. Bactrian, or two-humped, camels, themselves exotic central Asian "visitors," were beasts of burden in the caravans that traversed the Silk Road. The stringed lute (which the Chinese called the *pipa*) came from central Asia to become a lasting part of Chinese music.

Stylistically, the statue reveals a new interest in naturalism, an important trend in both painting and sculpture. Compared with the rigid, staring ceramic soldiers of the first emperor of Qin, this Tang band is alive with gesture and expression. The majestic camel throws its head back; the musicians are vividly captured in mid-performance. Ceramic figurines such as this, produced by the thousands for Tang tombs, offer glimpses into the gorgeous variety of Tang life. The statue's three-color glaze technique was a specialty of Tang ceramicists. The glazes—usually chosen from a restricted palette of amber-yellow, green, and blue— were splashed freely and allowed to run over the surface during firing to convey a feeling of spontaneity. The technique is emblematic

of Tang culture itself in its robust, colorful, and cosmopolitan expressiveness.

The Silk Road had first flourished in the second century CE. A 5,000-mile network of caravan routes from the Han capital (near present-day Luoyang, Henan, on the Yellow River) to Rome, it brought Chinese luxury goods to Western markets.

The journey began at the Jade Gate (Yumen) at the westernmost end of the Great Wall, where Chinese merchants turned their goods over to central Asian traders. Goods would change hands many more times before reaching the Mediterranean. Caravans headed first for the nearby desert oasis of Dunhuang. Here northern and southern

routes diverged to skirt the vast Taklamakan Desert. At Khotan, in western China, farther west than the area shown in MAP 10–1, travelers on the southern route could turn off toward a mountain pass into Kashmir, in northern India. Or they could continue on, meeting up with the northern route at Kashgar, on the western border of the Taklamakan, before proceeding over the Pamir Mountains into present-day Afghanistan. There, travelers could turn off into present-day Pakistan and India, or travel west through present-day Uzbekistan, Iran, and Iraq, arriving finally at Antioch, in Syria, on the coast of the Mediterranean. From there, land and sea routes led to Rome.

CAMEL CARRYING A GROUP OF MUSICIANS
From a tomb near Xi'an, Shanxi. Tang dynasty, c. mid 8th century CE. Earthenware with three-color glazes, height 26⅛" (66.5 cm). National Museum, Beijing.

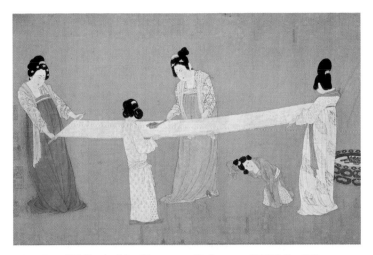

10-17 • Attributed to Emperor Huizong DETAIL OF LADIES PREPARING NEWLY WOVEN SILK
Copy after a lost Tang dynasty painting by Zhang Xuan. Northern Song dynasty, early 12th century CE. Handscroll, ink and colors on silk, 14½ × 57½″ (36 × 145.3 cm). Museum of Fine Arts, Boston. Chinese and Japanese Special Fund (12.886)

Confucius said of himself, "I merely transmit, I do not create; I love and revere the ancients." In this spirit, Chinese painters regularly copied paintings of earlier masters. Painters made copies both to absorb the lessons of their great predecessors and to perpetuate the achievements of the past. In later centuries, they took up the practice of regularly executing a work "in the manner of" some particularly revered ancient master. This was at once an act of homage, a declaration of artistic allegiance, and a way of reinforcing a personal connection with the past.

FIGURE PAINTING

Later artists looking back on their heritage recognized the Tang dynasty as China's great age of figure painting. Unfortunately, very few scroll paintings that can be definitely identified as Tang still exist. We can get some idea of the character of Tang figure painting from the wall paintings of Dunhuang (SEE FIG. 10–14). Another way to savor the particular flavor of Tang painting is to look at copies made by later, Song-dynasty artists. An outstanding example can be seen in *Ladies Preparing Newly Woven Silk*, attributed to Huizong (r. 1101–1126 CE), the last emperor of the Northern Song dynasty **(FIG. 10–17)**. A long handscroll, it depicts the activities of court women as they weave and iron silk. An inscription on the scroll informs us that the painting is a copy of a famous work by Zhang Xuan, an eighth-century painter known for his depictions of women at the Tang court. The original no longer exists, so we cannot know how faithful the copy is. Still, its refined lines and bright colors seem to share the grace and dignity of Tang sculpture and architecture. Two horses and riders **(FIG. 10–18)**, a man and a woman, made for use as tomb furnishings, reveal more of the robust naturalism and exuberance achieved during the Tang period. Accurate in proportion and lively in demeanor, the figures are not glazed (as is the tomb figure in "The Silk Road during the Tang Period," opposite) but are "cold-painted" using pigments after firing to render details of costume and facial features. The pair are indicative of the lively participation of women as well as men in sport and riding.

10–18 • TWO EQUESTRIAN FIGURES
Tang dynasty, first half 8th century CE. Molded, reddish-buff earthenware with cold-painted pigments over white ground, height (male figure) 14½″ (37 cm). Arthur M. Sackler Museum, Harvard Art Museum, Cambridge, Massachusetts. Gift of Anthony M. Solomon (2003.207.1-2)

The figures, one male, one female, each have pointed boots and are mounted on a standing, saddled and bridled horse; their hands are positioned to hold the reins. The male figure wears a tall, elaborately embellished hat, and the female figure has her hair arranged in a topknot.

SONG DYNASTY

A brief period of disintegration followed the fall of the Tang before China was again united, this time under the Song dynasty (960–1279), which established a new capital at Bianjing (present-day Kaifeng), near the Yellow River. In contrast to the outgoing confidence of the Tang, the mood during the Song was more introspective, a reflection of China's weakened military situation. In 1126 the Jurchen tribes of Manchuria invaded China, sacked the capital, and took possession of much of the northern part of the country. Song forces withdrew south and established a new capital at Hangzhou. From this point on, the dynasty is known as the Southern Song (1127–1179), with the first portion called in retrospect the Northern Song (960–1126).

Although China's territory had diminished, its wealth had increased because of advances in agriculture, commerce, and technology begun under the Tang. Patronage was plentiful, and the arts flourished.

SEATED GUANYIN BODHISATTVA.   In spite of changing political fortunes in the eleventh and twelfth centuries, artists continued to create splendid works. No hint of political disruption or religious questioning intrudes on the sublime grace and beauty of this seated Guanyin bodhisattva (FIG. 10–19). Bodhisattvas, beings who are close to enlightenment but who voluntarily remain on earth to help others achieve enlightenment, are represented as young princes wearing royal garments and jewelry, their finery indicative of their worldly but virtuous lives. Guanyin is the Bodhisattva of Infinite Compassion, who appears in many guises, in this case as the Water and Moon Guanyin. He sits on rocks by the sea, in the position known as royal ease. His right arm rests on his raised and

10-19 • SEATED GUANYIN BODHISATTVA
Liao dynasty, 10th–12th century CE. Wood with paint and gold, 95 × 65″ (241.3 × 165.1 cm). The Nelson-Atkins Museum of Art, Kansas City, Missouri. Purchase, Nelson Trust (34–10)

Pagodas developed from Indian stupas as Buddhism spread northeast along the Silk Road. Stupas merged with the watchtowers of Han-dynasty China in multi-storied stone or wood structures with projecting tiled roofs. This transformation culminated in wooden pagodas with upward-curving roofs supported by elaborate bracketing in China, Korea, and Japan. Buddhist pagodas retain the *axis mundi* masts of stupas. Like their south Asian prototypes, early east Asian pagodas were symbolic rather than enclosing structures. Later examples often provided access to the ground floor and sometimes to upper levels.

early stupa
India, 2nd century BCE

later stupa
Central Asia,
5th–6th century CE

watchtower
China, Han dynasty,
c. 206 BCE–220 CE

stone pagoda
northwestern China,
c. 5th century CE

wooden pagoda
Japan, 7th century CE

SEE MORE: View a simulation about pagodas www.myartslab.com

bent right knee and his left arm and foot hang down, the foot touching a lotus blossom. The wooden figure was carved in the eleventh or twelfth century in a territory on the northern border of Song China, a region ruled by the Liao dynasty (907–1125); the painting and gilding were restored in the sixteenth century.

Song culture is noted for its refined taste and intellectual grandeur. Where the Tang had reveled in exoticism, eagerly absorbing influences from Persia, India, and Central Asia, Song culture was more self-consciously Chinese. Philosophy experienced its most creative era since the "one hundred schools" of the Zhou. Song scholarship was brilliant, especially in history, and its poetry is noted for its depth. Perhaps the finest expressions of the Song are in art, especially painting and ceramics.

PHILOSOPHY: NEO-CONFUCIANISM

Song philosophers continued the process, begun during the Tang, of restoring Confucianism to dominance. In strengthening Confucian thought, they drew on Daoist and especially Buddhist ideas, even as they openly rejected Buddhism itself as foreign. These innovations provided Confucianism with a metaphysical aspect it had previously lacked, allowing it to propose a more satisfying, all-embracing explanation of the universe. This new synthesis of China's three main paths of thought is called Neo-Confucianism.

Neo-Confucianism teaches that the universe consists of two interacting forces known as *li* (principle or idea) and *qi* (matter). All pine trees, for example, consist of an underlying *li* we might call "Pine Tree Idea" brought into the material world through *qi*. All the *li* of the universe, including humans, are but aspects of an eternal first principle known as the Great Ultimate (*taiji*), which is completely present in every object. Our task as human beings is to rid our *qi* of impurities through education and self-cultivation so that our *li* may realize its oneness with the Great Ultimate. This lifelong process resembles the striving to attain buddhahood, and if we persist in our attempts, one day we will be enlightened—the term itself comes directly from Buddhism.

NORTHERN SONG PAINTING

The Neo-Confucian ideas found visual expression in art, especially in landscape, which became the most highly esteemed subject for painting. Northern Song artists studied nature closely to master its many appearances—the way each species of tree grew, the distinctive character of each rock formation, the changes of the seasons, the myriad birds, blossoms, and insects. This passion for realistic detail was the artist's form of self-cultivation: Mastering outward forms showed an understanding of the principles behind them.

Yet despite the convincing accumulation of detail, the paintings

10-20 • Fan Kuan TRAVELERS AMONG MOUNTAINS AND STREAMS
Northern Song dynasty, early 11th century CE. Hanging scroll, ink and colors on silk, height 6′9½″ (2.06 m). National Palace Museum, Taibei, Taiwan, Republic of China.

do not record a specific site. The artist's goal was to paint the eternal essence of "mountain-ness," for example, not to reproduce the appearance of a particular mountain. Painting a landscape required an artist to orchestrate his cumulative understanding of *li* in all its aspects—mountains and rocks, streams and waterfalls, trees and grasses, clouds and mist. A landscape painting thus expressed

the desire for the spiritual communion with nature that was the key to enlightenment. As the tradition progressed, landscape also became a vehicle for conveying human emotions, even for speaking indirectly of one's own deepest feelings.

In the earliest times, art reflected the mythocentric worldview of the ancient Chinese. Later, as religion came to dominate people's lives, the focus of art shifted, and religious images and human actions became important subjects. Subsequently, during the Song dynasty, artists developed landscape as the chief means of expression, preferring to avoid direct depiction of the human condition and to show ideals in a symbolic manner. The major form of Chinese artistic expression thus moved from the mythical, through the religious and ethical, and finally to the philosophical and aesthetic.

FAN KUAN.   One of the first great masters of Song landscape was the eleventh-century painter Fan Kuan (active c. 990–1030 CE), whose surviving major work, **TRAVELERS AMONG MOUNTAINS AND STREAMS**, is regarded as one of the great monuments of Chinese art **(FIG. 10–20)**. The work is physically large—almost 7 feet high—but the sense of monumentality also radiates from the composition itself, which makes its impression even when much reduced.

The composition unfolds in three stages, comparable to three acts of a drama. At the bottom a large, low-lying group of rocks, taking up about one-eighth of the picture surface, establishes the extreme foreground. The rest of the landscape pushes back from this point. In anticipating the shape and substance of the mountains to come, the rocks introduce the main theme of the work, much as the first act of a drama introduces the principal characters. In the middle ground, travelers and their mules are coming from the right. Their size confirms our human scale—how small we are, how vast is nature. This middle ground takes up twice as much picture surface as the foreground, and, like the second act of a play, shows variation and development. Instead of a solid mass, the rocks here are separated into two groups by a waterfall that is spanned by a bridge. In the hills to the right, the rooftops of a temple stand out above the trees.

Mist veils the transition to the background, with the result that the mountain looms suddenly. This background area, almost twice as large as the foreground and middle ground combined, is the climactic third act of the drama. As our eyes begin their ascent, the mountain solidifies. Its ponderous weight increases as it billows upward, finally bursting into the sprays of energetic brushstrokes that describe the scrubby growth on top. To the right, a slender waterfall plummets, not to balance the powerful upward thrust of the mountain but simply to enhance it by contrast. The whole painting, then, conveys the feeling of climbing a high mountain, leaving the human world behind to come face to face with the Great Ultimate in a spiritual communion.

All the elements are depicted with precise detail and in proper scale. Jagged brushstrokes describe the contours of rocks and trees and express their rugged character. Layers of short, staccato strokes

10–21 • Xu Daoning SECTION OF FISHING IN A MOUNTAIN STREAM
Northern Song dynasty, mid 11th century CE. Handscroll, ink on silk, 19″ × 6′10″ (48.9 cm × 2.09 m).
The Nelson-Atkins Museum of Art, Kansas City, Missouri. Purchase, Nelson Trust (33–1559)

(translated as "raindrop texture" from the Chinese) accurately mimic the texture of the rock surface. Spatial recession from foreground through middle ground to background is logically and convincingly handled, if not quite continuous.

Although it contains realistic details, the landscape represents no specific place. In its forms, the artist expresses the ideal forms behind appearances; in the rational, ordered composition, he expresses the intelligence of the universe. The arrangement of the mountains, with the central peak flanked by lesser peaks on each side, seems to reflect both the ancient Confucian notion of social hierarchy, with the emperor flanked by his ministers, and the Buddhist motif of the Buddha with bodhisattvas at his side. The landscape, a view of nature uncorrupted by human habitation, expresses a kind of Daoist ideal. Thus we find the three strains of Chinese thought united, much as they are in Neo-Confucianism itself.

The ability of Chinese landscape painters to take us out of ourselves and to let us wander freely through their sites is closely linked to the avoidance of perspective as it is understood in the West. Fifteenth-century European painters, searching for fidelity to appearances, developed a scientific system for recording exactly the view that could be seen from a single, fixed vantage point. The goal of Chinese painting is precisely to avoid such limits and show a totality beyond what we are normally given to see. If the ideal for centuries of Western painters was to render what can be seen from a fixed viewpoint, that of Chinese artists was to reveal nature through a distant, all-seeing, and mobile viewpoint.

XU DAONING.   The sense of shifting perspective is clearest in the handscroll, where our vantage point changes constantly as we move through the painting. One of the finest handscrolls to survive from the Northern Song is **FISHING IN A MOUNTAIN STREAM (FIG. 10–21)**, a painting executed in the middle of the eleventh century by Xu Daoning (c. 970–c. 1052). Starting from a thatched hut in the right foreground, we follow a path that leads to a broad, open view of a deep vista dissolving into distant mists and mountain peaks. (Remember that viewers observed only a small section of the scroll at a time. To mimic this effect, use two pieces of paper to frame a small viewing area, then move them slowly leftward.) Crossing over

a small footbridge, we are brought back to the foreground with the beginning of a central group of high mountains that show extraordinary shapes. Again our path winds back along the bank, and we have a spectacular view of the highest peaks from another small footbridge the artist has placed for us. At the far side of the bridge, we find ourselves looking up into a deep valley, where a stream lures our eyes far into the distance. We can imagine ourselves resting for a moment in the small pavilion halfway up the valley on the right. Or perhaps we may spend some time with the fishers in their boats as the valley gives way to a second, smaller group of mountains, serving both as an echo of the spectacular central group and as a transition to the painting's finale, a broad, open vista. As we cross the bridge here, we meet travelers coming toward us who will have our experience in reverse. Gazing out into the distance and reflecting on our journey, we again feel that sense of communion with nature that is the goal of Chinese artistic expression.

Such handscrolls have no counterpart in the Western visual arts and are often compared instead to the tradition of Western music, especially symphonic compositions. Both are generated from opening motifs that are developed and varied, both are revealed over time, and in both our sense of the overall structure relies on memory, for we do not see the scroll or hear the composition all at once.

ZHANG ZEDUAN.   The Northern Song fascination with precision extended to details within landscape. The emperor Huizong, whose copy of *Ladies Preparing Newly Woven Silk* was seen in FIGURE 10–17, gathered around himself a group of court painters who shared his passion for quiet, exquisitely detailed, delicately colored paintings of birds and flowers. Other painters specialized in domestic and wild animals, still others in palaces and buildings. One of the most spectacular products of this passion for observation is **SPRING FESTIVAL ON THE RIVER**, a long handscroll painted in the late eleventh or early twelfth century by Zhang Zeduan, an artist connected to the court **(FIG. 10–22)**. Beyond its considerable visual delights, the painting is also a valuable record of daily life in the Song capital.

The painting depicts a festival day when local inhabitants and visitors from the countryside thronged the streets. One high

10-22 • Zhang Zeduan SECTION OF SPRING FESTIVAL ON THE RIVER
Northern Song dynasty, late 11th–early 12th century CE. Handscroll, ink and colors on silk, 9½″ ×
7′4″ (24.8 × 2.28 m). The Palace Museum, Beijing.

point is the scene reproduced here, which takes place at the
Rainbow Bridge. The large boat to the right is probably bringing
goods from the southern part of China up the Grand Canal that
ran through the city at that time. The sailors are preparing to pass
beneath the bridge by lowering the sail and taking down the
mast. Excited figures on ship and shore gesture wildly, shouting
orders and advice, while a noisy crowd gathers at the bridge
railing to watch. Stalls on the bridge are selling food and other
merchandise; wine shops and eating places line the banks of the
canal. Everyone is on the move. Some people are busy carrying
goods, some are shopping, some are simply enjoying themselves.
Each figure is splendidly animated and full of purpose; the
depiction of buildings and boats is highly detailed, almost
encyclopedic.

Little is known about the painter Zhang Zeduan other than
that he was a member of the scholar-official class, the highly
educated elite of imperial China. His painting demonstrates skill in
the fine-line architectural drawing called *jiehua* ("ruled-line")
painting. Interestingly, some of Zhang Zeduan's peers were already

beginning to cultivate quite a different attitude toward painting as
a form of artistic expression, one that placed overt display of
technical skill at the lowest end of the scale of values. This
emerging scholarly aesthetic, developed by China's literati, later
came to dominate Chinese thinking about art.

SOUTHERN SONG PAINTING AND CERAMICS

Landscape painting took a very different course after the fall of the
north to the Jurchen in 1127, and the removal of the court to its
new capital in the south, Hangzhou.

XIA GUI. A new sensibility is reflected in the extant portion of
TWELVE VIEWS OF LANDSCAPE (FIG. 10–23) by Xia Gui (fl. c.
1195–1235), a member of the newly established Academy of
Painters. In general, academy members continued to favor such
subjects as birds and flowers in the highly refined, elegantly colored
court style patronized earlier by Huizong (SEE FIG. 10–17). Xia
Gui, however, was interested in landscape and cultivated his own
style. Only the last four of the 12 views that originally made up

10-23 • Xia Gui SECTION OF TWELVE VIEWS OF LANDSCAPE
Southern Song dynasty, early 13th century CE. Handscroll, ink on silk, height 11″ (28 cm); length of extant portion 7′7½″
(2.31 m). The Nelson-Atkins Museum of Art, Kansas City, Missouri. Purchase, Nelson Trust (32-159/2)

this long handscroll have survived, but they are enough to illustrate the unique quality of his approach.

In contrast to the majestic, austere landscapes of the Northern Song painters, Xia Gui presents an intimate and lyrical view of nature. Subtly modulated, perfectly controlled ink washes evoke a landscape veiled in mist, while a few deft brushstrokes suffice to indicate the details showing through the mist—the grasses growing by the bank, the fishers at their work, the trees laden with moisture, the two bent-backed figures carrying their heavy loads along the path that skirts the hill. Simplified forms, stark contrasts of light and dark, asymmetrical composition, and great expanses of blank space suggest a fleeting world that can be captured only in glimpses. The intangible has more presence than the tangible. By limiting himself to a few essential details, the painter evokes a deep feeling for what lies beyond.

This development in Song painting from the rational and intellectual to the emotional and intuitive, from the tangible to the intangible, had a parallel in philosophy. During the late twelfth century a new school of Neo-Confucianism called School of the Mind insisted that self-cultivation could be achieved through contemplation, which might lead to sudden enlightenment. The idea of sudden enlightenment may have come from Chan Buddhism, better known in the West by its Japanese name, Zen. Chan Buddhists rejected formal paths to enlightenment such as scripture, knowledge, and ritual, in favor of meditation and techniques designed to "short-circuit" the rational mind. Xia Gui's painting seems also to suggest this intuitive approach.

The subtle and sophisticated paintings of the Song were created for a highly cultivated audience who were equally discerning in other arts such as ceramics. Building on the considerable accomplishments of the Tang, Song potters achieved a technical and aesthetic perfection that has made their wares models of excellence throughout the world. Like their painter contemporaries, Song potters turned away from the exuberance of Tang styles to create more quietly beautiful pieces.

GUAN WARE.   Among the most prized of the many types of Song ceramics is Guan ware, made mainly for imperial use **(FIG. 10–24)**. The everted lip, high neck, and rounded body of this simple vase show a strong sense of harmony. Enhanced by a

10-24 • GUAN WARE VASE
Southern Song dynasty, 13th century CE. Gray stoneware with crackled grayish-blue glaze, height 6⅝″ (16.8 cm). Percival David Foundation of Chinese Art, British Museum, London.

SEE MORE: View a video about the process of ceramic making **www.myartslab.com**

lustrous grayish-blue glaze, the form flows without break from base to lip. The piece has an introspective quality as eloquent as the blank spaces in Xia Gui's painting. The aesthetic of the Song is most evident in the crackle pattern on the glazed surface. The crackle technique was probably discovered accidentally, but came to be used deliberately in some of the most refined Song wares. In the play of irregular, spontaneous crackles over a perfectly regular, perfectly planned form we can sense the same spirit that hovers behind the self-effacing virtuosity and freely intuitive insights of Xia Gui's landscape.

In 1279 the Southern Song dynasty fell to the conquering forces of the Mongol leader Kublai Khan (1215–1294). China was subsumed into the vast Mongol Empire. Mongol rulers founded the Yuan dynasty (1279–1368), setting up their capital in the northeast in what is now Beijing. Yet the cultural center of China remained in the south, in the cities that rose to prominence during the Song, especially Hangzhou. This separation of political and cultural centers, coupled with a lasting resentment toward "barbarian" rule, created the climate for later developments in the arts.

THE ARTS OF KOREA

Set between China and Japan, Korea occupies a peninsula in northeast Asia. Inhabited for millennia, the peninsula gave rise to a distinctively Korean culture during the Three Kingdoms period.

THE THREE KINGDOMS PERIOD

Traditionally dated 57 BCE to 668 CE, the Three Kingdoms period saw the establishment of three independent nation-states: Silla in the southeast, Baekje in the southwest, and Goguryeo in the north. Large tomb mounds built during the fifth and sixth centuries are enduring monuments of this period.

A GOLD HEADDRESS. The most spectacular items recovered from these tombs are trappings of royal authority (FIG. 10–25). Made expressly for burial, this elaborate crown was assembled from cut pieces of thin gold sheet, held together by gold wire. Spangles of gold embellish the crown, as do comma-shaped ornaments of green and white jadeite—a form of jade mineralogically distinct from the nephrite prized by the early Chinese. The tall, branching forms rising from the crown's periphery resemble trees and antlers. Within the crown is a conical cap woven of narrow strips of sheet gold and ornamented with appendages that suggest wings or feathers.

HIGH-FIRED CERAMICS. The tombs have also yielded ceramics in abundance. Most are containers for offerings of food placed in the tomb to nourish the spirit of the deceased. These items generally are of unglazed **stoneware**, a high-fired ceramic ware that is impervious to liquids, even without glaze.

The most imposing ceramic shapes are the tall stands that were used to support round-bottomed jars (FIG. 10–26). Such stands typically have a long, cylindrical shaft set on a bulbous base. Cut into the moist clay before firing, their openwork apertures lighten what otherwise would be rather ponderous forms. Although few examples of Three Kingdoms ceramics exhibit surface ornamentation, other than an occasional combed wave pattern or an incised configuration of circles and **chevrons** (v-shapes), here snakes inch their way up the shaft of the stand.

10-25 • CROWN
Korea. Three Kingdoms period, Silla kingdom, probably 6th century CE. From the Gold Crown Tomb, Gyeongju, North Gyeongsang Province. Gold with jadeite ornaments, height 17½" (44.5 cm). National Museum of Korea, Seoul, Republic of Korea.

10-26 • CEREMONIAL STAND WITH SNAKE, ABSTRACT, AND OPENWORK DECORATION
Korean. Three Kingdoms period, Silla kingdom, 5th–6th century CE. Gray stoneware with combed, stamped, applied, and openwork decoration and with traces of natural ash glaze, height 23⅛″ (58.7 cm). Reportedly recovered in Andong, North Gyeongsang Province. Arthur M. Sackler Museum, Harvard University, Cambridge, Massachusetts. Partial gift of Maria C. Henderson and partial purchase through the Ernest B. and Helen Pratt Dane Fund for the Acquisition of Oriental Art (1991.501)

A BODHISATTVA SEATED IN MEDITATION. Buddhism was introduced into the Goguryeo kingdom from China in 372 CE and into Baekje by 384. Although it probably reached Silla in the second half of the fifth century, Buddhism gained recognition as the official religion of the Silla state only in 527.

At first, Buddhist art in Korea was a mere imitation of Chinese art. However, by the late sixth century, Korean sculptors had created a style of their own, as illustrated by a magnificent gilt bronze image of a bodhisattva (probably the bodhisattva Maitreya) seated in meditation that likely dates to the early seventh century (**FIG. 10–27**). Although the pose links it to Chinese sculpture of the late sixth century, the slender body, elliptical face, elegant drapery folds, and trilobed crown distinguish it as Korean.

Buddhism was introduced to Japan from Korea—from the Baekje kingdom, according to literary accounts. In fact, historical sources indicate that numerous Korean sculptors were active in

10-27 • BODHISATTVA SEATED IN MEDITATION
Korean. Three Kingdoms period, probably Silla kingdom, early 7th century CE. Gilt bronze, height 35⅞″ (91 cm). National Museum of Korea, Seoul, Republic of Korea (formerly in the collection of the Toksu Palace Museum of Fine Arts, Seoul).

Japan in the sixth and seventh centuries; several early masterpieces of Buddhist art in Japan show pronounced Korean influence (SEE FIG. 11–6).

main hall **(FIG. 10–28)**. Seated on a lotus pedestal, the image represents the historical Buddha Shakyamuni at the moment of his enlightenment, as indicated by his earth-touching gesture, or *bhumisparsha mudra*. The full, taut forms, diaphanous drapery, and anatomical details of his chest relate this image to eighth-century Chinese sculptures. Exquisitely carved low-relief images of bodhisattvas and lesser deities grace the walls of the antechamber, vestibule, and main hall.

GORYEO DYNASTY

Established in 918, the Goryeo dynasty eliminated the last vestiges of Unified Silla rule in 935; it would continue until 1392, ruling from its capital at Gaeseong—to the northwest of present-day Seoul and now in North Korea. A period of courtly refinement, the Goryeo dynasty is best known for its celadon-glazed ceramics.

CELADON-GLAZED CERAMICS. The term **celadon** refers to a high-fired, transparent glaze of pale bluish-green hue, typically applied over a pale gray stoneware body. Chinese potters invented celadon glazes

10-28 • SEATED SHAKYAMUNI BUDDHA
Seokguram Grotto, near Gyeongju, North Gyeongsang Province, Korea. Unified Silla period, c. 751 CE. Granite, height of Buddha 11′2½″ (342 cm).

The Buddha's hands are in the *bhumisparsha mudra*, the earth-touching gesture symbolizing his enlightenment.

THE UNIFIED SILLA PERIOD

In 660, the Silla kingdom conquered Baekje, and, in 668, through an alliance with Tang-dynasty China, it vanquished Goguryeo, uniting the peninsula under the rule of the Unified Silla dynasty, which lasted until 935. Buddhism prospered under Unified Silla, and many large, important temples were erected in and around Gyeongju, the Silla capital.

SEOKGURAM. The greatest monument of the Unified Silla period is Seokguram, an artificial cave-temple constructed under royal patronage atop Mount Toham, near Gyeongju. The temple is modeled after Chinese cave-temples of the fifth, sixth, and seventh centuries, which were in turn inspired by the Buddhist cave-temples of India.

Built in the mid eighth century of cut blocks of granite, Seokguram consists of a small rectangular antechamber joined by a narrow vestibule to a circular main hall with a domed ceiling. More than 11 feet in height, a huge seated Buddha dominates the

10-29 • MAEBYEONG BOTTLE WITH DECORATION OF BAMBOO AND BLOSSOMING PLUM TREE
Korea. Goryeo dynasty, late 12th–early 13th century CE. Inlaid celadon ware: light gray stoneware with decoration inlaid with black and white slips under celadon glaze, height 13¼″ (33.7 cm). Tokyo National Museum, Tokyo, Japan. (TG-2171)

10-30 • SEATED WILLOW-BRANCH GWANSE'EUM BOSAL (THE BODHISATTVA AVALOKITESHVARA)
Korea. Goryeo dynasty, late 14th century CE. Hanging scroll, ink, colors, and gold pigment on silk, height 62½" (159.6 cm). Arthur M. Sackler Museum, Harvard University, Cambridge, Massachusetts. Bequest of Grenville L. Winthrop (1943.57.12)

techniques of decoration. Most notable among their inventions was inlaid decoration, in which black and white slips, or finely ground clays, were inlaid into the intaglio lines of decorative elements incised or stamped in the body, creating underglaze designs in contrasting colors. The bottle in **FIGURE 10–29** displays three different pictorial scenes inlaid in black and white slips. The scene featured here depicts a clump of bamboo growing at the edge of a lake, the stalks intertwined with the branches of a blossoming plum tree (which flowers in late winter, before donning its leaves). Geese swim in the lake and butterflies flutter above, linking the several scenes around the bottle. Called *maebyeong* ("plum bottle"), such broad-shouldered vessels were used as storage jars for wine, vinegar, and other liquids. A small, bell-shaped cover originally capped the bottle, protecting its contents and complementing its curves.

BUDDHIST PAINTING. Buddhism, the state religion of Goryeo, enjoyed royal patronage; many temples were thus able to commission the very finest architects, sculptors, and painters. The most sumptuous Buddhist works produced during the Goryeo period were paintings. Wrought in ink and colors on silk, the fourteenth-century hanging scroll illustrated in **FIGURE 10–30** depicts Gwanse'eum Bosal (whom the Chinese called Guanyin), the bodhisattva of compassion. The flesh tones used for the bodhisattva's face and hands, along with the rich colors and gold pigment used for the deity's clothing, reflect the luxurious taste of the period. Numerous paintings of this type were exported to Japan, where they influenced the course of Buddhist painting.

and had initiated the continuous production of celadon-glazed wares as early as the first century CE. Korean potters began to experiment with such glazes in the eighth and ninth centuries; their earliest celadons reflect the strong imprint of Chinese ware. Soon, the finest Goryeo celadons rivaled the best Chinese court ceramics. These wares were used by people of various socioeconomic classes during the Goryeo dynasty, with the finest examples going to the palace, nobles, or the powerful Buddhist clergy.

Prized for their classic simplicity, Korean celadons of the eleventh century often have little decoration, while those of the twelfth century frequently sport incised, carved, or molded decoration, thus generally mimicking the style and ornamentation of contemporaneous Chinese ceramics. By the mid twelfth century, Korean potters began to explore new styles and

THINK ABOUT IT

10.1 Examine the *guang* (fig. 10–5) and consider how its iconography may have related to a ritual-oriented culture in Bronze Age China.

10.2 Summarize the main tenets of Confucianism. Then select a work from the chapter that gives visual form to Confucian philosophy and explain how it does so.

10.3 Select one of the Song-era Chinese landscape paintings included in the chapter and explain how it may embody Daoist ideals.

10.4 Compare and contrast the Chinese seated Guanyin bodhisattva (FIG. 10–19) and the Korean bodhisattva seated in meditation (FIG. 10–27). Define the meaning of bodhisattva, and examine how the artists gave visual expression to the deity's attributes.

10.5 Based on examples illustrated in the chapter, identify parallel developments in painting and sculpture from the Han through the Song dynasty.

PRACTICE MORE: Compose answers to these questions, get flashcards for images and terms, and review chapter material with quizzes
www.myartslab.com

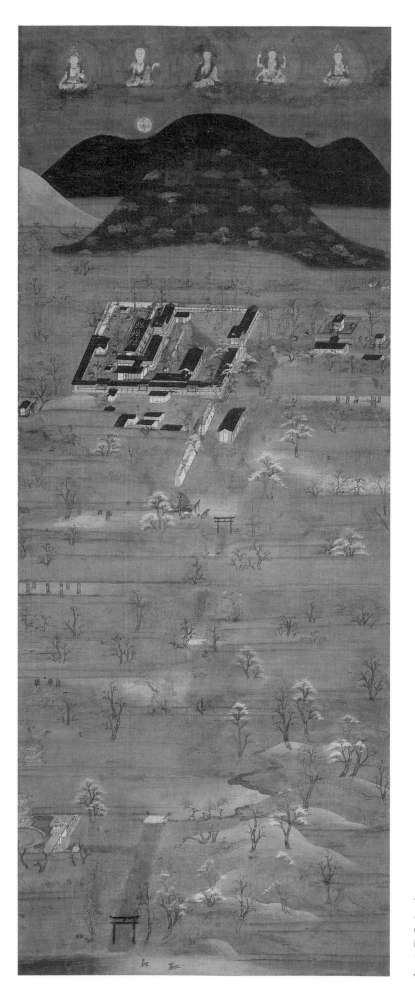

11–1 • KASUGA SHRINE MANDALA Kamakura period, early 14th century CE. Hanging scroll, ink, color, and gold on silk, 39½ × 15⅝″ (100.3 × 39.8 cm). Mary and Jackson Burke Collection.

JAPANESE ART BEFORE 1333

A group of Buddhist deities hovers in the sky across the top of this painting (FIG. 11–1), above verdant hills and meadows filled with blossoming cherry and plum trees, and a diagrammatic, bird's-eye view of a religious compound. The sacred site depicted in recognizable, but partially idealized, form is the Kasuga Shrine in Nara, dedicated to deities, known as *kami*, of Japan's native Shinto religion. It served as the family shrine for the most powerful aristocratic clan in ancient Japan, the Fujiwara, who chose the site because of its proximity to their home as well as for its natural beauty. As life in Japan revolved around natural seasonal rhythms, so too did conceptions of *kami*, who give and protect life and embody the life-sustaining forces of nature. The Japanese believe that *kami* descend from mysterious heavens at supremely beautiful places such as majestic mountains, towering waterfalls, old and gnarled trees, or unusual rock formations, thus rendering such locations holy. They consider them as places where they can go to commune with *kami*. The deer glimpsed scampering about the grounds are sacred messengers of *kami*, and freely roam the area even today.

That foreign deities associated with Buddhism preside over a native Shinto shrine presents no anomaly to the Japanese. By the Heian period (794–1185 CE), the interaction of Buddhist and Shinto doctrines resulted in the belief that *kami* were emanations of Buddhist deities who were their original forms. When Buddhism first entered Japan in the sixth century, efforts began to integrate that new faith with the indigenous Japanese religious belief system centered around *kami*, which only later came to be called Shinto. Until the government forcibly separated the two religions in the latter part of the nineteenth century, and elevated Shinto to bolster worship of the emperor, the two religions were intimately intertwined and evolved in a co-mingled manner. The two faiths could exist side by side because of their complementary values. Shinto explains the origins of the Japanese people and its deities protect them, while Buddhism offers salvation after death.

This painting encapsulates various aspects of the essential character of Japanese art and culture in the ancient and early medieval eras. Like all religious art from early Japan, it was created to aid religious teachings and beliefs. In its own time it was not considered a work of art. It testifies to the importance of nature in the Japanese worldview and how reverence for the natural world informed religious practice and visual vocabulary. Additionally, it shows how the Japanese integrated the foreign religion of Buddhism with indigenous belief systems without sacrificing either one. Finally, it reveals the existence at this early date of a sophisticated and uniquely Japanese courtly style aesthetic.

LEARN ABOUT IT

11.1 Recognize the native elements in early Japanese art.

11.2 Understand Japan's cultural relationship with China and Korea.

11.3 Summarize the transformation of Japanese Buddhist sculpture.

11.4 Discuss the ways Shinto influences Japanese aesthetic perceptions.

11.5 Distinguish different uses of Buddhist paintings in connection with the different sects of Buddhism for which they were made.

HEAR MORE: Listen to an audio file of your chapter **www.myartslab.com**

PREHISTORIC JAPAN

Human habitation in Japan dates to around 30,000 years ago (MAP 11–1). Sometime after 15,000 years ago Paleolithic peoples gave way to Neolithic hunter-gatherers, who gradually developed the ability to make and use ceramics. Recent scientific dating methods have shown that some works of Japanese pottery date to earlier than 10,000 BCE, making them the oldest now known.

JOMON PERIOD

The early potters lived during the Jomon period (c. 11,000–400 BCE), named for the patterns on much of the pottery they produced. They made functional earthenware vessels, probably originally imitating reed baskets, by building them up with coils of clay, then firing them in bonfires at relatively low temperatures. They also created small humanoid figures known as **dogu**, which were probably effigies that manifested a kind of sympathetic magic. Around 5000 BCE agriculture emerged with the planting and harvesting of beans and gourds.

YAYOI PERIOD

During the succeeding Yayoi era (c. 400 BCE–300 CE), the introduction of rice cultivation by immigrants from Korea helped transform Japan into an agricultural nation. As it did elsewhere in the world, this shift to agriculture brought larger permanent settlements, class structure with the division of labor into agricultural and nonagricultural tasks, more hierarchical forms of social organization, and a more centralized government. Korean settlers also brought metal technology. Bronze was used to create weapons as well as ceremonial objects such as bells. Iron metallurgy developed later in this period, eventually replacing stone tools in everyday life.

KOFUN PERIOD

Centralized government developed further during the ensuing Kofun ("old tombs") period (c. 300–552 CE), named for the large royal tombs that were built then. With the emergence of a more complex social order, the veneration of leaders grew into the beginnings of an imperial system. Still in existence today in Japan, this system eventually explained that the emperor (or, very rarely, empress) descended directly from Shinto deities. When an emperor died, chamber tombs were constructed following Korean examples. Various grave goods were placed inside the tomb chambers, including large amounts of pottery, presumably to pacify the spirits of the dead and to serve them in their next life. As part of a general cultural transfer from China through Korea, fifth-century potters in Japan gained knowledge of finishing techniques and improved kilns, and began to produce high-fired ceramic ware.

The Japanese government has never allowed the major sacred tombs to be excavated, but much is known about the mortuary practices of Kofun-era Japan. Some of the huge tombs of the fifth and sixth centuries were constructed in a shape resembling a large

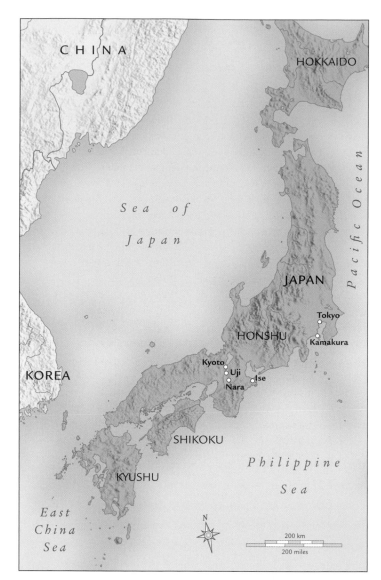

MAP 11–1 • JAPAN

Melting glaciers at the end of the Ice Age in Japan 15,000 years ago raised the sea level and formed the four main islands of Japan: Hokkaido, Honshu, Shikoku, and Kyushu.

keyhole and surrounded by moats dug to protect the sacred precincts. Tomb sites might extend over more than 400 acres, with artificial hills built over the tombs themselves. On the top of the hills were placed ceramic works of sculpture called **haniwa**.

HANIWA.   The first *haniwa* were simple cylinders that may have held jars with ceremonial offerings. By the fifth century, these cylinders came to be made in the shapes of ceremonial objects, houses, and boats. Gradually, living creatures were added to the repertoire of *haniwa* subjects, including birds, deer, dogs, monkeys, cows, and horses. By the sixth century, **HANIWA** in human shapes were crafted, including males and females of various types, professions, and classes (FIG. 11–2).

Haniwa illustrate several enduring characteristics of Japanese aesthetic taste. Unlike Chinese tomb ceramics, which were often

ART AND ITS CONTEXTS

Writing, Language, and Culture

Chinese culture enjoyed great prestige in east Asia. Written Chinese served as an international language of scholarship and cultivation, much as Latin did in medieval Europe. Educated Koreans, for example, wrote almost exclusively in Chinese until the fifteenth century. In Japan, Chinese continued to be used for certain kinds of writing, such as Buddhist *sutras*, philosophical and legal texts, and Chinese poetry (by Japanese writers), into the nineteenth century.

When it came to writing their own language, the Japanese initially borrowed Chinese characters, or *kanji*. Differences between the Chinese and Japanese languages made this system extremely unwieldy, so during the ninth century they developed two syllabaries, or *kana*, from simplified Chinese characters. (A syllabary is a system of lettering in which each symbol stands for a syllable.) *Katakana*, consisting of angular symbols, was developed to aid pronunciation of Chinese Buddhist texts and now is generally used for foreign words. *Hiragana*, comprised of graceful, cursive symbols, was the written language the Japanese first used to write native poetry and prose. Eventually it came to be used to represent only the grammatical portions of the written Japanese language in conjunction with Chinese characters that convey meaning. Japanese written in *hiragana* was once called "women's hand" because its rounded forms looked feminine. During the Heian period *hiragana* were used to create a large body of literature, written either by women or sometimes for women by men.

A charming poem originated in Heian times to teach the new writing system. In two stanzas of four lines each, it uses almost all of the syllable sounds of spoken Japanese and thus almost every *kana* symbol. It was memorized as we would recite our ABCs. The first stanza translates as:

> Although flowers glow with color
> They are quickly fallen,
> And who in this world of ours
> Is free from change?
> (Translation by Earl Miner)

Like Chinese, Japanese is written in columns from top to bottom and across the page from right to left. (Following this logic, Chinese and Japanese narrative paintings also read from right to left.) Below is the stanza written three ways. At the right, it appears in *katakana* glossed with the original phonetic value of each symbol. (Modern pronunciation has shifted slightly.) In the center, the stanza appears in flowing *hiragana*. To the left is the mixture of *kanji* and *hiragana* that eventually became standard.

kanji hiragana mixed

常ならむ
我世誰ぞ
散りぬるを
色は匂へど

hiragana

つねならむ
わかよたれそ
ちりぬるを
いろにほへと

katakana

Tsu-ne-na-ra-mu ツネナラム
Wa-ka-yo-ta-re-so ワカヨタレソ
Chi-ri-nu-ru-wo チリヌルヲ
I-ro-ha-ni-he-to イロハニホヘト

JAPANESE ART BEFORE 1333 **CHAPTER 11** 357

11–2 • *HANIWA*
Kyoto. Kofun period, 6th century CE. Earthenware, height 27″ (68.5 cm). Collection of the Tokyo National Museum. Important Cultural Property.

There have been many theories as to the function of *haniwa*. The figures seem to have served as some kind of link between the world of the dead, over which they were placed, and the world of the living, from which they could be viewed. This figure has been identified as a seated female shaman, wearing a robe, belt, and necklace and carrying a mirror at her waist. In early Japan, shamans acted as agents between the natural and the supernatural worlds, just as *haniwa* figures were links between the living and the dead.

glazed, *haniwa* were left with their clay bodies unglazed. Nor do *haniwa* show a preoccupation with technical skill seen in Chinese ceramics. Instead, their makers explored the expressive potentials of simple and bold form. *Haniwa* are never perfectly symmetrical; their slightly off-center eye slits, irregular cylindrical bodies, and unequal arms impart the idiosyncrasy of life and individuality.

SHINTO.   As described at the outset of this chapter, Shinto is Japan's indigenous religious belief system. It encompasses a variety of ritual practices that center around family, village, and national devotion to *kami* (Shinto deities). The term Shinto was not coined until after the arrival of Buddhism in the sixth century CE, and as *kami* worship was influenced by and incorporated into Buddhism it became more systematized, with shrines, a hierarchy of deities, and more strictly regulated ceremonies.

THE ISE SHRINE.   One of the great Shinto monuments is the Grand Shrine of Ise, on the coast southwest of Tokyo **(FIG. 11–3)**, where the main deity worshiped is the sun goddess Amaterasu-o-mi-*kami*, the legendary progenitor of Japan's imperial family. Japan's earliest written historical texts recorded by the imperial

court in the eighth century state that the Ise Shrine dates to the first century CE. Although we do not know for certain if this is true, it is known that it has been ritually rebuilt, alternately on two adjoining sites at 20-year intervals with few breaks since the year 690, a time when the imperial family was solidifying its hegemony. Its most recent rebuilding took place in 1993, by carpenters who train for the task from childhood. After the *kami* is ceremonially escorted to the freshly copied shrine, the old shrine is dismantled. Thus—like Japanese culture itself—this exquisite shrine is both ancient and constantly renewed. In this sense it embodies one of the most important characteristics of Shinto faith—ritual purification—derived from respect for the cycle of the seasons in which pure new life emerges in springtime and gives way to death in winter, yet is reborn again in the following year.

Although Ise is visited by millions of pilgrims each year, only members of the imperial family and a few Shinto priests are allowed within the enclosure that surrounds its inner shrine. Although detailed documents on its appearance date back to the tenth century, shrine authorities never allowed photographers access to its inner compound until 1953, when the iconic photograph of it reproduced in FIGURE 11–3 was taken by a photographer officially

11-3 • MAIN HALL, INNER SHRINE, ISE
Mie Prefecture. Last rebuilt 1993. Photograph by Watanabe Yoshio (1907–2000), 1953. National Treasure.

engaged by a quasi-governmental cultural relations agency. The reluctance of shrine officials to permit photography even then may stem from beliefs that such intimate pictures would violate the privacy of the shrine's most sacred spaces.

The Ise Shrine has many aspects that are typical of Shinto architecture, including wooden piles raising the building off the ground, a thatched roof held in place by horizontal logs, the use of unpainted cypress wood, and the overall feeling of natural simplicity rather than overwhelming size or elaborate decoration. The building's shape is indebted to raised granaries used by the Yayoi people, which are known from drawings on bronze artifacts of the Yayoi period. The sensitive use of wood and thatch in the Ise Shrine suggests an early origin for the Japanese appreciation of natural materials that persists to the present day.

ASUKA PERIOD

During the Asuka period's single century (552–645 CE), new forms of philosophy, medicine, music, food, clothing, agriculture, city planning, religion, visual art, and architecture entered Japan from Korea and China at an astonishing pace. Most significant among these were the Buddhist religion, a centralized governmental structure, and a system of writing. Each was adopted and gradually modified to suit Japanese conditions, and each has had an enduring legacy.

Buddhism reached Japan in Mahayana form, with its many buddhas and bodhisattvas (see "Buddhism," page 297). After being accepted by the imperial family, it was soon adopted as a state religion. Buddhism represented not only different gods from Shinto but an entirely new concept of religion. Worship of Buddhist deities took place inside worship halls of temples situated in close proximity to imperial cities. The temples looked like nothing constructed in Japan before, with Chinese-influenced buildings housing anthropomorphic Buddhist icons possessing an elaborate iconography (see "Buddhist Symbols," page 362). At that time, *kami* were not portrayed in human form. Yet Buddhism attracted followers because it offered a rich cosmology with profound teachings of meditation and enlightenment, and the protective powers of its deities enabled the ruling elites to justify their own power, through association with Buddhism. They called upon Buddhist deities to nurture and protect the populace over whom they ruled. Many highly developed aspects of continental Asian art accompanied the new religion, including new methods of painting and sculpture.

HORYUJI

The most significant surviving early Japanese temple is Horyuji, located on Japan's central plains not far from Nara. The temple was founded in 607 by Prince Shotoku (574–622), who ruled Japan as a regent and became the most influential early proponent of Buddhism. Rebuilt after a fire in 670, Horyuji is the oldest wooden temple in the world. It is so famous that visitors are often surprised at its modest size. Yet its just proportions and human scale, together with the artistic treasures it contains, make Horyuji an enduringly beautiful monument to Buddhist faith in early Japan.

The main compound of Horyuji consists of a rectangular courtyard surrounded by covered corridors, one of which contains a gateway. Within the compound are only two buildings, the **kondo** (golden hall), and a five-story pagoda. Within a simple asymmetrical layout, the large *kondo* perfectly balances the tall, slender pagoda (**FIG. 11–4**). The *kondo* is filled with Buddhist images and is used for worship and ceremonies. The pagoda serves as a reliquary and is not entered. Other monastery buildings lie outside the main compound, including an outer gate, a lecture hall, a repository for sacred texts, a belfry, and dormitories for monks.

Among the many treasures still preserved in Horyuji is a shrine decorated with paintings in lacquer. It is known as the Tamamushi Shrine after the *tamamushi* beetle, whose iridescent wings were originally affixed to the shrine to make it glitter, much

11–5 • HUNGRY TIGRESS JATAKA
Panel of the Tamamushi Shrine, Horyuji. Asuka period, c. 650 CE. Lacquer on wood, height of shrine 7′7½″ (2.33 m). Horyuji Treasure House, Nara. National Treasure.

11-6 • Tori Busshi BUDDHA SHAKA AND ATTENDANT BODHISATTVAS IN THE HORYUJI *KONDO*
Asuka period, c. 623 CE. Gilt bronze, height of seated figure 34½″ (87.5 cm). Horyuji, Nara. National Treasure.

like mother-of-pearl. Its architectural form replicates an ancient palace-form building type that predates Horyuji itself.

HUNGRY TIGRESS JATAKA. Paintings on the sides of the Tamamushi Shrine are among the few two-dimensional works of art to survive from the Asuka period. Most celebrated among them are two that illustrate Jataka tales, stories about former lives of the Buddha. One depicts the future Buddha nobly sacrificing his life in order to feed his body to a starving tigress and her cubs (FIG. 11–5). The tigers are at first too weak to eat him, so he must jump off a cliff to break open his flesh. The anonymous artist has created a full narrative within a single frame. The graceful form of the Buddha appears three times, harmonized by the curves of the rocky cliff and tall sprigs of bamboo. First, he hangs his shirt on a tree, then he dives downward onto the rocks, and finally starving animals devour his body. The elegantly slender renditions of the figure and the somewhat abstract treatment of the cliff, trees, and bamboo represent an international Buddhist style that was

transmitted to Japan via China and Korea. These illustrations of Jataka tales helped popularize Buddhism in Japan.

SHAKA TRIAD. Another example of the international style of early Buddhist art at Horyuji is the sculpture called the Shaka Triad, traditionally identified as being made by Tori Busshi (FIG. 11–6). (Shaka is the Japanese name for Shakyamuni, the historical Buddha.) Tori Busshi (Busshi means Buddhist image-maker) may have been a descendant of Korean craftsmen who emigrated to Japan as part of an influx of Buddhists and artisans from Korea. The Shaka Triad reflects the strong influence of Chinese art of the Northern Wei dynasty (SEE FIG. 10–12). The frontal pose, the outsized face and hands, and the linear treatment of the drapery all suggest that the maker of this statue was well aware of earlier continental models, while the fine bronze casting of the figures shows his advanced technical skill. The Shaka Triad and the Tamamushi Shrine reveal the importance of Buddhist imagery to the transmission of the faith.

NARA PERIOD

The Nara period (645–794) is named for Japan's first permanent imperial capital, founded in 710. Previously, an emperor's death was thought to taint his entire capital city, so for reasons of purification (and perhaps also of politics), his successor usually selected a new site. As the government adopted ever more complex aspects of the Chinese political system, necessitating construction of huge administrative complexes, it abandoned this custom in the eighth century when Nara was founded. During this period, divisions of the imperial bureaucracy grew exponentially and hastened the swelling of the city's population to perhaps 200,000 people.

One result of the strong central authority was the construction in Nara of magnificent Buddhist temples and Shinto shrines that dwarfed those built previously. The expansive park in the center of Nara today is the site of the largest and most important of these, including the Shinto Kasuga Shrine illustrated in FIGURE 11–1. The grandest of the Buddhist temples in Nara Park is Todaiji, which Emperor Shomu (r. 724–749) conceived as the headquarters of a vast network of branch temples throughout the nation. He had it constructed because of his deep faith in Buddhism. Todaiji served as both a state-supported central monastic training center and as the setting for public religious ceremonies. The most spectacular of these took place in 752 and celebrated the consecration of the main Buddhist statue of the temple in a traditional "eye-opening" ceremony, in its newly constructed Great Buddha Hall (*Daibutsuden*; see "The Great Buddha Hall," page 364). The statue, a giant gilt bronze image of the Buddha Birushana (Vairochana in Sanskrit), was inspired by the Chinese tradition of erecting monumental stone Buddhist statues in cave-temples (SEE, FOR EXAMPLE, FIG. 10–12).

The ceremony, which took place in the vast courtyard in front of the Great Buddha Hall, was presided over by an illustrious

Buddhist Symbols

A few of the most important Buddhist symbols, which have myriad variations, are described here in their most generalized forms.

Lotus flower: Usually shown as a white waterlily, the lotus (Sanskrit, *padma*) symbolizes spiritual purity, the wholeness of creation, and cosmic harmony. The flower's stem is an *axis mundi* ("axis of the world").

Lotus throne: Buddhas are frequently shown seated on an open lotus, either single or double, a representation of *nirvana* (SEE FIG. 11–10).

Chakra: An ancient sun symbol, the *chakra* (wheel) symbolizes both the various states of existence (the Wheel of Life) and the Buddhist doctrine (the Wheel of the Law). A *chakra*'s exact meaning depends on how many spokes it has (SEE FIG. 9–7).

Marks of a buddha: A buddha is distinguished by 32 physical attributes (*lakshana*s). Among them are a bulge on top of the head (*ushnisha*), a tuft of hair between the eyebrows (*urna*), elongated earlobes, and 1,000-spoked *chakra*s on the soles of the feet.

Mandala: *Mandala*s are diagrams of cosmic realms, representing order and meaning within the spiritual universe. They may be simple or complex, three- or two-dimensional, and in a wide array of forms—such as an Indian stupa (SEE FIG. 9–8) or a Womb World *mandala* (SEE FIG. 11–8), an early Japanese type.

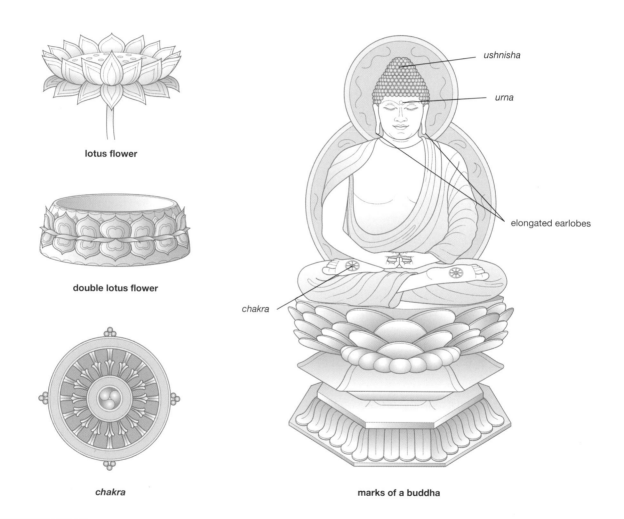

lotus flower

double lotus flower

chakra

marks of a buddha

Indian monk and included *sutra* chanting by over 10,000 Japanese Buddhist monks and sacred performances by 4,000 court musicians and dancers. Vast numbers of Japanese courtiers and emissaries from the Asian continent comprised the audience. Numerous ritual objects used in the ceremony came from exotic Asian and Near Eastern lands. The resulting cosmopolitan atmosphere reflected the position Nara then held as the eastern terminus of the Central Asian Silk Road.

Many of these treasures have been preserved in the Shosoin Imperial Repository at Todaiji, which today contains some 9,000

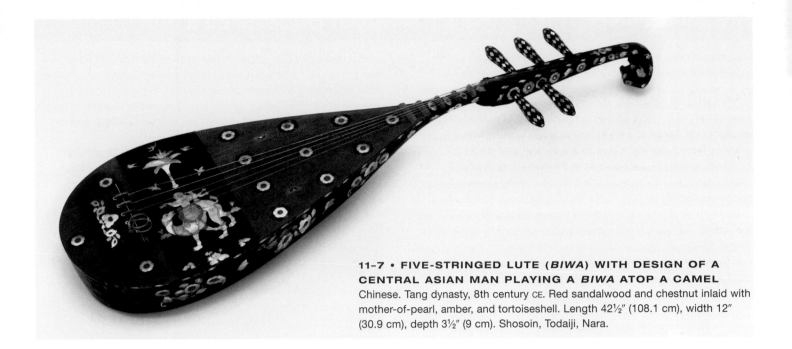

11-7 • FIVE-STRINGED LUTE (*BIWA*) WITH DESIGN OF A CENTRAL ASIAN MAN PLAYING A *BIWA* ATOP A CAMEL
Chinese. Tang dynasty, 8th century CE. Red sandalwood and chestnut inlaid with mother-of-pearl, amber, and tortoiseshell. Length 42½″ (108.1 cm), width 12″ (30.9 cm), depth 3½″ (9 cm). Shosoin, Todaiji, Nara.

objects. The Shosoin came into being in the year 756, when Emperor Shomu died and his widow donated some 600 of his possessions to the temple, including a number of objects used during the Great Buddha's consecration ceremony. Many years later, objects used in Buddhist rituals and previously stored elsewhere at Todaiji were added to these. The objects formerly owned by Emperor Shomu consisted mainly of his personal possessions, such as documents, furniture, musical instruments, games, clothing, medicine, weapons, food and beverage vessels of metal, glass, and lacquer, and some Buddhist ritual objects. Some of these were made in Japan while others were clearly not and came from as far away as China, India, Iran, Greece, Rome, and Egypt. They reflect the vast international trade network that existed at this early date.

One of the items Emperor Shomu's widow donated in 756 is a magnificently crafted five-stringed lute (*biwa*) made of lacquered red sandalwood and chestnut, and inlaid with mother-of-pearl, amber, and tortoiseshell. Its plectrum guard features a design of a man of central Asian origin (apparent from his clothing and physical features) sitting atop a camel and playing a lute (**FIG. 11–7**). This instrument is the only existing example of an ancient five-stringed lute. Its form was invented in India and transmitted to China and Japan via the Silk Road. The Shosoin piece is generally identified as Chinese. However, as with many of the objects preserved in the Shosoin, the location of its manufacture is not absolutely certain. While it was most likely crafted in China and imported to Japan for use in the consecration ceremony (researchers have recently conclusively determined that it was indeed played), it is also plausible that Chinese (or Japanese) craftsmen made it in Japan using imported materials. Its meticulous workmanship reveals the high level of crafts production that artists of this era achieved. Such consummate skill has been a hallmark of Japanese crafts since then.

Influenced by Emperor Shomu, the Buddhist faith permeated all aspects of court society of the Nara period. Indeed, in 749 Shomu abdicated the throne to retire as a monk. His daughter, who succeeded him as empress, was also a devout Buddhist and wanted to cede her throne to a Buddhist monk. This dismayed her advisors and prompted them to move the capital city away from Nara, where they felt Buddhist influence had become overpowering, and establish a new one, Kyoto, within whose bounds, at first, only a few Buddhist temples would be allowed. The move of the capital to Kyoto marked the end of the Nara period.

HEIAN PERIOD

The Japanese fully absorbed and transformed their cultural borrowings from China and Korea during the Heian period (794–1185). Generally peaceful conditions contributed to a new air of self-reliance. The imperial government severed ties to China in the ninth century, a time when the power of related aristocratic families increased. An efficient method of writing the Japanese language was developed, and the rise of vernacular literature generated such prose masterpieces as Lady Murasaki's *The Tale of Genji*. During these four centuries of splendor and refinement, two major streams of Buddhism emerged—first, esoteric sects and, later, those espousing salvation in the Pure Land Western Paradise of the Buddha Amida.

ESOTERIC BUDDHIST ART

With the removal of the capital to Kyoto, the older Nara temples lost their influence. Soon two new Esoteric sects of Buddhism, Tendai and Shingon, grew to dominate Japanese religious life. Strongly influenced by polytheistic religions such as Hinduism,

The Great Buddha Hall (*Daibutsuden*) is distinguished today as the largest wooden structure in the world. To give a sense of its unprecedented scale, it was so large that the area surrounding only one of the two pagodas that flanked it, within its own cloistered compound, could accommodate the entire main compound of Horyuji. Yet the present Great Buddha Hall, dating to a reconstruction of 1707, is 30 percent smaller than the original, which towered nearly 90 feet in height. Since it was first erected in 752 CE natural disasters and intentional destruction by foes of the imperial family necessitated its reconstruction four times. It was first destroyed during civil wars in the twelfth century and rebuilt in 1203, then destroyed in yet another civil war in 1567. Reconstruction did not occur until the late seventeenth century under the direction of a charismatic monk who solicited funds not from the government, which was then impoverished, but through popular subscription. This building, completed in 1707, is essentially the structure that stands on the site today. However, by the late nineteenth century its condition had deteriorated so profoundly that restoration finally undertaken between 1906 and 1913 entailed completely dismantling it and putting it back together, this time utilizing steel (imported from England) and concrete to provide invisible support to the roof, which had nearly collapsed. Architects adapted this nontraditional solution mainly because no trees of sufficiently large dimensions could be found, and no traditional carpenters then living possessed knowledge of ancient construction techniques. This project occurred only after laws were enacted in 1897 to preserve ancient architecture. Since then, another major restoration on the building took place between 1973 and 1980.

Like the building, the Great Buddha Daibutsu statue has not survived intact. Its head was completely destroyed in the late sixteenth century and replaced as part of the hall's reconstruction in the late seventeenth century, when its torso and lotus petal throne also required extensive restoration. The present statue, though impressive in scale, appears stiff and rigid. Its more lyrical original appearance can be approximated from that of engraved images of seated Buddhist deities found on a massive cast-bronze lotus petal from the original statue that has survived in fragmentary form. The petal features a buddha with a narrow waist, broad shoulders, and elegantly flowing robes that characterize the style of contemporaneous buddha images of the Tang dynasty (see, for example, the central buddha in FIG. 10–14).

THE BUDDHA SHAKA, DETAIL OF A PARADISE SCENE
Engraved bronze lotus petal from the original Great Buddha (Daibutsu) statue of the Buddha Birushana. 8th century CE. Height of petal 79″ (200 cm). *Daibutsuden*, Todaiji. National Treasure.

GREAT BUDDHA HALL (*DAIBUTSUDEN*), TODAIJI, NARA
Original structure completed in 752 CE. Destroyed and rebuilt in 1707. Extensively restored 1906–13. UNESCO World Heritage Site, National Treasure.

11-8 • WOMB WORLD *MANDALA*
Heian period, late 9th century CE. Hanging scroll, colors on silk, 6′ × 5′1½″
(1.83 × 1.54 m). Toji, Kyoto. National Treasure.

*Mandala*s are used not only in teaching, but also as vehicles for practice. A monk, initiated into secret teachings, may meditate upon and assume the gestures of each deity depicted in the *mandala*, gradually working out from the center, so that he absorbs some of each deity's powers. The monk may also recite magical phrases, called *mantra*s, as an aid to meditation. The goal is to achieve enlightenment through the powers of the different forms of the Buddha. *Mandala*s are created in sculptural and architectural forms as well as in paintings (SEE FIG. 9–29). Their integration of the two most basic shapes, the circle and the square, is an expression of the principles of ancient geomancy (divining by means of lines and figures) as well as Buddhist cosmology.

Esoteric Buddhism (known as Tantric Buddhism in Nepal and Tibet) included a daunting number of deities, each with magical powers. The historical Buddha was no longer very important. Instead, most revered was the universal Buddha, called Dainichi ("Great Sun") in Japanese, who was believed to preside over the universe. He was accompanied by buddhas and bodhisattvas, as well as guardian deities who formed fierce counterparts to the more benign gods.

Esoteric Buddhism is hierarchical, and its deities have complex relationships to one another. Learning all the different gods and their interrelationships was assisted greatly by works of

art, especially *mandalas*, cosmic diagrams of the universe that portray the deities in schematic order. The Womb World *mandala* from Toji, for example, is entirely filled with depictions of gods. Dainichi is at the center, surrounded by buddhas of the four directions (**FIG. 11–8**). Other deities, including some with multiple heads and limbs, branch out in diagrammatical order, each with a specific symbol of power. To believers, the *mandala* represents an ultimate reality beyond the visible world.

Perhaps the most striking attribute of many Esoteric Buddhist images is their sense of spiritual force and potency, especially in depictions of the wrathful deities, which are often surrounded by flames, like those visible in the Womb World *mandala* just below the main circle of Buddhas. Esoteric Buddhism, with its intricate theology and complex doctrines, was a religion for the educated aristocracy, not for the masses. Its intricate network of deities, hierarchy, and ritual found a parallel in the elaborate social divisions of the Heian court.

PURE LAND BUDDHIST ART

Rising militarism, political turbulence, and the excesses of the imperial court marked the beginning of the eleventh century in Japan. To many Japanese of this century, the unsettled times seemed to confirm the coming of *Mappo*, a long-prophesied dark age of spiritual degeneration. Japanese of all classes reacted by increasingly turning to the promise of salvation after death through simple faith in the existence of a Buddhist realm known as the Western

Paradise of the Pure Land, a resplendent place filled with divine flowers and music. Amida (Amithaba in Sanskrit) and his attendant bodhisattvas preside there as divine protectors who compassionately accept into their land of bliss all who submit wholeheartedly to their benevolent powers. Pure Land beliefs had spread to Japan from China by way of Korea, where they also enjoyed great popularity. They offered a more immediate and easy means to achieve salvation than the elaborate rituals of the Esoteric sects. The religion held that merely by chanting *Namu Amida Butsu* ("Hail to Amida Buddha"), the faithful would be reborn into the Western Paradise.

TECHNIQUE | Joined-Block Wood Sculpture

Wood is a temperamental material because fluctuations in moisture content cause it to swell and shrink. Cut from a living, sap-filled tree, it takes many years to dry to a state of stability. While the outside of a piece of wood dries fairly rapidly, the inside yields its moisture only gradually, causing a difference in the rates of shrinkage between the inside and the outside, which induces the wood to crack. Consequently, a large statue carved from a single log must inevitably crack as it ages. Natural irregularities in wood, such as knots, further accentuate this problem. Thus, wood with a thinner cross section and fewer irregularities is less susceptible to cracking because it can dry more evenly. (This is the logic behind sawing logs into boards before drying.)

Japanese sculptors developed an ingenious and unique method, the joined-block technique, to reduce cracking in heavy wooden statues. This allowed them to create larger statues in wood than ever before, enabled standardization of body proportions, and encouraged division of labor among teams of carvers, some of whom became specialists in certain parts, such as hands or crossed legs or lotus thrones. To create large statues seated in the lotus pose, sculptors first put four blocks together vertically two by two in front and back, to form the main body, then added several blocks horizontally at what would become the front of the statue for the lap and knees. After carving each part, they assembled the figure and hollowed out the interior. This cooperative approach also had the added benefit of enabling workshops to produce large statues more quickly to meet a growing demand. Jocho is credited as the master sculptor who perfected this technique. The diagram shows how he assembled the Amida Buddha at the Byodoin (SEE FIG. 11–10).

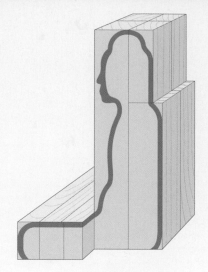

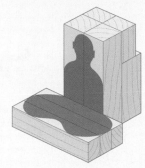

Diagram of the joined-block wood sculpture technique used on the Amida statue by Jocho (SEE FIG. 11–10).

SEE MORE: View a simulation about the joined-block technique **www.myartslab.com**

11–9 • PHOENIX HALL, BYODOIN, UJI
Kyoto Prefecture. Heian period, c. 1053 CE. Unesco World Heritage Site, National Treasure.

11-10 • Jocho AMIDA BUDDHA
Phoenix Hall, Byodoin. Heian period, c. 1053 CE. Gold leaf and lacquer on wood, height 9′8″ (2.95 m). National Treasure.

The Byodoin's central image of Amida, carved by the master sculptor Jocho (d. 1057), exemplifies the serenity and compassion of this Buddha **(FIG. 11–10)**. When reflected in the water of the pond before it, the Amida image seems to shimmer in its private mountain retreat. The figure was not carved from a single block of wood like earlier sculpture, but from several blocks in Jocho's new **joined-block** method of construction (see "Joined-Block Wood Sculpture," opposite). This technique allowed sculptors to create larger and lighter statuary. It also reflects the growing importance of wood as the medium of choice for Buddhist sculpture, reflecting the Japanese love for this natural material.

Surrounding the Amida on the walls of the Byodoin are smaller wooden figures of bodhisattvas and angels, some playing musical instruments. Everything about the Byodoin was designed to simulate the appearance of the paradise that awaits the believer after death. Its remarkable state of preservation after more than 900 years allows visitors to experience the late Heian religious ideal at its most splendid.

SECULAR PAINTING AND CALLIGRAPHY

Alongside the permeation of Buddhism during the Heian era (794–1185), a refined secular culture also arose at court. Gradually, over the course of these four centuries, the pervasive influence of Chinese culture in aristocratic society gave rise to new, uniquely Japanese developments. Above all, Heian court culture greatly valued refinement: Pity any man or woman at court who was not accomplished in several forms of art. A woman would be admired merely for the way she arranged the 12 layers of her robes by color, or a man for knowing which kind of incense was being burned. Concurrently, court life became preoccupied by the poetical expression of human love. In this climate, women became a vital force in Heian society. Although the status of women was to decline in later periods, they contributed greatly to art at the Heian court and became famous for their prose and poetry.

Although male couriers continued to be required to read and write Chinese, both men and women of court society wrote prose and poetry in their native Japanese language using the newly devised *kana* script (see "Writing, Language, and Culture," page 357). They also used *kana* on text portions of new types of small-scale secular paintings—handscrolls or folding albums designed to be appreciated in private settings.

At the beginning of the eleventh century, the lady-in-waiting Lady Murasaki transposed the lifestyle of Heian aristocrats into fiction for the amusement of her fellow court ladies, in *The Tale of Genji*, which some experts consider the world's first novel. The Japanese today admire this book as the pinnacle of their culture's

BYODOIN. One of the most beautiful temples of Pure Land Buddhism is the Byodoin, located in the Uji Mountains not far from Kyoto **(FIG. 11–9)**. The temple itself was originally a secular palace whose form was intended to suggest the appearance of the palatial residence of Amida in his Western Paradise (SEE FIG. 10–14). It was built for a member of the powerful Fujiwara family who served as the leading counselor to the emperor. After the counselor's death in the year 1052, his descendants converted the palace into a memorial temple to honor his spirit. The Byodoin is often called the Phoenix Hall, not only for the pair of phoenix images on its roof, but also because the shape of the building itself suggests the mythical bird. Its thin columns give the Byodoin a sense of airiness, as though the entire temple could easily rise up through the sky to Amida's Western Paradise. The hall rests gently in front of an artificial pond created in the shape of the Sanskrit letter A, the sacred symbol for Amida.

A CLOSER LOOK

The Tale of Genji ▸

Scene from *The Tale of Genji*, Kashiwagi chapter.
Heian period, 12th century CE. Handscroll, ink and colors on paper, 8⅝ × 18⅞″
(21.9 × 47.9 cm). Tokugawa Art Museum, Nagoya. National Treasure.

Only 19 illustrated scenes from this earliest known example of an illustrated hand-scroll of *The Tale of Genji*, created about 100 years after the novel was written, have been preserved. Scholars assume that it once contained illustrations from the entire novel of 54 chapters, approximately 100 pictures in all. Each scroll seems to have been produced by a team of artists. One was the calligrapher, most likely a member of the nobility. Another was the master painter, who outlined two or three illustrations per chapter in fine brushstrokes and indicated the color scheme. Next, colorists went to work, applying layer after layer of color to build up patterns and textures. After they had finished, the master painter returned to reinforce outlines and apply the finishing touches, among them the details of the faces.

Thickly applied mineral colors are now cracking and flaking.

A "line for an eye, hook for a nose" style is used for facial features.

The building interior is seen from a bird's-eye perspective via a "blown-away roof".

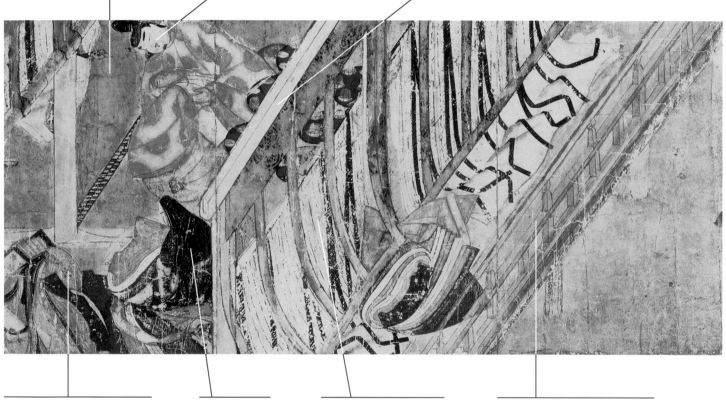

A court lady beneath 12 layers of robes holds a fan to shield her face.

Court ladies have long, flowing hair.

A free-standing curtain screen creates privacy.

Wooden verandas surround Japanese houses, merging interior and exterior.

SEE MORE: View the Closer Look feature for the Scene from *The Tale of Genji* www.myartslab.com

literary achievements (in 2009, the official 1,000-year anniversary of its completion, numerous exhibitions and celebrations took place throughout Japan). Underlying the story of the love affairs of Prince Genji and his companions is the Japanese conception of fleeting pleasures and ultimate sadness in life, an echo of the Buddhist view of the vanity of earthly pleasures.

YAMATO-E HANDSCROLLS—*THE TALE OF GENJI*. One of the earliest extant secular paintings from Japan in a new native style is a series of scenes from an illustrated handscroll that depicts *The Tale of Genji*, which unknown artists painted in the twelfth century. The painting of Japanese native subjects in Japanese rather than Chinese styles is known as *yamato-e* (native Japanese–style pictures; Yamato is the old Japanese word for Japan). The type of *yamato-e* painting in the handscroll alternated sections of text with illustrations of scenes from the story and featured delicate lines, strong (but sometimes muted) mineral colors, and asymmetrical compositions. The *Genji* paintings have a refined, subtle emotional impact. They generally show court figures in architectural settings, with the frequent addition of natural elements, such as sections of gardens, that help to convey the mood of the scene. Thus a blossoming cherry tree appears in a scene of happiness, while unkempt weeds appear in a depiction of loneliness. Such correspondence between nature and human emotion is an enduring feature of Japanese poetry and art. The figures in *The Tale of Genji* paintings do not show their emotions directly on their faces, which are rendered with a few simple lines. Instead, their feelings are conveyed by colors, poses, and the total composition of the scenes.

One scene evokes the seemingly happy Prince Genji holding a baby boy borne by his wife, Nyosan. In fact, the baby was fathered by another court noble. Since Genji himself has not been faithful to Nyosan, who appears in profile below him, he cannot complain; meanwhile the true father of the child has died, unable to acknowledge his only son (see "A Closer Look," opposite). Thus, what should be a joyful scene has undercurrents of irony and sorrow. The irony is even greater because Genji himself is the illegitimate son of an emperor.

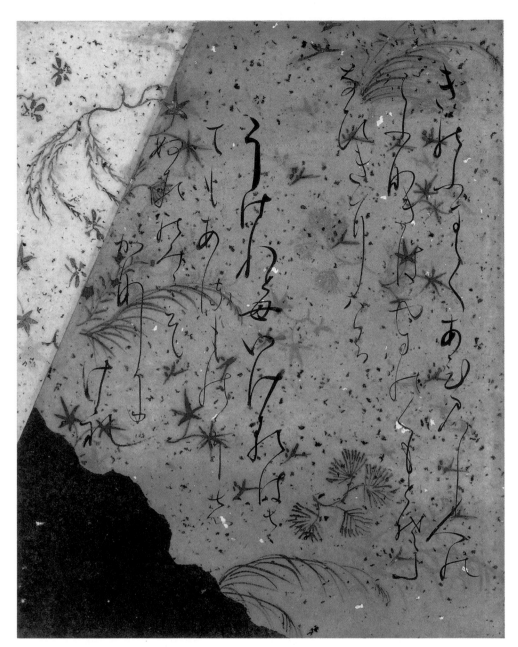

11–11 • ALBUM LEAF FROM THE *ISHIYAMA-GIRE* (DISPERSED VOLUMES, ONCE OWNED BY THE ISHIYAMA TEMPLE, OF THE ANTHOLOGY OF THE THIRTY-SIX IMMORTAL POETS)

Heian period, early 12th century CE. Ink with gold and silver on decorated and collaged paper, 52 × 17⅓" (131.8 × 44 cm). Freer Gallery of Art, Smithsonian Institution, Washington, D.C. (F1969.4)

One might expect a painting of such an emotional scene to focus on the people involved. Instead, they are rendered in rather small size, and the scene is dominated by a screen that effectively squeezes Genji and his wife into a corner. This composition deliberately represents how their positions in courtly society have forced them into this unfortunate situation.

CALLIGRAPHY IN JAPANESE. The text portions of the *The Tale of Genji* handscroll were written in *kana* script, which was also used to write poetry in Japanese. In the Heian period, the most popular form of native poetry was a 31-syllable format known as *waka*,

which had first been composed in the eighth century. During the Heian era, the finest *waka* by various writers were collected together and hand-copied in albums, the most popular of which, compiled in the eleventh century, featured writers collectively known as the Thirty-Six Immortal Poets, which is still appreciated by educated Japanese today. The earliest of many surviving examples of this iconic collection originally contained 39 volumes of poems. Two volumes were taken apart and sold in 1929, and now survive in single page sections **(FIG. 11–11)**. Collectively these separated volumes are known as the *Ishiyama-gire* (Ishiyama fragments, named after Ishiyamadera, the temple that originally owned the volumes).

11–12 • Attributed to Toba Sojo ***DETAIL OF*** ***FROLICKING ANIMALS***
Heian period, 12th century CE. Handscroll, ink on paper, height 12″ (30.5 cm). Kozanji, Kyoto. National Treasure.

With its simple, flowing symbols interspersed occasionally with more complex Chinese characters, this style of writing created a distinctive asymmetrical balance to the appearance of the written words, entirely different from the formal symmetry of Chinese calligraphy. In these album leaves, the poems seem to float elegantly on fine colored papers decorated with painting, block printing, scattered gold and silver, and sometimes paper collage. Often, as in FIGURE 11–11, the irregular pattern of torn paper edges adds a serendipitous element. The page shown here reproduces two verses by the eighth-century courtier Ki no Tsurayuki that express melancholy emotions. One reads:

> Until yesterday
> I could meet her,
> But today she is gone—
> Like clouds over the mountain
> She has been wafted away.

The spiky, flowing calligraphy and the patterning of the papers, the rich use of gold, and the suggestions of natural imagery match the elegance of the poetry, epitomizing courtly Japanese taste.

YAMATO-E HANDSCROLLS—*FROLICKING ANIMALS.* In its sedate portrayal of courtly life, *The Tale of Genji* scroll represents one side of *yamato-e*. But another style of native painting emerged contemporaneously. Characterized by bold, rapid strokes of the brush, and little or no use of color, it most often depicted subjects outside the court, in playful and irreverent activities. One of the early masterpieces of this style is *Frolicking Animals*, a set of handscrolls satirizing the life of many different levels of society. Painted entirely in ink,

the scrolls are attributed to Toba Sojo, the abbot of a Buddhist temple, and they represent the humor of Japanese art to the full.

In one scene, a frog buddha sits upon an altar while a monkey dressed as a monk prays proudly to him; in other scenes frogs, donkeys, foxes, and rabbits play, swim, and wrestle, with one frog boasting of his prowess when he flings a rabbit to the ground **(FIG. 11–12)**. Unlike the *Genji* scroll, there is no text to *Frolicking Animals*, so it is hard to know exactly what was being satirized. Nevertheless, the universality of the humorous antics portrayed in this scroll highlights an important aspect of Japanese art that makes it instantly engaging to viewers everywhere.

KAMAKURA PERIOD

The courtiers of the Heian era became so engrossed in their own refinement that they neglected their responsibilities for governing the country. Clans of warriors—samurai—from outside the capital grew increasingly strong. Two of these, the Taira and Minamoto, wielded the most power and took opposing sides in the factional conflicts of the imperial court, in order to control the weakened emperor and take charge of running the country.

The Kamakura era (1185–1333) began when the head of the Minamoto clan, Yoritomo (1147–1199), defeated the Taira family and ordered the emperor to appoint him as shogun (general-in-chief). To resist the softening effects of courtly life in Kyoto, he established his military capital in Kamakura, while the emperor continued to reside in Kyoto. Although Yoritomo's newly invented title of shogun nominally respected the authority of the emperor, at the same time it assured him of supreme military and political

ART AND ITS CONTEXTS

Arms and Armor

Battles such as the one depicted in *Night Attack on the Sanjo Palace* (SEE FIG. 11–13) were fought largely by archers on horseback. Samurai archers charged the enemy at full gallop and loosed their arrows just before they wheeled away. The scroll clearly shows their distinctive bow, with its asymmetrically placed handgrip. The lower portion of the bow is shorter than the upper so it can clear the horse's neck. The samurai wear a long, curved sword at the waist.

By the tenth century, Japanese swordsmiths had perfected techniques for crafting their legendarily sharp swords. Sword-makers face a fundamental difficulty: steel hard enough to hold a razor-sharp edge is brittle and breaks easily, but steel resilient enough to withstand rough use is too soft to hold a keen edge. The Japanese ingeniously forged a blade which laminated a hard cutting edge within less brittle support layers.

The earliest form of samurai armor, illustrated here, known as *yoroi*, was intended for use by warriors on horseback, as seen in FIGURE 11–13. It was made of overlapping iron and lacquered leather scales, punched with holes and laced together with leather thongs and brightly colored silk braids. The principal piece wrapped around the chest, left side, and back. Padded shoulder straps hooked it together back to front. A separate piece of armor was tied to the body to protect the right side. The upper legs were protected by a four-sided skirt that attached to the body armor, while two large rectangular panels tied on with cords guarded the arms. The helmet was made of iron plates riveted together. From it hung a neckguard flared sharply outward to protect the face from arrows shot at close range as the samurai wheeled away from an attack.

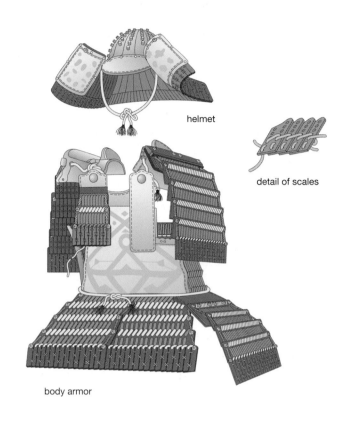

helmet

detail of scales

body armor

---

power. This tradition of rule by shogun that Yoritomo initiated lasted in various forms until 1868.

A BATTLE HANDSCROLL. The battles for domination between the Minamoto and the Taira became famous not only in medieval Japanese history but also in literature and art. One of the great painted handscrolls depicting these battles is **NIGHT ATTACK ON THE SANJO PALACE (FIG. 11–13)**. Painted perhaps 100 years after the actual event, the scroll conveys a sense of eye-witness reporting even though the anonymous artist had to imagine the scene from verbal (and at best semifactual) descriptions. The style of the painting includes some of the brisk and lively linework of *Frolicking Animals* and also traces of the more refined brushwork, use of color, and bird's-eye viewpoint of *The Tale of Genji* scroll. The main element, however, is the savage depiction of warfare (see "Arms and Armor," above). Unlike the *Genji* scroll, *Night Attack* is full of action: flames engulf the palace, horses charge, warriors behead their enemies, court ladies try to hide, and a sense of

energy and violence is conveyed with great sweep and power. The era of poetic refinement was now over in Japan, and the new world of the samurai began to dominate the secular arts.

PURE LAND BUDDHIST ART

By the beginning of the Kamakura period, Pure Land Buddhist beliefs had swept throughout Japan, and several charismatic priests founded new sects to preach this ideology. They traveled all around the country spreading the new gospel, which appealed to people of all levels of education and sophistication. They were so successful that since the Kamakura period, Pure Land Buddhist sects have remained the most popular form of Buddhism in Japan.

A PORTRAIT SCULPTURE. The itinerant monk Kuya (903–972), famous for urging country folk to join him in singing chants in praise of the Buddha Amida, was one of the early proponents of Pure Land practices. Kamakura-period Pure Land Buddhist followers regarded him as a founder of their religious tradition.

11–13 • SECTION OF *NIGHT ATTACK ON THE SANJO PALACE*

Kamakura period, late 13th century CE. Handscroll, ink and colors on paper, 16¼ × 275½" (41.3 × 699.7 cm). Museum of Fine Arts, Boston. Fenollosa-Weld Collection (11.4000)

The battles between the Minamoto and Taira clans were fought primarily by mounted and armored warriors, who used both bows and arrows, and the finest swords. In the year 1160, some 500 Minamoto rebels opposed to the retired emperor Go-Shirakawa carried out a daring raid on the Sanjo Palace. In a surprise attack in the middle of the night, they abducted the emperor. The scene was one of great carnage, much of it caused by the burning of the wooden palace. Despite the drama of the scene, this was not the decisive moment in the war. The Minamoto rebels would eventually lose more important battles to their Taira enemies. Yet Minamoto forces, heirs to those who carried out this raid, would eventually prove victorious, destroying the Taira clan in 1185.

Believers would have immediately recognized Kuya in this thirteenth-century portrait statue by Kosho (**FIG. 11–14**): The traveling clothes, the small gong, the staff topped by deer horns (symbolic of his slaying a deer, whose death converted him to Buddhism), clearly identify the monk, whose sweetly intense expression gives this sculpture a radiant sense of faith. As for Kuya's chant, Kosho's solution to the challenge of putting words into sculptural form was simple but brilliant: He carved six small buddhas emerging from Kuya's mouth, one for each of the six syllables of *Na-mu-A-mi-da-Buts(u)* (the final u is not articulated). Believers would have understood that these six small buddhas embodied the Pure Land chant.

RAIGO PAINTINGS. Pure Land Buddhism taught that even one sincere invocation of the sacred chant could lead the most wicked sinner to the Western Paradise. Paintings called **raigo** ("welcoming approach") were created depicting the Amida Buddha, accompanied by bodhisattvas, coming down to earth to welcome the soul of the dying believer. Golden cords were often attached to these paintings, which were taken to the homes of the dying. A person near death held onto these cords, hoping that Amida would escort the soul directly to paradise.

Raigo paintings differ significantly in style from the complex *mandala*s and fierce guardian deities of esoteric Buddhism. The

11–14 • Kosho KUYA PREACHING
Kamakura period, before 1207 CE. Painted wood with inlaid eyes, height 46½" (117.5 cm). Rokuhara Mitsuji, Kyoto. Important Cultural Property.

11–15 • DESCENT OF AMIDA AND THE TWENTY-FIVE BODHISATTVAS
Kamakura period, 13th century CE. Hanging scroll, colors and gold on silk, 57¼ × 61½″ (145 × 155.5 cm).
Chionin, Kyoto. National Treasure.

earliest known example of this subject is found on the walls and doors of the Phoenix Hall, surrounding Jocho's sculpture of Amida (SEE FIG. 11–10). Like that statue, they radiate warmth and compassion. In the Kamakura period, *raigo* paintings were made in great numbers, reflecting the popularity of Pure Land Buddhism at that time. One magnificent example portrays Amida Buddha and 25 bodhisattvas swiftly descending over mountains. The artist used gold paint and thin slivers of gold leaf cut in elaborate patterning to suggest the divine radiance of the deities (FIG. 11–15). This

painstaking cut-gold leaf technique, known as *kirikane*, is one of the great achievements of early Japanese Buddhist artists. It originated in China, but Japanese artists refined and perfected it. In this painting, the darkened silk behind the figures heightens the sparkle of their golden aura. In the flickering light of oil lamps and torches, *raigo* paintings would have appeared magical in a temple or a dying person's home.

One of the most remarkable aspects of this painting is its sensitive rendering of the landscape, full of rugged peaks and

Daruma, Founder of Zen

Zen monks modeled their behavior on that of the patriarch or founder of their lineage, the mythical Indian Buddhist sage Daruma (Bodhidharma in Sanskrit), who emigrated to China in the sixth century CE, and famously transmitted his teachings to a Chinese disciple, who became the second Chan patriarch. This portrait of *Daruma* (FIG. A) is one of the earliest surviving examples of a Japanese Zen painting. Using fine ink outlines and a touch of color for the robe and the figure's sandals, the artist portrays the Zen master seated meditating atop a rock, with an unwavering focused gaze that is intended to convey his inner strength and serenity. At the top of the scroll is an inscription in Chinese by Yishan Yining (1247–1317), one of several influential early Chinese Chan masters to emigrate to Japan. He had actually planned only to visit in his role as head of an official diplomatic delegation from China in 1299, but he wound up staying for the duration of his life. Although wary of him at first, his sincere intentions to teach Zen and his erudite abilities quickly attracted influential supporters, to whom he taught Chinese religious practices and cultural traditions. Thus soon after arrival, Yishan was appointed as the tenth head abbot of the large Zen temple of Kenchoji in Kamakura, a post he held briefly, before moving on to head several other Zen temples.

Kenchoji had been founded in 1253 by another emigrant Chan master, Lanxi Daolong (1213–1278). Lanxi had been the first Chan master to travel to Japan. There, he was warmly received by the fifth Minamoto shogun who helped him plan construction of Kenchoji where, for the first time, authentic Chinese Chan Buddhism was to be taught in Japan. Kenchoji remains one of the most important Zen monasteries in Japan today. The temple owns many formal portraits of its founder, including this one (FIG. B), considered by many to be the best, in that it seems to capture Daolong's inner spirit as well as his outer form. This type of painting is peculiar to Chan and Zen sects and is known as *chinso*. These paintings were often gifts given by a master to disciples when they completed their formal training and departed his presence to officiate at their

own temples. They served as personal reminders of their master's teachings and tangible evidence of their right to transmit Zen teachings to their own pupils (like a diploma). Lanxi Daolong dedicated the inscription of this painting to an important regent (samurai official), a confidant of the shogun, and not an ordained Zen monk. This shows that Zen, from its early days in Japan, also strove to attract followers from among those in power who could not abandon their secular life for the rigorous, cloistered existence required of Zen monks who lived in temples.

B. PORTRAIT OF THE CHINESE ZEN MASTER LANXI DAOLONG
Inscription by Lanxi Daolong. Kamakura period, dated 1271 CE. Hanging scroll, colors on silk, 41⅓ × 18″ (105 × 46.1 cm). Kenchoji, Kamakura. National Treasure.

A. DARUMA
Artist unknown, inscription by Chinese Chan (Zen) master Yishan Yining (1247–1317). Kamakura period, early 14th century CE. Hanging scroll, ink and colors on silk, 39⅝ × 20″ (100.8 × 50.8 cm). Tokyo National Museum. Important Cultural Property.

flowering trees. These natural elements reveal that the Japanese possessed great appreciation for the beautiful land in which they dwelled, an appreciation that stems from Shinto beliefs. Coincidence cannot account for the fact that Shinto pictures portraying the landscape of Japan as divine first appeared in the Kamakura period, just when Pure Land Buddhism grew popular. One of these paintings is the Kasuga Shrine *mandala* of FIGURE 11–1. It illustrates how artists contributed to the merging of the two faiths of Buddhism and Shinto at that time. The artist of this work intentionally made the shrine buildings resemble those of the palatial abode of Amida in his Western Paradise and rendered the landscape details with the radiant charm of Amida's heaven.

ZEN BUDDHIST ART

Toward the latter part of the Kamakura period, Zen Buddhism was introduced to Japan from China where it was already highly developed and known as Chan. Zen had been slow to reach Japan because of the interruption of relations between the two countries during the Heian period. But during the Kamakura era, both emigrant Chinese (see "Daruma, Founder of Zen," opposite) and Japanese monks who went to China to study Buddhism, and returned home enthused about the new teachings they learned there, brought Zen to Japan. The monk Kuya, represented in the statue by Kosho (SEE FIG. 11–14), epitomized the itinerant life of a Pure Land Buddhist monk who wandered the countryside and relied on the generosity of believers to support him. Zen monks lived very differently. They secluded themselves in monasteries, leading an austere life of simplicity and self-responsibility.

In some ways, Zen resembles the original teachings of the historical Buddha in that it emphasizes individual enlightenment through meditation, without the help of deities or magical chants. It especially appealed to the self-disciplined spirit of samurai warriors, who were not satisfied with the older forms of Buddhism connected with the Japanese court. Zen was the last major form of Buddhism to reach Japan from the Asian mainland and it had a profound and lasting impact on Japanese arts and culture.

Just as the *Night Attack* (SEE FIG. 11–13) reveals a propensity for recording the consequences of political turbulence through representation of gruesome battle scenes in vivid colors, Kamakura-era Buddhist sculpture and painting also emphasized realism. Various factors account for this new taste. Society was dominated by samurai warriors, who possessed a more pragmatic outlook on the world than the Heian-period courtiers who lived a dreamlike existence at court. In addition, renewed contacts with China introduced new styles for Buddhist art that also emphasized realism. Finally, forging personal connections with heroic exploits and individuals, both past and present, political and religious, greatly concerned the people of the Kamakura period. Representing these figures in arresting pictorial and sculpted images helped reinforce legends and perpetuate their influence, which accounts for the predominance of these subjects in the period's art.

As the Kamakura era ended, the seeds of the future were planted both politically and culturally: The coming age witnessed the nation's continued dominance by the warrior class and the establishment of Zen as the religion of choice among those warriors who wielded power at the highest levels. As before, the later history of Japanese art continued to be marked by an intriguing interplay between native traditions and imported foreign culture.

THINK ABOUT IT

11.1 Discuss Japan's relationship with China during the Kamakura period with respect to patterns of influence. Include specific examples related to society, as well as art techniques learned, referring to Chapter 10 as necessary.

11.2 Discuss the development of Japanese native-style arts during the Heian period. Define the main characteristics of native traditions of writing and secular painting. Describe how the innovations in new forms of Buddhist sculpture then differed from older forms in appearance, technique, and materials used.

11.3 Discuss the development of Buddhist practice and Buddhist sculpture over the course of time in Japan by selecting an image or object from three of the following four periods: Asuka, Nara, Heian, Kamakura. Explain each work in the context of its respective culture, including its relation to particular practices of Buddhism, for example Zen.

11.4 Summarize the beliefs of the Shinto religion and discuss the integration of Shinto and Buddhist traditions in Japanese culture.

11.5 Distinguish the defining characteristics of esoteric and Pure Land Buddhist painting and explain these differences with reference to one work of each from the chapter.

PRACTICE MORE: Compose answers to these questions, get flashcards for images and terms, and review chapter material with quizzes **www.myartslab.com**

12-1 • OFFERING 4, LA VENTA Mexico. Olmec culture, c. 900–400 BCE. Jade, greenstone, and sandstone, height of figures 6¼–7″ (16–18 cm). Museo Nacional de Antropología, Mexico City.

ART OF SOUTH AND SOUTHEAST ASIA AFTER 1200

Upon entering the gateway that today serves as the entrance to the great Taj Mahal complex, the visitor beholds the majestic white marble structure that is one of the world's best-known monuments. Its reflection shimmers in the pools of the garden meant to evoke a vision of paradise as described in the Qur'an, the holy book of Islam. The building's façades are delicately inlaid with inscriptions designed by India's foremost calligrapher of the time, Amanat Khan, and floral arabesques in semiprecious stones—carnelian, agate, coral, turquoise, garnet, lapis, and jasper. Above, its luminous, white marble dome reflects each shift in light, flushing rose at dawn, dissolving in its own brilliance in the noonday sun. This extraordinary building, originally and appropriately called the Illuminated Tomb and only from the nineteenth century known as the **TAJ MAHAL (FIG. 23–1)**, was built between 1632 and 1648 by the Mughal ruler Shah Jahan as a mausoleum for his favorite wife, Mumtaz Mahal, who died in childbirth, and likely as a tomb for himself.

Inside, the Taj Mahal invokes the *hasht behisht* ("eight paradises"), a plan named for the eight small chambers that ring the interior—one at each corner and one behind each *iwan*, a vaulted opening with an arched portal, that is a typical feature of eastern Islamic architecture. In two stories (for a total of 16 chambers), the rooms ring the octagonal central area, which rises the full two stories to a domed ceiling that is lower than the outer dome. In this central chamber, surrounded by a finely carved octagonal openwork marble screen, are the exquisite inlaid **cenotaphs** (funerary monuments) of Shah Jahan and his wife, whose actual tombs lie in the crypt below.

The Taj Mahal includes much more than the white marble tomb. On one side is a mosque, while opposite and very similar in appearance is a building that may have served as a rest house. The enormous garden, both in front of the building and in its continuation on the opposite side of the Jamuna River, lends a lush setting consistent with Islamic notions of paradise. Both the side buildings and the two parts of the garden provide a sense of perfect symmetry to the entire complex.

A dynasty of central Asian origin, the Mughals were the most successful of the many Islamic groups that established themselves in India beginning in the twelfth century. Under their patronage, Persian and central Asian influences mingled with older traditions of the South Asian subcontinent, adding yet another dimension to the already ancient and complex artistic heritage of India.

LEARN ABOUT IT

23.1 Understand the impact of Islam on the art of India and Southeast Asia.

23.2 Understand how exogenous influences affect the form of a nation's arts.

23.3 Recognize how nationalism can be expressed in art.

23.4 Understand the way global styles can address indigenous themes.

23.5 Recognize the ways in which art of diverse religions is produced simultaneously in the same nation.

HEAR MORE: Listen to an audio file of your chapter **www.myartslab.com**

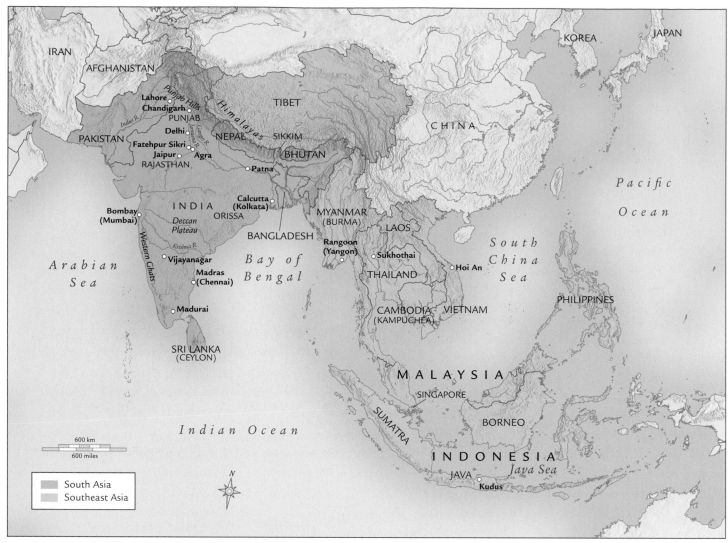

MAP 23-1 • SOUTH AND SOUTHEAST ASIA

Throughout its history, the kingdoms comprising the Indian subcontinent engaged—sometimes peacefully, sometimes militarily—with neighboring and more distant people, contributing significantly to the development of its art.

INDIA AFTER 1200

By 1200 India was already among the world's oldest civilizations (see "Foundations of Indian Culture," page 774). The art that survives from its earlier periods is almost exclusively sacred, most of it inspired by the three principal religions: Buddhism, Hinduism, and Jainism. These three religions remained a primary focus for Indian art, even as dynasties arriving from the northwest began to establish the new religious culture of Islam.

BUDDHIST ART

After many centuries of prominence, Buddhism had been in decline as a cultural force in India since the seventh or eighth century. By 1200, the principal Buddhist centers were concentrated in the northeast, in the region that had been ruled by the Pala dynasty (c. 750–1199). There, in great monastic universities that attracted monks from as far away as China, Korea, and Japan, was cultivated a form of Buddhism known as Tantric (Vajrayana) Mahayana.

ICONOGRAPHY OF A TANTRIC BODHISATTVA. The practices of Tantric Buddhism, which include techniques for visualizing deities, encourage the development of images with precise iconographic details such as the twelfth-century gilt-bronze sculpture of **THE BODHISATTVA AVALOKITESHVARA** in **FIGURE 23–2** from the site of Kurkihar in eastern India. Bodhisattvas are beings who are well advanced on the path to buddhahood (enlightenment), the goal of Mahayana Buddhists, and who have vowed out of compassion to help others achieve enlightenment. Avalokiteshvara, the bodhisattva of greatest compassion, whose vow is to forgo buddhahood until all others become buddhas, became the most popular of these saintly beings in India and in East Asia.

Characteristic of bodhisattvas, Avalokiteshvara is distinguished in art by his princely garments, unlike a buddha, who wears a monk's robes. Avalokiteshvara is specifically recognized by the lotus flower he holds and by the presence in his crown of his "parent" Buddha, in this case Amitabha, the Buddha of the Western Pure

Land (the Buddhist paradise). Other marks of Avalokiteshvara's extraordinary status are the third eye (symbolizing the ability to see in miraculous ways) and the wheel on his palm (signifying the ability to teach the Buddhist truth).

Avalokiteshvara is shown here in the relaxed pose known as the posture of royal ease. One leg angles down; the other is drawn up onto the lotus seat, itself considered an emblem of spiritual purity. His body bends gracefully, if a bit stiffly, to one side. The chest scarf and lower garment cling to his body, fully revealing its shape. Delicate floral patterns enliven the textiles, and closely set parallel folds provide a wiry, linear tension that contrasts with the hard but silken surfaces of the body. Linear energy continues in the sweep of the tightly pleated hem emerging from under the right thigh, in the sinuous lotus stalks on each side, and in the fluttering ribbons of the elaborate crown. A profusion of details and varied textures creates an ornate effect—the lavish jewelry, the looped hair piled high and cascading over the shoulders, the ripe blossoms, the rich layers of the lotus seat. Though still friendly and human, the image is somewhat formalized. The features of the face, where we instinctively look for a human echo, are treated abstractly, and despite its reassuring smile the statue's expression remains remote. Through richness of ornament and tension of line, this style expresses the heightened power of a perfected being.

With the fall of the Pala dynasty in the late twelfth century, the last centers of Buddhism in northern India collapsed, and most

23-3 • DETAIL OF A LEAF WITH THE BIRTH OF MAHAVIRA
Kalpa Sutra, western Indian school (probably Gujarat). c. 1375–1400. Gouache on paper, 3⅜ × 3″ (8.5 × 7.6 cm). Prince of Wales Museum, Bombay.

23-2 • THE BODHISATTVA AVALOKITESHVARA
From Kurkihar, Bihar. Pala dynasty, 12th century. Gilt-bronze, height 10″ (25.5 cm). Patna Museum, Patna.

of the monks dispersed, mainly into Nepal and Tibet (SEE MAP 23–1). From that time, Tibet has remained the principal stronghold of Tantric Buddhist practice and its arts (see "Tantric Influence in the Art of Nepal and Tibet," page 776). The artistic style perfected under the Palas, however, became an influential international style throughout East and Southeast Asia.

JAIN ART

The Jain religion traces its roots to a spiritual leader called Mahavira (c. 599–527 BCE), whom it regards as the final in a series of 24 saviors known as pathfinders (*tirthankaras*). Devotees seek through purification to become worthy of rebirth in the heaven of the pathfinders, a zone of pure existence at the zenith of the universe. Jain monks live a life of austerity, and even laypersons avoid killing any living creature.

A MANUSCRIPT LEAF FROM THE *KALPA SUTRA*. Muslim dynasties brought with them a rich tradition of book illustration, and non-Islamic religions began to write and illustrate their own sacred books, previously intended largely for memorization. The Jains of western India, primarily in the region of Gujarat, created many illustrated manuscripts, such as this *Kalpa Sutra*, which explicates the lives of the pathfinders (FIG. 23–3). Produced during the late fourteenth century, it is one of the first Jain manuscripts on

Foundations of Indian Culture

The earliest civilization on the Indian subcontinent flourished toward the end of the third millennium BCE along the Indus River in present-day Pakistan. Remains of its expertly engineered brick cities have been uncovered, together with works of art that intriguingly suggest spiritual practices and reveal artistic traits known in later Indian culture.

The decline of the Indus civilization during the mid second millennium BCE coincides with (and may be related to) the arrival from the northwest of a seminomadic people who spoke an Indo-European language and referred to themselves as Aryans. Over the next millennium they were influential in formulating the new civilization that gradually emerged. The most important Aryan contributions to this new civilization included the Sanskrit language and the sacred texts called the Vedas. The evolution of Vedic thought under the influence of indigenous Indian beliefs culminated in the mystical, philosophical texts called the Upanishads, which took shape sometime after 800 BCE.

The Upanishads teach that the material world is illusory; only Brahman, the universal soul, is real and eternal. We—that is, our individual souls—are trapped in this illusion in a relentless cycle of birth, death, and rebirth. The ultimate goal of religious life is to liberate ourselves from this cycle and to unite our individual soul with Brahman.

Buddhism and Jainism are two of the many religions that developed in the climate of Upanishadic thought. Buddhism (see "Buddhism" page 297) is based on the teachings of Shakyamuni Buddha, who lived in central India about 500 BCE; Jainism was shaped about the same time by the followers of the spiritual leader Mahavira. Both religions acknowledged the cyclical nature of existence and taught a means of liberation from it, but they rejected the authority,

rituals, and social strictures of Vedic religion. Whereas the Vedic religion was in the hands of a hereditary priestly class, Buddhist and Jain communities welcomed all members of society, which gave them great appeal. The Vedic tradition eventually evolved into the many sects now collectively known as Hinduism (see "Hinduism" page 298).

Through most of its history India was a mosaic of regional dynastic kingdoms, but from time to time empires emerged that unified large parts of the subcontinent. The first was that of the Maurya dynasty (c. 322–185 BCE), whose great king Ashoka patronized Buddhism. From this time Buddhist doctrines spread widely and its artistic traditions were established.

In the first century CE the Kushans, a central Asian people, created an empire extending from present-day Afghanistan down into central India. Buddhism prospered under Kanishka, the most powerful Kushan king, and spread into central Asia and to east Asia. At this time, under the evolving thought of Mahayana Buddhism, traditions first evolved for depicting the image of the Buddha in art.

Later, under the Gupta dynasty (c. 320–550 CE) in northern India, Buddhist art and culture reached their high point. However, Gupta monarchs also patronized Hindu art, and from this time Hinduism grew to become the dominant Indian religious tradition, with its emphasis on the great gods Vishnu, Shiva, and the Goddess—all with multiple forms.

After the tenth century, numerous regional dynasties prevailed, some quite powerful and long-lasting. Hindu temples, in particular, developed monumental and complex forms that were rich in symbolism and ritual function, with each region of India producing its own variation.

---

paper rather than palm leaf, the material that had previously been used for written documents.

With great economy, the illustration, inserted between blocks of Sanskrit text, depicts the birth of Mahavira. He is shown cradled in his mother's arms as she reclines in her bed under a canopy |connoting royalty, attended by three ladies-in-waiting. Decorative pavilions and a shrine with peacocks on the roof suggest a luxurious palace setting. Everything appears two-dimensional against the brilliant red or blue ground. Vibrant colors and crisp outlines impart an energy to the painting that suggests the arrival of the divine in the mundane world. Transparent garments with variegated designs reveal the swelling curves of the figures, whose alert postures and gestures convey a sense of the importance and excitement of the event. Strangely exaggerated features, such as the protruding eyes, contribute to the air of the extraordinary. With its angles and tense curves, the drawing is closely linked to the aesthetics of Sanskrit calligraphy, and the effect is as if the words themselves had suddenly flared into color and image.

HINDU ART

With the increasing popularity of Hindu sects came the rapid development of Hindu temples. Spurred by the ambitious building programs of wealthy rulers, well-formulated regional styles had evolved by about 900 CE. The most spectacular structures of the era were monumental, with a complexity and grandeur of proportion rarely equaled even in later Indian art.

Emphasis on monumental individual temples gave way to the building of vast temple complexes and more moderately scaled, yet more richly ornamented, individual temples. These developments took place largely in the south of India, although some of the largest temples are in the north, for example, the Sun Temple at Konarak, built in the thirteenth century, and the Govind Deva Temple in Brindavan, built in the sixteenth century under the patronage of the Mughal emperor Akbar. The mightiest of the southern Indian kingdoms was Vijayanagar (c. 1336–1565), whose rulers successfully countered the potential incursions of neighboring dynasties, both Hindu and Muslim, for more than 200 years. Under the patronage of the Vijayanagar kings and their successors, the Nayaks, some of India's most spectacular Hindu architecture was created.

TEMPLE AT MADURAI. The enormous temple complex at Madurai, one of the capitals of the Nayaks, is an example of this fervent expression of Hindu faith. Founded around the thirteenth century, it is dedicated to the goddess Minakshi (the local name for Parvati, the consort of the god Shiva) and to Sundareshvara (the local name for Shiva himself). The temple complex stands in the center of the city and is the focus of Madurai life. At its heart are the two oldest shrines, one to Minakshi and the other to Sundareshvara. Successive additions over the centuries gradually expanded the complex around these small shrines and came to dominate the visual landscape of the city. The most dramatic features of this and similar "temple cities" of the south were the thousand-pillar halls, large ritual-bathing pools, and especially the entrance gateways, **gopuras** in Sanskrit, that tower above the temple site and the surrounding city like modern skyscrapers (**FIG. 23–4**).

Gopuras proliferated as a temple city grew, necessitating new and bigger enclosing walls, and thus new gateways. Successive rulers, often seeking to outdo their predecessors, donated taller and taller *gopuras*. As a result, the tallest structures in temple cities are often at the periphery, rather than at the central temples, which are sometimes totally overwhelmed by the height of the surrounding structures. The temple complex at Madurai has 11 *gopuras*, the largest over 160 feet tall.

Formally, the *gopura* has its roots in the pyramidal tower characteristic of the seventh-century southern temple style. As the *gopura* evolved, it took on the graceful concave silhouette shown here. The exterior is embellished with thousands of sculpted figures, evoking a teeming world of gods and goddesses. Inside, stairs lead to the top for an extraordinary view.

23-4 • OUTER GOPURA OF THE MINAKSHI-SUNDARESHVARA TEMPLE
Madurai, Tamil Nadu, south India. Nayak dynasty, mostly 13th to mid 17th century, with modern renovations.

Tantric Influence in the Art of Nepal and Tibet

The legacy of India's Tantric Buddhist art can be traced in the regions of Nepal and Tibet. Artistic expression of Esoteric Buddhist ideals reached a high point in the seventeenth and eighteenth centuries. Indeed, even today, artists worldwide continue to explore aspects of this tradition.

Inlaid Devotional Sculpture. In Nepal, where Hinduism intermingled with Buddhism, sculptors developed a metalwork style in which a traditional artistic use of polished stones became prevalent in devotional sculptures as well. Inlaid gems and semiprecious stones often enlivened their copper or bronze sculptures, which were almost always brightly gilded. Complex representations of deities, often multiarmed and adorned with celestial attributes, predominated, but some themes from early Buddhism were revived. In one particularly fine eighteenth-century example (FIG. A), Maya, the Mother of the Buddha, holds the legendary tree branch while the Buddha emerges from her side. The cast and **chased** (ornamented by hammering or incising the metal surface) details of the regal costume of Queen Maya, including fluttering scarves, elaborate jewelry, and a large crown, are studded with real jewels, pearls, and semiprecious stones. The tree, also, is richly inlaid, symbolizing the auspicious nature of the event. Both the tree and the figure rise from a pedestal shaped to suggest the blossoming lotus, a reference to the appearance of the Buddha's purity in the muddy pond of the material world.

***Tangka* Painting.** Buddhism was established relatively late in Tibet, but the region has since become almost wholly identified with the religion. With the rule of a lineage of Dalai Lamas established in the seventeenth century and continuing through to the twentieth century, and a related expansion of monasteries, the arts associated with Tantric Buddhism flourished. Wrathful manifestations of powerful deities were evoked in sculpted and painted forms, with the scroll-like *tangka* emerging as a major format. A nineteenth-century painting of Achala (FIG. B), one of a group of wrathful deities associated with truth, resolve, and the overcoming of obstacles, exemplifies this major aspect of Tibetan art. The deity exudes brilliant red flames while brandishing a sword and posing as if to strike. Following traditional practice, the artist—or artists, as such paintings may have employed highly specialized craftsmen—positions the terrifying figure on a lotus pedestal, establishing his ethereal nature. The background suggests the green hills and blue sky of the material world as well as the cosmic geometry envisioned in Tantric Buddhism. Repeated representations of the deity emphasize the efficacious function and conspicuous power of the image.

A. MAYA, MOTHER OF BUDDHA, HOLDING A TREE BRANCH
From Nepal. 18th century. Gilt bronze with inlaid precious stones, height 22″ (56 cm). Musée Guimet, Paris.

B. ACHALA
From Tibet. 19th century. Gouache on cotton, 33½ × 23⅔″ (85 × 60 cm). Musée Guimet, Paris.

23-5 • SHWE-DAGON STUPA (PAGODA)
Yangon.15th century. Construction at the site dates from at least the 14th century, with continuous replastering and redecoration to the present.

THE BUDDHIST AND HINDU INHERITANCE IN SOUTHEAST ASIA

India's Buddhist and Hindu traditions influenced Southeast Asia (discussed in Chapter 9), where they were absorbed by newly rising kingdoms in the regions now comprising Burma (Myanmar), Thailand, Cambodia, Vietnam, and Indonesia.

THERAVADA BUDDHISM IN BURMA AND THAILAND

In northern Burma, from the eleventh to the thirteenth century, rulers raised innumerable religious monuments—temples, monasteries, and stupas—in the Pagan Plain, following the Scriptures of Theravada Buddhism (also called Hinayana Buddhism, see Chapter 9). To the south arose the port city of Yangon (formerly known as Rangoon, called Dagon in antiquity), the nation's present-day capital. Established by Mon rulers (SEE FIG. 9–29) at least by the eleventh century, Yangon is site of the **SHWE-DAGON STUPA** (FIG. 23–5), which enshrines relics of the Buddha. The modern structures of Shwe-dagon ("Golden Dagon") rise from an ancient core—fourteenth century or earlier—and reflect centuries of continual restoration and enhancement. The site

continues to be a center of Theravada devotion amid symbolic ornamentation—especially lotus elements symbolic of the Buddha's purity—and splendid decoration in gilding and precious stones supplied by pious contributions. Images of the Buddha, and sometimes his footprints alone, provide focal points for devotion.

In Thailand, the Sukhothai kingdom (mid thirteenth to late fourteenth century) also embraced Theravada Buddhism, although Hindu shrines were constructed as well in its capital city, Sukhothai (ancient name Sukhodaya). Artisans working under royal patrons developed a classic statement of Theravada ideals in bronze sculptures of the Buddha. Notable was their development of a free-standing walking Buddha. Especially evocative of the ascetic simplicity of Theravada Buddhism, however, are their many renditions of the Buddha Calling the Earth to Witness (FIG. 23–6). Inspired by devotional texts and poetry, and further refined through reference to models from Sri Lanka, the iconographic and stylistic elements became notably formalized. The Buddha's cranial protuberance is interpreted as a flame of divine knowledge, as it was in southern India and Sri Lanka, and details of his ecclesiastical garb are reduced to a few elegant lines. The *mudras* (see page 304), or hand gestures, are quietly eloquent.

23-6 • SEATED SUKHOTAI BRONZE BUDDHA
Leaded bronze, height 35⅜" (90 cm). The Walters Art Museum, Baltimore. Bequest of A.B. Griswold, 1992. 54.2775

23-7 • GROUP OF VIETNAMESE CERAMICS FROM THE HOI AN HOARD
Late 15th to early 16th century, porcelain with underglaze blue decoration; barbed-rim dishes: (left) diameter 14″ (35.1 cm); (right) diameter 13¼″ (34.7 cm). Phoenix Art Museum. (2000.105–109)

More than 150,000 blue-and-white ceramic items were found in the hold of a sunken ship excavated in the late 1990s under commission from the Vietnamese government, which later sent many of the retrieved items for public auction. The 23 small cups among the works shown here were found packed inside the jar.

VIETNAMESE CERAMICS

Both the Burmese and Thai kingdoms produced ceramics, often inspired by stonewares and porcelains from China. Sukhothai potters, for example, made green-glazed and brown-glazed wares, called Sawankhalok wares. Even more widespread were the wares of Vietnamese potters. For example, excavation of the Hoi An "hoard" (FIG. 23–7), actually the contents of a sunken ship laden with ceramics for export, brought to light an impressive variety of ceramic forms made by Vietnamese potters of the late fifteenth to early sixteenth century. Painted in underglaze cobalt blue and further embellished with overglaze enamels, these wares were shipped throughout Southeast Asia and beyond, as far east as Japan and as far west as England and the Netherlands.

INDONESIAN TRADITIONS

Indonesia, now the world's most populous Muslim country, experienced a Hindu revival in the centuries following its Buddhist period, which came to a close in the eighth or ninth century (see Chapter 9). As a consequence, it has maintained unique traditions that build upon the Hindu epics, especially the *Ramayana*. Islamic monuments in Indonesia, like the Hindu and Buddhist ones, draw from a rich and diverse repertoire of styles and motifs. The **MINARET MOSQUE** of Kudus in central Java (FIG. 23–8) was built in 1549. The minaret serves as the tower from which Muslims are

called to worship five times daily, but the minaret's red brick, general shape, and the niches that adorn its façade all recall Hindu temples built in east Java about two centuries earlier. As in India, Javanese artists worked in a consistent style, independent of the religion of the patron. Their architecture did, of course, accommodate the specific ritual functions of the building.

MUGHAL PERIOD

Islam first touched the South Asian subcontinent in the eighth century, when Arab armies captured a small territory near the Indus River. Later, beginning around 1000, Turkic factions from central Asia, relatively recent converts to Islam, began military campaigns into north India, at first purely for plunder, then seeking territorial control. From 1193, various Turkic and Afghan dynasties ruled portions of the subcontinent from the northern city of Delhi. These sultanates, as they are known, constructed forts, mausoleums, monuments, and mosques. Although these early dynasties left their mark, it was the Mughal dynasty that made the most inspired and lasting contribution to the art of India.

The Mughals, too, came from central Asia. Muhammad Zahir-ud-Din, known as Babur ("Lion" or "Panther"), was the first Mughal emperor of India (r. 1526–30). He emphasized his Turkic

23-8 • MINARET MOSQUE
1549. Kudus, Java.

heritage, though he had equally impressive Mongol ancestry. After some initial conquests in central Asia, he amassed an empire stretching from Afghanistan to Delhi, which he conquered in 1526. Akbar (r. 1556–1605), the third ruler, extended Mughal control over most of north India, and under his two successors, Jahangir and Shah Jahan, northern India was generally unified by 1658. The Mughal Empire lasted until 1858, when the last Mughal emperor was deposed and exiled to Burma by the British.

MUGHAL ARCHITECTURE

Mughal architects were heir to a 300-year-old tradition of Islamic building in India. The Delhi sultans who preceded them had great forts housing government and court buildings. Their architects had introduced two fundamental Islamic structures, the mosque and the tomb, along with construction based on the arch and the dome. (Earlier Indian architecture had been based primarily on post-and-lintel construction.) They had also drawn freely on Indian architecture, borrowing both decorative and structural elements to create a variety of hybrid styles, and had especially benefited from the centuries-old Indian virtuosity in stonecarving and masonry. The Mughals followed in this tradition, synthesizing Indian, Persian, and central Asian elements for their forts, palaces, mosques, tombs, and cenotaphs (tombs or monuments to someone whose remains are actually somewhere else).

Akbar, an ambitious patron of architecture and city planning, constructed a new capital at a place he named Fatehpur Sikri ("City of Victory at Sikri"), celebrating his military conquests and the birth of his son Salim, who subsequently took on the throne name of Jahangir. The palatial and civic buildings, built primarily during Akbar's residence there from about 1572 to 1585, have drawn much admiration. There are two major components to Fatehpur Sikri: a religious section including the Jami Mosque and the administrative and residential section. Among the most extraordinary buildings in the administrative and residential section is the private audience hall (Diwan-i Khas) (see "A Closer Look," page 780). In the center of the hall is a tall pillar supporting a circular platform on which Akbar could sit as he received his nobles and dispensed justice. The structure recalls, perhaps consciously, the pillars erected by Ashoka (see Chapter 9) to promulgate his law.

THE TAJ MAHAL. Perhaps the most famous of all Indian Islamic structures, the Taj Mahal is sited on the bank of the Jamuna River at Agra, in northern India. Built between 1631 and 1648, it was commissioned as a mausoleum for his wife by the emperor Shah Jahan (r. 1628–58), who is believed to have taken a major part in overseeing its design and construction.

Visually, the Taj Mahal never fails to impress (SEE FIG. 23–1). As visitors enter through a monumental, hall-like gate, the tomb rises before them across a spacious garden set with long reflecting pools. Measuring some 1,000 by 1,900 feet, the enclosure is unobtrusively divided into quadrants planted with trees and flowers, and framed by broad walkways and stone inlaid in geometric patterns. In Shah Jahan's time, fruit trees and cypresses—symbolic of life and death, respectively—lined the walkways, and fountains played in the shallow pools. Truly, the senses were beguiled in this earthly evocation of paradise.

The garden in which the mausoleum is set is comprised of two parts divided by the Jamuna River. Thus while the structure appears to visitors to be set at the end of a garden, it is in fact in the center of a four-part garden, a traditional Mughal tomb setting used for earlier Mughal tombs. The tomb is flanked by two smaller structures not visible here, one a mosque and the other a hall designed in mirror image. They share a broad base with the tomb and serve visually as stabilizing elements. Like the entrance hall, they are made mostly of red sandstone, rendering even more startling the full glory of the tomb's white marble, a material previously reserved for the tombs of saints and so here implying an elevated religious stature for Shah Jahan and Mumtaz Mahal. The tomb is raised higher than these structures on its own marble platform. At each corner of the platform, a minaret defines the surrounding space. The minarets' three levels correspond to those of the tomb, creating a bond between them. Crowning each minaret is a **chattri** (pavilion). Traditional embellishments of Indian palaces, *chattris* quickly passed into the vocabulary of Indian Islamic architecture, where they appear prominently. Minarets occur in architecture throughout the Islamic world; from their heights, the faithful are called to prayer.

A CLOSER LOOK

Private Audience Hall, Fatehpur Sikri › c.1570, north-central India.

The circular throne. Here Akbar sat, probably on a large cushion, able to look down on those petitioning for justice.

Ramps to the four directions. These gave Akbar access to his throne. They were also probably intended to recall the rivers that flowed to the four corners of the world, conveying Akbar's justice.

Closely spaced brackets serve as the capital for the pillar and structural base for the throne

One of the four doorways providing access to the private audience hall.

This pillar, reminiscent of Ashoka's pillars, supported the throne from which Akbar dispensed justice.

SEE MORE: View the Closer Look feature for the Private Audience Hall at Fatehpur Sikri **www.myartslab.com**

A lucid geometric symmetry pervades the tomb. It is basically square, but its **chamfered** (sliced-off) corners create a subtle octagon. Measured to the base of the **finial** (the spire at the top), the tomb is almost exactly as tall as it is wide. Each façade is identical, with a central *iwan* flanked by two stories of smaller *iwans*. By creating voids in the façades, these *iwans* contribute markedly to the building's sense of weightlessness. On the roof, four octagonal *chattris*, one at each corner, create a visual transition to the lofty, bulbous dome, the crowning element that lends special power to this structure. Framed but not obscured by the *chattris*, the dome rises more gracefully and is lifted higher by its drum than in

earlier Mughal tombs, allowing the swelling curves and elegant lines of its beautifully proportioned, surprisingly large form to emerge with perfect clarity.

By the seventeenth century, India was well known for exquisite craftsmanship and luxurious decorative arts (see "Luxury Arts," page 782). The pristine surfaces of the Taj Mahal are embellished with utmost subtlety (**FIG. 23–9**). Even the sides of the platform on which the Taj Mahal stands are carved in relief with a **blind arcade** (decorative arches set into a wall) motif and carved relief panels of flowers. The portals are framed with verses from the Qur'an and inlaid in black marble, while the spandrels are

23-10 • AKBAR INSPECTING THE CONSTRUCTION OF FATEHPUR SIKRI
Akbarnama. c. 1590. Opaque watercolor on paper, 14¾ × 10″ (37.5 × 25 cm). Victoria & Albert Museum, London. (I.S.2-1896 91/117)

Many of the painters in the Mughal imperial workshops are recorded in texts of the period. Based on those records and on signatures that occur on some paintings, the design of this work has been attributed to Tulsi Kalan (Tulsi the Elder), the painting to Bandi, and the portraits to Madhu Kalan (Madhu the Elder) or Madhu Khurd (Madhu the Younger).

decorated with floral arabesques inlaid in colored semiprecious stones, a technique known by its Italian name **pietra dura**. Not strong enough to detract from the overall purity of the white marble, the embellishments enliven the surfaces of this impressive yet delicate masterpiece.

MUGHAL PAINTING

Probably no one had more control over the solidification of the Mughal Empire and the creation of Mughal art than the emperor Akbar. A dynamic, humane, and just leader, Akbar enjoyed religious discourse and loved the arts, especially painting. He created an imperial atelier (workshop) of painters, which he placed under the direction of two artists from the Persian court. Learning from these two masters, the Indian painters of the atelier soon transformed Persian styles into the more vigorous, naturalistic styles that mark Mughal painting (see "Indian Painting on Paper," page 784). At Akbar's cosmopolitan court, pictorial sources from Europe also became inspiration for Mughal artists.

PAINTING AT THE COURT OF AKBAR.   Akbar's court artists also produced paintings documenting Akbar's own life and accomplishments recorded in the *Akbarnama*, a text written by Akbar's court biographer, Abul Fazl. Among the most fascinating in this imperial manuscript are those that record Akbar's supervision of the construction of Fatehpur Sikri. One painting (**FIG. 23–10**) documents his inspection of the stonemasons and other craftsmen.

PAINTING IN THE COURTS OF JAHANGIR AND SHAH JAHAN. Jahangir (r. 1605–1627), Akbar's son and successor, was a connoisseur of painting; he had his own workshop, which he

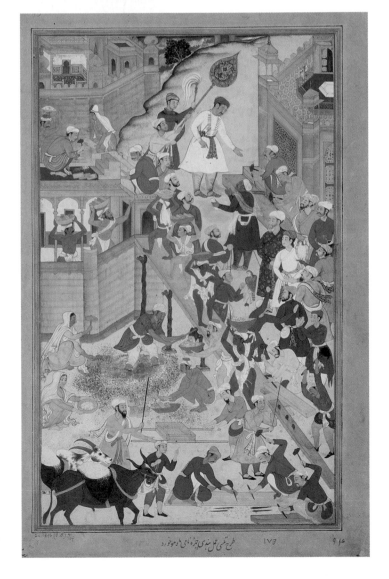

Luxury Arts

The decorative arts of India have been widely appreciated since the first century CE. An Indian ivory carving was found at Pompeii, while other Indian works of the time have been found along the Silk Route connecting China with Rome. For centuries Indian textiles have been made for export and copied in Europe for domestic consumption. Technically superb and crafted from precious materials, tableware, jewelry, furniture, and containers enhance the prestige of their owners and give visual pleasure as well. Metalwork and work in rock crystal, agate, and jade, carving in ivory, and intricate jewelry are all characteristic Indian arts. Because of the intrinsic value of their materials, however, pieces have been disassembled, melted down, and reworked, making the study of Indian luxury arts very difficult. Many pieces, like the carved ivory panel illustrated here, have no date or records of manufacture or ownership. And, like it, many such panels have been removed from a larger container or piece of furniture.

Carved in ivory against a golden ground, where openwork, stylized vines with spiky leaves weave an elegant arabesque, loving couples dally under the arcades of a palace courtyard, whose thin columns and cusped arches resemble the arcades of the palace of Tirumala Nayak (r. 1623–1659) in Madurai (present-day Tamil Nadu). Their huge eyes under heavy brows suggest the intensity of their gaze, and the artist's choice of the profile view shows off their long noses and sensuously thick lips. Their hair is tightly controlled; the men have huge buns, and the women long braids hanging down their backs. Are they divine lovers? After all, Krishna lived and loved on earth among the cowherd maidens. Or are we observing scenes of courtly romance?

The rich jewelry and well-fed look of the couples indicate a high station in life. Men as well as women have voluptuous figures—rounded buttocks and thighs, abdomens hanging over jeweled belts, and sharply indented slim waists that emphasize seductive breasts. Their smooth flesh contrasts with the diaphanous fabrics that swath their plump legs, and their long arms and elegant gestures seem designed to show off their rich jewelry—bracelets, armbands, necklaces, huge earrings, and ribbons. Such amorous couples symbolize harmony as well as fertility.

The erotic imagery suggests that the panel illustrated here might have adorned a container for personal belongings such as jewelry, perfume, or cosmetics. In any event, the ivory relief is a brilliant example of south Indian secular arts.

PANEL FROM A BOX
From Tamil Nadu, south India. Nayak dynasty, late 17th–18th century. Ivory backed with gilded paper, 6 × 12⅜ × ⅛″ (15.2 × 31.4 × 0.3 cm). Virginia Museum of Fine Arts.
The Arthur and Margaret Glasgow Fund. 80.171

established even before he became emperor. His focus on detail was much greater than that of his father. In his memoirs, he claimed:

> My liking for painting and my practice in judging it have arrived at such a point that when any work is brought before me, either of deceased artists or of those of the present day, without their names being told me I say on the spur of the moment that it is the work of such and such a man, and if there be a picture containing many portraits, and each face be the work of a different master, I can discover which face is the work of each of them. And if any other person has put in the eye and eyebrow of a face, I can perceive whose work the original face is and who has painted the eye and eyebrows.

Portraits become a major art under Jahangir. The portrait Jahangir commissioned of himself with the Safavid-dynasty Persian emperor Shah Abbas **(FIG. 23–11)** demonstrates his sense of his superiority: Jahangir is depicted much larger than Shah Abbas, who appears to bow deferentially to the Mughal emperor; Jahangir's head is centered in the halo; and he stands on the lion, whose body

23-12 • Nadir al-Zaman (Abu'l Hasan) PRINCE KHURRAM, THE FUTURE SHAH JAHAN AT AGE 25 From the Minto Album. Mughal period, c. 1616–1617. Opaque watercolor, gold and ink on paper, 18⅛ × 4½″ (20.6 × 11.5 cm); page 15¼ × 10½″ (39 × 26.7 cm). Victoria & Albert Museum, London

23-11 • Nadir al-Zaman (Abu'l Hasan) JAHANGIR AND SHAH ABBAS From the St. Petersburg Album. Mughal period, c. 1618. Opaque watercolor, gold and ink on paper, 9⅜ × 6″ (23.8 × 15.4 cm). Freer Museum of Art, Smithsonian Institution, Washington, DC. Purchase, F1945.9. Freer Gallery, Washington

spans a vast territory, including Shah Abbas's own Persia. We can only speculate on the target audience for this painting. Because it is small, it certainly would not be intended for Jahangir's subjects; a painting of this size could not be publicly displayed. But because we know that paintings were commonly sent by embassies from one kingdom to another, it may have been intended as a gift for Shah Abbas, one with a message of clear strength and superiority cloaked in the diplomatic language of cordiality.

Jahangir was succeeded by his son, Prince Khurram, who took the title Shah Jahan. Although Shah Jahan's greatest artistic achievements were in architecture, painting continued to flourish during his reign. A portrait of Prince Khurram bears an inscription indicating that he considered it "a very good likeness of me at age 25" **(FIG. 23–12)**. Like all portraits of Shah Jahan, this one depicts him in profile, the view that has least likelihood of distortion. Holding an exquisite turban ornament, the prince stands quite

Before the fourteenth century most painting in India had been on walls or palm leaves. With the introduction of paper, about the same time in India as in Europe, Indian artists adapted painting techniques from Persia and over the ensuing centuries produced jewel-toned works on paper.

Painters usually began their training early. As young apprentices, they learned to make brushes and grind pigments. Brushes were made from the curved hairs of a squirrel's tail, arranged to taper from a thick base to a single hair at the tip. Paint came from pigments of vegetables and minerals—lapis lazuli to make blue, malachite for pale green—that were ground to a paste with water, then bound with a solution of gum from the acacia plant. Paper was made by crushing fibers of cotton and jute to a pulp, pouring the mixture onto a woven mat, drying it, and then burnishing with a smooth piece of agate, often achieving a glossy finish.

Artists frequently worked from a collection of sketches belonging to a master painter's atelier. Sometimes, to transfer the drawing to a blank sheet beneath, sketches were pricked with small, closely spaced holes that were then daubed with wet color. The resulting dots were connected into outlines, and the process of painting began.

First, the painter applied a thin wash of a chalk-based white, which sealed the surface of the paper while allowing the underlying sketch to show through. Next, outlines were filled with thick washes of brilliant, opaque, unmodulated color. When the colors were dry, the painting was laid face down on a smooth marble surface and burnished with a rounded agate stone, rubbing first up and down, then side to side. The indirect pressure against the marble polished the pigments to a high luster. Then outlines, details, and modeling—depending on the style— were added with a fine brush.

Sometimes certain details were purposely left for last, such as the eyes, which were said to bring the painting to life. Gold and raised details were applied when the painting was nearly finished. Gold paint, made from pulverized, 24-carat gold leaf bound with acacia gum, was applied with a brush and burnished to a high shine. Raised details such as the pearls of a necklace were made with thick, white, chalk-based paint, with each pearl a single droplet hardened into a tiny raised mound.

formally against a dark background, allowing nothing in the painting to compete for the viewer's attention.

RAJPUT PAINTING

Outside of the Mughal strongholds at Delhi and Agra, much of northern India was governed regionally by local Hindu princes, descendants of the so-called Rajput warrior clans, who were allowed to keep their lands in return for allegiance to the Mughals. Like the Mughals, Rajput princes frequently supported painters at their courts, and in these settings a variety of strong, indigenous Indian painting styles were perpetuated. Rajput painting, more abstract than the Mughal style, included subjects like those treated by Mughal painters, royal portraits and court scenes, as well as indigenous subjects such as Hindu myths, love poetry, and Ragamala illustrations (illustrations of musical modes).

The Hindu devotional movement known as *bhakti*, which had done much to spread the faith in the south from around the seventh century, now experienced a revival in the north. As it had earlier in the south, *bhakti* inspired an outpouring of poetic literature, this time devoted especially to Krishna, the popular human incarnation of the god Vishnu. Most renowned is the *Gita Govinda*, a cycle of rhapsodic poems about the love between God and humans expressed metaphorically through the love between the young Krishna and the cowherd Radha.

The illustration here (**FIG. 23–13**) is from a manuscript of the *Gita Govinda* probably produced in present-day Rajasthan about 1525–50. The blue god Krishna sits in dalliance with a group of cowherd women. Standing with her maid and consumed with love for Krishna, Radha peers through the trees, overcome by jealousy. Her feelings are indicated by the cool blue color behind her, while the crimson red behind the Krishna grouping suggests passion. The curving stalks and bold patterns of the flowering vines and trees express not only the exuberance of springtime, when the story unfolds, but also the heightened emotional tensions of the scene. Birds, trees, and flowers are as brilliant as fireworks against the black, hilly landscape edged in an undulating white line. As in the Jain manuscript earlier (SEE FIG. 23–3), all the figures are of a single type, with plump faces in profile and oversized eyes. Yet the resilient line of the drawing gives them life, and the variety of textile patterns provides some individuality. The intensity and resolute flatness of the scene seem to thrust all of its energy outward, irrevocably engaging the viewer in the drama.

Quite a different mood pervades **HOUR OF COWDUST**, a work from the Kangra School in the Punjab Hills, foothills of the Himalayas north of Delhi (**FIG. 23–14**). Painted around 1790, some 250 years later than the *Gita Govinda* illustration, it shows the influence of Mughal naturalism on the later schools of Indian painting. The theme is again Krishna. Wearing his peacock crown, garland of flowers, and yellow garment—all traditional iconography of Krishna-Vishnu—he returns to the village with his fellow cowherds and their cattle. All eyes are upon him as he plays his flute, said to enchant all who hear it. Women with water jugs on their heads turn to look; others lean from windows to watch and call out to him. We are drawn into this charming village scene by the diagonal movements of the cows as they surge through the gate and into the courtyard beyond. Pastel houses and walls create a sense of space, and in the distance we glimpse other villagers going about their work or peacefully sitting in their houses. A rim of dark trees softens the horizon, and an atmospheric sky completes the aura of enchanted naturalism. Again, all the figures are similar in

23–13 • KRISHNA AND THE *GOPIS*

From the *Gita Govinda*, Rajasthan, India. Mughal period,
c. 1525–1550. Gouache on paper, 4⅞ × 7½″ (12.3 × 19 cm). Prince of
Wales Museum, Bombay.

The lyrical poem *Gita Govinda*, by the poet-saint Jayadeva, was
probably written in eastern India during the latter half of the twelfth
century. The episode illustrated here occurs early in the relationship
of Radha and Krishna, which in the poem is a metaphor for the
connection between humans and God. The poem traces the progress
of their love through separation, reconciliation, and fulfillment.
Intensely sensuous imagery characterizes the entire poem, as in the
final song, when Krishna welcomes Radha to his bed. (Narayana is the
name of Vishnu in his role as cosmic creator.)

Leave lotus footprints on my bed of tender shoots, loving Radha!
Let my place be ravaged by your tender feet!
Narayana is faithful now. Love me Radhika!
I stroke your feet with my lotus hand—you have come far.
Set your golden anklet on my bed like the sun.
Narayana is faithful now. Love me Radhika!
Consent to my love. Let elixir pour from your face!
To end our separation I bare my chest of the silk that bars your breast.
Narayana is faithful now. Love me Radhika!

(Translated by Barbara Stoler Miller)

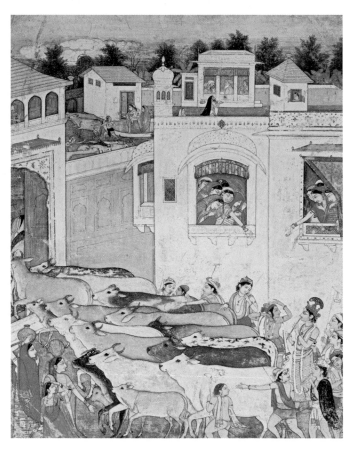

23–14 • HOUR OF COWDUST

From Punjab Hills, India. Mughal period, Kangra School,
c. 1790. Gouache on paper, 14¹⁵⁄₁₆ × 12⁹⁄₁₆″ (36 × 31.9 cm). Museum
of Fine Arts, Boston. Denman W. Ross Collection (22.683)

type, this time with a perfection of proportion and a gentle, lyrical movement that complement the idealism of the setting. The scene embodies the sublime purity and grace of the divine, which, as in so much Indian art, is evoked into our human world to coexist with us as one.

INDIA'S ENGAGEMENT WITH THE WEST

By the time *Hour of Cowdust* was painted, India's regional rulers, both Hindu and Muslim, had reasserted themselves, and the vast Mughal Empire had shrunk to a small area around Delhi. At the same time, however, a new power, Britain, was making itself felt, inaugurating a markedly different period in Indian history.

BRITISH COLONIAL PERIOD

First under the mercantile interests of the British East India Company in the seventeenth and eighteenth centuries, and then under the direct control of the British government as a part of the British Empire in the nineteenth century, India was brought forcefully into contact with the West and its culture, a very different situation from its long-standing role in a world system that had included trade in both commodities and culture. The political concerns of the British Empire extended even to the arts, especially architecture. Over the course of the nineteenth century, the great cities of India, such as Calcutta (present-day Kolkata), Madras (Chennai), and Bombay (Mumbai), took on a European aspect as British architects built in the revivalist styles favored in England.

NEW DELHI. In 1911, the British announced its intention to move the seat of government from Calcutta to a newly constructed Western-style capital city to be built at New Delhi, a move intended to capitalize on the long-standing association of Delhi with powerful rulers such as the Mughals. Two years later, Sir Edwin Lutyens (1869–1944) was appointed joint architect for New Delhi (with Herbert Baker), and was charged with laying out the new city and designing the Viceroy's House, the present-day Rashtrapati Bhavan (President's House). Drawing inspiration from Classical antiquity—as well as from more recent urban models, such as Paris and Washington, D.C.—Lutyens sited the Viceroy's House as a focal point along with the triumphal arch that he designed as the All India War Memorial, now called the **INDIA GATE** (**FIG. 23–15**). In these works Lutyens sought to maintain the tradition of Classical architecture—he developed a "Delhi order" based on the Roman Doric—while incorporating massing, detail, and ornamentation derived from Indian architecture as well. The new capital was inaugurated in 1931.

MOTHER INDIA. Far prior to Britain's consolidation of imperial power in New Delhi a new spirit asserting Indian independence and pan-Asiatic solidarity was awakening. For example, working near Calcutta, the painter Abanindranath Tagore (1871–1951)—nephew of the poet Rabindranath Tagore (1861–1941), who went on to win the Nobel Prize for Literature in 1913—deliberately rejected the medium of oil painting and the academic realism of Western art. Like the Nihonga artists of Japan (SEE FIG. 25–15) with whom he was in contact, Tagore strove to create a style that reflected his ethnic origins. In **BHARAT MATA** (Mother India) he invents a nationalistic icon by using Hindu symbols while

23–15 • Sir Edwin Lutyens INDIA GATE
Originally the All India War Memorial. New Delhi. British colonial period, 20th century.

23-16 • Abanindranath Tagore
BHARAT MATA (MOTHER INDIA)
1905. Watercolor on paper, 10½ × 6″
(26.7 × 15.3 cm). Rabindra Bharati Society,
Calcutta.

also drawing upon the format and techniques of Mughal and Rajput painting **(FIG. 23–16)**.

THE MODERN PERIOD

In the wake of World War II, the imperial powers of Europe began to shed their colonial domains. The attainment of self-rule had been five long decades in the making, when finally—chastened by the nonviolent example of Mahatma Gandhi (1869–1948)—the British Empire relinquished its "Jewel in the Crown," which was partitioned to form two modern nations: India and Pakistan. After independence in 1947, the exuberant young nation welcomed a modern, internationalist approach to art and architecture.

JAWAHAR KALA KENDRA.   Architect Charles Correa often draws on traditional Indian architectural forms. One example is his impressive **JAWAHAR KALA KENDRA**, a center for the visual and performing arts in Jaipur that was completed in 1992 **(FIG. 23–17)**. Like the original design of Jaipur, the building's design is based on a nine-square plan, and its elevation makes visual reference to the city's historic buildings. Correa's work is not confined to India, but

23-17 • Charles Correa JAWAHAR KALA KENDRA
1992. Jaipur. Like many of Correa's buildings, this arts center draws upon traditional Indian motifs and forms. Its many open spaces provide a feeling of connected space rather than individual rooms.

includes buildings in Europe and the United States, for example the Cognitive Sciences Complex at MIT completed in 2005.

TWO MODERN ARTISTS. Artists working after Indian independence have continued to study and work abroad, but often draw upon India's distinctive literary and religious traditions as well as regional and folk art traditions. One example is Manjit Bawa (b. 1941), who worked in Britain as a silkscreen artist before returning to India to settle in New Delhi. His distinctive canvases, painted meticulously in oil, juxtapose illusionistically modeled figures and animals against brilliantly colored backgrounds of flat, unmodulated color. The composite result, for example in **DHARMA AND THE GOD (FIG. 23–18)**, brings a strikingly new interpretation to the heroic figures of Indian tradition.

With Anish Kapoor (b. 1954), as with so many artists living abroad, we must consider issues of identity. Although some of his work draws inspiration from his Indian origins, for example, his 1981 composition **AS IF TO CELEBRATE, I DISCOVERED A MOUNTAIN BLOOMING WITH RED FLOWERS (23–19)**, whose red and ocher mounds recall the vermilion and other pigments beautifully piled for sale outside Indian temples, other works make no reference to India. Kapoor represented Britain, where he now lives and works, at the Venice Biennale in 1990, further complicating the issue of his identity.

23-18 • Manjit Bawa DHARMA AND THE GOD
1984. Oil on canvas, 85 × 72¹⁵⁄₁₆″ (216 × 185.4 cm). Peabody Essex Museum, Salem, Massachusetts. The Davida and Chester Herwitz Collection

23-19 • Anish Kapoor **AS IF TO CELEBRATE, I DISCOVERED A MOUNTAIN BLOOMING WITH RED FLOWERS**
1981. Wood, cement, polystyrene and pigment, 3 elements, 38¼ (highest point) × 30 (widest point) × 63″ (97 × 76.2 × 160 cm); 13 × 28 × 32″ (33 × 71.1 × 81.3 cm); 8¼ × 6 × 18½″ (21 × 15.3 × 47 cm), overall dimensions variable. Arts Council Collection, South Bank Centre, London.

THINK ABOUT IT

23.1 Explain some of the ways that Islamic art and culture impacted that of the Indian subcontinent. Explain how the Taj Mahal demonstrates influence from building styles studied in Chapter 8, and indicate how it departs from prior styles on the Indian subcontinent.

23.2 Analyze the Shwe-Dagon Stupa (Pagoda) in Yangon, and determine how the structure incorporates influence from Indian buildings. In your answer, compare the stupa to at least one Indian building.

23.3 Analyze the form of the India Gate (SEE FIG. 23–15) and explain how the ancient Roman form of the triumphal arch (see, for example, the Arch of Titus (SEE FIG. 6–32) is used within a new Indian context.

23.4 Explain how the artist Anish Kapoor utilizes Indian themes in his work *As if to Celebrate, I Discovered a Mountain Blooming with Red Flowers* (SEE FIG. 23–19). What other ideas can you infer from this work?

23.5 From the works discussed in this chapter, select a two-dimensional religious artwork from each of two religions practiced in India. Compare and contrast both directly, determining similarities in regional style and technique as well as differences due to their varying religious contexts.

PRACTICE MORE: Compose answers to these questions, get flashcards for images and terms, and review chapter material with quizzes **www.myartslab.com**

24–1 • Wang Hui A THOUSAND PEAKS AND MYRIAD RAVINES
Qing dynasty, 1693. Hanging scroll, ink on paper, 8′2½″ × 3′4½″ (2.54 × 1.03 m). National Palace Museum, Taibei, Taiwan, Republic of China.

EXPLORE MORE: Gain insight from a primary source related to *A Thousand Peaks and Myriad Ravines* www.myartslab.com

CHINESE AND KOREAN ART AFTER 1279

A THOUSAND PEAKS AND MYRIAD RAVINES (FIG. 24–1), painted by Wang Hui (1632–1717) in 1693, exemplifies the subjects of Chinese landscape painting: mountains, rivers, waterfalls, trees, rocks, temples, pavilions, houses, bridges, boats, wandering scholars, fishers—familiar motifs from a tradition now many centuries old. On it, the artist has written:

> Moss and weeds cover the rocks and mist hovers over the water.
> The sound of dripping water is heard in front of the temple gate.
> Through a thousand peaks and myriad ravines the spring flows,
> And brings the flying flowers into the sacred caves.

> In the fourth month of the year 1693, in an inn in the capital, I painted this based on a Tang-dynasty poem in the manner of [the painters] Dong [Yuan] and Ju[ran].
>
> (Translation by Chu-tsing Li)

The inscription refers to the artist's inspiration found in the lines of a Tang-dynasty poem, which offered the subject, and in the paintings of tenth-century painters Dong Yuan and Juran, on which he based his style. Wang Hui's art reflects ideals of the scholar in imperial China.

China's scholar class was unique, the product of an examination system designed to recruit the finest minds in the country for government service. Instituted during the Tang dynasty (618–907) and based on even earlier traditions, the civil service examinations were excruciatingly difficult, but for the tiny percentage who passed at the highest level, the rewards were prestige, position, power, and wealth. Steeped in philosophy, literature, and history, China's scholars—often called *wenren* (literati)—shared a common outlook. Following Confucianism, they became officials to fulfill their obligation to the world; pulled by Daoism, they retreated from society in order to come to terms with nature and the universe: to create a garden, to write poetry, to paint.

During the Song dynasty (960–1279) the examinations were expanded and regularized. More than half of all government positions came to be filled by scholars. In the subsequent Yuan and Ming periods, the tradition of **literati painting** (a style that reflected the taste of the educated class) further developed. When the Yuan period of foreign rule came to an end, the new Ming ruling house revived the court traditions of the Song. The Ming became the model for the rulers of Korea's Joseon dynasty, under whose patronage these styles achieved a distinctive and austere beauty.

In the Qing era, China was again ruled by an outside group, this time the Manchus. While maintaining their traditional connections to Tibet and inner Asia through their patronage of Tibetan Buddhism, the Manchu rulers also embraced Chinese ideals, especially those of the literati. Practicing painting and calligraphy, composing poetry in Chinese, and collecting esteemed Chinese works of art, these rulers amassed the great palace collections that can now be seen in Beijing and Taibei.

LEARN ABOUT IT

24.1 Analyze the continued importance of the three ways of thought (Daoism, Confucianism, and Buddhism) in Chinese art of the thirteenth century to the present.

24.2 Assess the influence of court life and patronage on art in China and Korea.

24.3 Examine the continuing relationship of calligraphy and painting in Chinese art.

24.4 Discuss literati values and the scholarly life in art in later China and Korea.

24.5 Assess the emergence of expression as a value of importance beyond representation in China and Korea, from the thirteenth century to the present.

HEAR MORE: Listen to an audio file of your chapter **www.myartslab.com**

THE MONGOL INVASIONS

At the beginning of the thirteenth century the Mongols, a nomadic people from the steppes north of China, began to amass an empire. Led first by Genghiz Khan (c. 1162–1227), then by his sons and grandsons, they swept westward into central Europe and overran Islamic lands from Central Asia through present-day Iraq. To the east, they quickly captured northern China, and in 1279, led by Kublai Khan, they conquered southern China as well. Grandson of the mighty Genghiz, Kublai proclaimed himself emperor of China and founder of the Yuan dynasty (1279–1368).

The Mongol invasions were traumatic, and their effect on China was long-lasting. During the Song dynasty, China had grown increasingly introspective. Rejecting foreign ideas and influences, intellectuals had focused on defining the qualities that constituted true "Chinese-ness." They drew a clear distinction between their own people, whom they characterized as gentle, erudite, and sophisticated, and the "barbarians" outside China's borders, whom they regarded as crude, wild, and uncivilized. Now, faced with the reality of barbarian occupation, China's inward gaze intensified in spiritual resistance. For centuries to come, long after the Mongols had gone, leading scholars continued to seek intellectually more challenging, philosophically more profound, and artistically more subtle expressions of all that could be identified as authentically Chinese (see "Foundations of Chinese Culture," opposite).

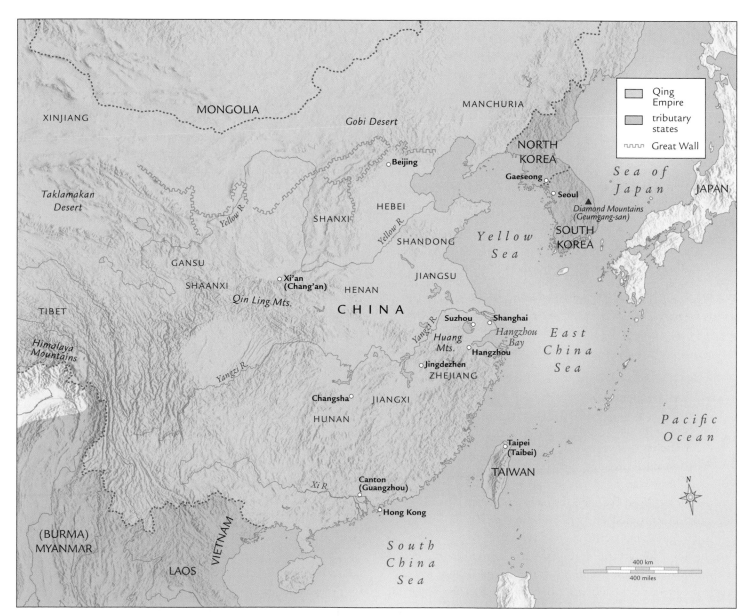

MAP 24-1 • CHINA AND KOREA

The map shows the borders of both contemporary China and Korea. The colored areas indicate the historical extent of the Qing dynasty empire (1644–1911) including its tributary states.

Foundations of Chinese Culture

Chinese culture is distinguished by its long and continuous development. Between 6000 and 2000 BCE a variety of Neolithic cultures flourished across China. Through long interaction these cultures became increasingly similar and they eventually gave rise to the three Bronze Age dynastic states with which Chinese history traditionally begins: the Xia, the Shang (c. 1700–1100 BCE), and the Zhou (1100–221 BCE).

The Shang developed traditions of casting ritual vessels in bronze, working jade in ceremonial shapes, and writing consistently in scripts that directly evolved into the modern Chinese written language. Society was stratified, and the ruling group maintained its authority in part by claiming power as intermediaries between the human and spirit worlds. Under the Zhou a feudal society developed, with nobles related to the king ruling over numerous small states.

During the latter part of the Zhou dynasty, states began to vie for supremacy through intrigue and increasingly ruthless warfare. The collapse of social order profoundly influenced China's first philosophers, who largely concerned themselves with the pragmatic question of how to bring about a stable society.

In 221 BCE, rulers of the state of Qin triumphed over the remaining states, unifying China as an empire for the first time. The Qin created the mechanisms of China's centralized bureaucracy, but their rule was harsh and the dynasty was quickly overthrown. During the ensuing Han dynasty (206 BCE–220 CE), China at last knew peace and prosperity. Confucianism was made the official state ideology, in the process assuming the form and force of a religion. Developed from the thought of Confucius (551–479 BCE), one of the many philosophers of the Zhou, Confucianism is an ethical system for the management of society based on establishing correct relationships among people. Providing a counterweight was Daoism, which also came into its own during the Han dynasty. Based on the thought of Laozi, a possibly legendary contemporary of Confucius, and the philosopher Zhuangzi (369–286 BCE), Daoism is a view of life that seeks to harmonize the individual with the Dao, or Way, the process of the universe. Confucianism and Daoism have remained central to Chinese thought—the one addressing the public realm of duty and conformity, the other the private world of individualism and creativity.

Following the collapse of the Han dynasty, China experienced a centuries-long period of disunity (220–589 CE). Invaders from the north and west established numerous kingdoms and dynasties, while a series of six precarious Chinese dynasties held sway in the south. Buddhism, which had begun to spread over trade routes from India during the Han era, now flourished. The period also witnessed the economic and cultural development of the south (previous dynasties had ruled from the north).

China was reunited under the Sui dynasty (581–618 CE), which quickly fell to the Tang (618–907), one of the most successful dynasties in Chinese history. Strong and confident, Tang China fascinated and, in turn, was fascinated by the cultures around it. Caravans streamed across central Asia to the capital, Chang'an, then the largest city in the world. Japan and Korea sent thousands of students to study Chinese culture, and Buddhism reached the height of its influence before a period of persecution signaled the start of its decline.

The mood of the Song dynasty (960–1279) was quite different. The martial vigor of the Tang gave way to a culture of increasing refinement and sophistication, and Tang openness to foreign influences was replaced by a conscious cultivation of China's own traditions. In art, landscape painting emerged as the most esteemed genre, capable of expressing both philosophical and personal concerns. With the fall of the north to invaders in 1126, the Song court set up a new capital in the south, which became the cultural and economic center of the country.

YUAN DYNASTY

The Mongols established their capital in the northern city now known as Beijing (MAP 24–1). The cultural centers of China, however, remained the great cities of the south, where the Song court had been located for the previous 150 years. Combined with the tensions of Yuan rule, this separation of China's political and cultural centers created a new dynamic in the arts.

Throughout most of Chinese history, the imperial court had set the tone for artistic taste: Artisans attached to the court produced architecture, paintings, gardens, and objects of jade, lacquer, ceramics, and silk especially for imperial use. Over the centuries, painters and calligraphers gradually moved higher up the social scale, for these "arts of the brush" were often practiced by scholars and even emperors, whose high status reflected positively on whatever interested them. With the establishment of an imperial painting academy during the Song dynasty, painters finally achieved a status equal to that of court officials. For the literati, painting came to be grouped with calligraphy and poetry as the trio of accomplishments suited to members of the cultural elite.

But while the literati elevated the status of painting by virtue of practicing it, they also began to develop their own ideas of what painting should be. Not needing to earn an income from their art, they cultivated an amateur ideal in which personal expression counted for more than "mere" professional skill. They created for themselves a status as artists totally separate from and superior to professional painters, whose art they felt was inherently compromised, since it was done to please others, and impure, since it was tainted by money.

The conditions of Yuan rule now encouraged a clear distinction between court taste, ministered to by professional

Marco Polo

China under Kublai Khan was one of four Mongol khanates that together extended west into present-day Iraq and through Russia to the borders of Poland and Hungary. For roughly a century, travelers moved freely across this vast expanse, making the era one of unprecedented cross-cultural exchange. Diplomats, missionaries, merchants, and adventurers flocked to the Yuan court, and Chinese envoys were dispatched to the West. The most celebrated European traveler of the time was a Venetian named Marco Polo (c. 1254–1324), whose descriptions of his travels were for several centuries the only firsthand account of China available in Europe.

Marco Polo was still in his teens when he set out for China in 1271. He traveled with his uncle and father, both merchants, bearing letters for Kublai Khan from Pope Gregory X. After a four-year journey the

Polos arrived at last in Beijing. Marco became a favorite of the emperor and spent the next 17 years in his service, during which time he traveled extensively throughout China. He eventually returned home in 1295.

Imprisoned later during a war between Venice and Genoa, rival Italian city-states, Marco Polo passed the time by dictating an account of his experiences to a fellow prisoner. The resulting book, *A Description of the World*, has fascinated generations of readers with its depiction of prosperous and sophisticated lands in the East. Translated into many European languages, it was an important influence in stimulating further exploration. When Columbus set sail across the Atlantic in 1492, one of the places he hoped to find was a country Marco Polo called Zipangu—Japan.

---

artists and artisans, and literati taste. The Yuan dynasty continued the imperial role as patron of the arts, commissioning buildings, murals, gardens, paintings, and decorative arts. Western visitors such as the Italian Marco Polo were impressed by the magnificence of the Yuan court (see "Marco Polo," above). But scholars, profoundly alienated from the new government, took little notice of these accomplishments. Nor did Yuan rulers have much use for scholars, especially those from the south. The civil service examinations were abolished, and the highest government positions were bestowed, instead, on Mongols and their foreign allies. Scholars now tended to turn inward, to search for solutions of their own and to try to express themselves in personal and symbolic terms.

ZHAO MENGFU. Zhao Mengfu (1254–1322) was a descendant of the imperial line of Song. Unlike many scholars of his time, he eventually chose to serve the Yuan government and was made a high official. A painter, calligrapher, and poet, all of the first rank,

Zhao was especially known for his carefully rendered paintings of horses. But he also cultivated another manner, most famous in his landmark painting **AUTUMN COLORS ON THE QIAO AND HUA MOUNTAINS** (FIG. 24–2).

Zhao painted this work for a friend whose ancestors came from Jinan, the present-day capital of Shandong Province, and the painting supposedly depicts the landscape there. Yet the mountains and trees are not painted in the accomplished naturalism of Zhao's own time but rather in the archaic yet oddly elegant manner of the earlier Tang dynasty (618–907). The Tang dynasty was a great era in Chinese history, when the country was both militarily strong and culturally vibrant. Through his painting Zhao evoked a nostalgia not only for his friend's distant homeland but also for China's past.

This educated taste for the "spirit of antiquity" became an important aspect of literati painting in later periods. Also typical of literati taste are the unassuming brushwork, the subtle colors sparingly used (many literati paintings forgo color altogether), the use of landscape to convey personal meaning, and even the

24-2 • Zhao Mengfu AUTUMN COLORS ON THE QIAO AND HUA MOUNTAINS
Yuan dynasty, 1296. Handscroll, ink and color on paper, 11¼ × 36¾" (28.6 × 9.3 cm). National Palace Museum, Taibei, Taiwan, Republic of China.

intended audience—a close friend. The literati did not paint for public display but for each other. They favored small formats such as **handscrolls**, **hanging scrolls**, or **album leaves** (book pages), which could easily be shown to friends or shared at small gatherings (see "Formats of Chinese Painting," page 797).

NI ZAN. Of the considerable number of Yuan painters who took up Zhao's ideas, several became models for later generations. One such was Ni Zan (1301–74), whose most famous surviving painting is **THE RONGXI STUDIO (FIG. 24–3)**. Done entirely in ink, the painting depicts the lake region in Ni's home district. Mountains, rocks, trees, and a pavilion are sketched with a minimum of detail using a dry brush technique—a technique in which the brush is not fully loaded with ink but rather is about to run out, so that white paper "breathes" through the ragged strokes. The result is a painting with a light touch and a sense of simplicity and purity. Literati styles were believed to reflect the painter's personality. Ni's spare, dry style became associated with a noble spirit, and many later painters adopted it or paid homage to it.

Ni Zan was one of those eccentrics whose behavior has become legendary in the history of Chinese art. In his early years he was one of the richest men in the region, the owner of a large estate. His pride and his aloofness from daily affairs often got him into trouble with the authorities. His cleanliness was notorious. In addition to washing himself several times daily, he also ordered his servants to wash the trees in his garden and to clean the furniture after his guests had left. He was said to be so unworldly that late in life he gave away most of his possessions and lived as a hermit in a boat, wandering on rivers and lakes.

Whether these stories are true or not, they were important elements of Ni's legacy to later painters, for Ni's life as well as his art served as a model. The painting of the literati was bound up with certain views about what constituted an appropriate life. The ideal, as embodied by Ni Zan and others, was of a brilliantly gifted scholar whose spirit was too refined for the dusty world of government service and who thus preferred to live as a recluse, or as one who had retired after having become frustrated by a brief stint as an official.

MING DYNASTY

The founder of the next dynasty, the Ming (1368–1644), came from a family of poor uneducated peasants. As he rose through the ranks in the army, he enlisted the help of scholars to gain power and solidify his following. Once he had driven the Mongols from Beijing and firmly established himself as emperor, however, he grew to distrust intellectuals. His rule was despotic, even ruthless. Throughout the nearly 300 years of Ming rule most emperors shared his attitude, so although the civil service examinations were reinstated, scholars remained alienated from the government they were trained to serve.

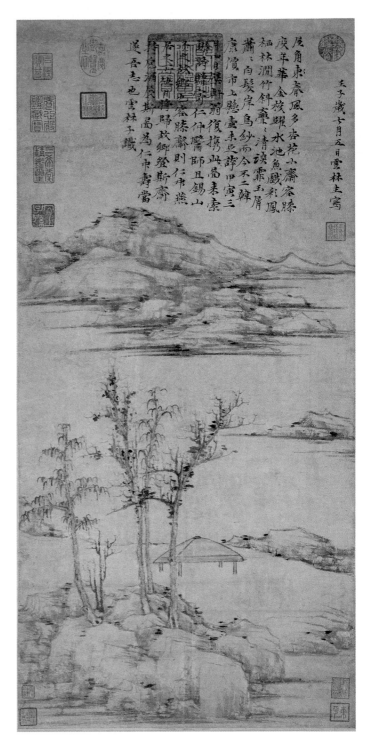

24-3 • Ni Zan THE RONGXI STUDIO
Yuan dynasty, 1372. Hanging scroll, ink on paper, height 29⅜″ (74.6 cm). National Palace Museum, Taibei, Taiwan, Republic of China.

The idea that a painting is not done to capture a likeness or to satisfy others but is executed freely and carelessly for the artist's own amusement is at the heart of the literati aesthetic. Ni Zan once wrote this comment on a painting: "What I call painting does not exceed the joy of careless sketching with a brush. I do not seek formal likeness but do it simply for my own amusement. Recently I was rambling about and came to a town. The people asked for my pictures, but wanted them exactly according to their own desires and to represent a specific occasion. [When I could not satisfy them,] they went away insulting, scolding, and cursing in every possible way. What a shame! But how can one scold a eunuch for not growing a beard?" (translated in Bush and Shih, p. 266).

24-4 • Yin Hong HUNDREDS OF BIRDS ADMIRING THE PEACOCKS
Ming dynasty, late 15th–early 16th century. Hanging scroll, ink and color on silk, 7'10½" × 6'5" (2.4 × 1.96 m). Cleveland Museum of Art. Purchase from the J. H. Wade Fund, 74.31

24-5 • Dai Jin RETURNING HOME LATE FROM A SPRING OUTING
Ming dynasty. Hanging scroll, ink on silk, 5½' × 2'8¾" (1.68 × 0.83 m). National Palace Museum, Taibei, Taiwan, Republic of China.

COURT AND PROFESSIONAL PAINTING

The contrast between the luxurious world of the court and the austere ideals of the literati continued through the Ming dynasty.

A typical example of Ming court taste is **HUNDREDS OF BIRDS ADMIRING THE PEACOCKS**, a large painting on silk by Yin Hong, an artist active during the late fifteenth and early sixteenth centuries (**FIG. 24–4**). A pupil of well-known courtiers, Yin most probably served in the court at Beijing. The painting is an example of the birds-and-flowers genre, which had been popular with artists

of the Song academy. Here the subject takes on symbolic meaning, with the homage of the birds to the peacocks representing the homage of court officials to the imperial state. The style goes back to Song academy models, although the large format and multiplication of details are traits of the Ming.

A related, yet bolder and less constrained, landscape style was also popular during this period. Sometimes called the Zhe style since its roots were in Hangzhou, Zhejiang Province, where the Southern Song court had been located, this manner especially influenced

24-6 • Qiu Ying SECTION OF SPRING DAWN IN THE HAN PALACE
Ming dynasty, 1500–1550. Handscroll, ink and color on silk, 1' × 18'13⁄16" (0.30 × 5.7 m). National Palace Museum, Taibei, Taiwan, Republic of China.

TECHNIQUE | Formats of Chinese Painting

With the exception of large wall paintings that typically decorated palaces, temples, and tombs, most Chinese paintings were done in ink and water-based colors on silk or paper. Finished works were generally mounted as **handscrolls**, **hanging scrolls**, or leaves in an album.

An album comprises a set of paintings of identical size mounted in a book. (A single painting from an album is called an **album leaf**.) The paintings in an album are usually related in subject, such as various views of a famous site or a series of scenes glimpsed on one trip.

Album-sized paintings might also be mounted as a handscroll, a horizontal format generally about 12 inches high and anywhere from a few feet to dozens of feet long. More typically, however, a handscroll would be a single continuous painting. Handscrolls were not meant to be displayed all at once, the way they are commonly presented today in museums. Rather, they were unrolled only occasionally, to be savored in much the same spirit as we might view a favorite film. Placing the scroll on a flat surface such as a table, a viewer would unroll it a foot or two at a time, moving gradually through the entire scroll from right to left, lingering over favorite details. The scroll was then rolled up and returned to its box until the next viewing.

Like handscrolls, hanging scrolls were not displayed permanently but were taken out for a limited time: a day, a week, a season. Unlike a handscroll, however, the painting on a hanging scroll was viewed as a whole—unrolled and put up on a wall, with the roller at the lower end acting as a weight to help the scroll hang flat. Although some hanging scrolls are quite large, they are still fundamentally intimate works, not intended for display in a public place.

Creating a scroll was a time-consuming and exacting process accomplished by a professional mounter. The painting was first backed with paper to strengthen it. Next, strips of paper-backed silk were pasted to the top, bottom, and sides, framing the painting on all four sides. Additional silk pieces were added to extend the scroll horizontally or vertically, depending on the format. The assembled scroll was then backed again with paper and fitted with a half-round dowel, or wooden rod, at the top of a hanging scroll or on the right end of a handscroll, with ribbons for hanging and tying, and with a wooden roller at the other end. Hanging scrolls were often fashioned from several patterns of silk, and a variety of piecing formats were developed and codified. On a handscroll, a painting was generally preceded by a panel giving the work's title and often followed by a long panel bearing **colophons**—inscriptions related to the work, such as poems in its praise or comments by its owners over the centuries. A scroll would be remounted periodically to better preserve it, and colophons and inscriptions would be preserved in each remounting. **Seals** added another layer of interest. A treasured scroll often bears not only the seal of its maker but also those of collectors and admirers through the centuries.

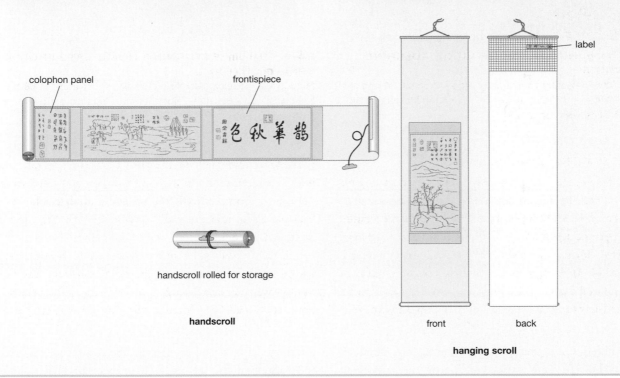

colophon panel

frontispiece

label

色 秋 華 鵲

handscroll rolled for storage

handscroll

front

back

hanging scroll

---

painters in Korea and Japan. A major example is **RETURNING HOME LATE FROM A SPRING OUTING (FIG. 24–5)**, unsigned but attributed to Dai Jin (1388–1462). This work reflects the Chinese sources for such artists as An Gyeon (SEE FIG. 24–17) and Sesshu (SEE FIG. 25–3).

QIU YING. A preeminent professional painter in the Ming period was Qiu Ying (1494–1552), who lived in Suzhou, a prosperous southern city. He inspired generations of imitators with exceptional works, such as a long handscroll known as **SPRING DAWN IN THE HAN PALACE (FIG. 24–6)**. The painting is based on Tang-dynasty depictions of women in the court of the Han dynasty (206 BCE–220 CE). While in the service of a well-known collector, Qiu Ying had the opportunity to study many Tang paintings, whose artists usually concentrated on the figures, leaving out the

A CLOSER LOOK

Spring Dawn in the Han Palace ▶

Ming dynasty, 1500–1550. Section of a handscroll, ink and color on silk, 1′ × 18′¹³⁄₁₆″ (0.30 × 5.7 m). National Palace Museum, Taibei, Taiwan, Republic of China.

Two ladies unwrap a *qin*, the zither or lute that was the most respected of musical instruments.

A seated lady plays the *pipa*, an instrument introduced from Central Asia during the Tang dynasty.

Antique vessels of bronze, lacquer, and porcelain adorn the room and suggest the ladies' refined taste.

A tray landscape featuring an eroded rock provides a sculptural counterpart to landscape (mountain-and-water) painting and suggests a place where immortals might dwell.

Two ladies dance together letting their sleeves and sashes swirl.

SEE MORE: View the Closer Look feature for the detail of *Spring Dawn in the Han Palace* **www.myartslab.com**

background entirely. Qiu's graceful and elegant figures—although modeled after those in Tang works—are portrayed in a setting of palace buildings, engaging in such pastimes as chess, music, calligraphy, and painting. With its antique subject matter, refined technique, and flawless taste in color and composition, *Spring Dawn in the Han Palace* brought professional painting to a new high point (see "A Closer Look," above).

DECORATIVE ARTS

Qiu Ying painted to satisfy his patrons in Suzhou. The cities of the south were becoming wealthy, and newly rich merchants collected

paintings, antiques, and art objects. The court, too, was prosperous and patronized the arts on a lavish scale. In such a setting, the decorative arts thrived.

MING BLUE-AND-WHITE WARES. The Ming became famous the world over for its exquisite ceramics, especially **porcelain** (see "The Secret of Porcelain," opposite). The imperial kilns in Jingdezhen, in Jiangxi Province, became the most renowned center for porcelain not only in all of China, but in all the world. Particularly noteworthy are the blue-and-white wares produced there during the ten-year reign of the ruler known as the Xuande

Marco Polo, it is said, was the one who named a new type of ceramic he found in China. Its translucent purity reminded him of the smooth whiteness of the cowry shell, *porcellana* in Italian. **Porcelain** is made from kaolin, an extremely refined white clay, and petuntse, a variety of the mineral feldspar. When properly combined and fired at a sufficiently high temperature, the two materials fuse into a glasslike, translucent ceramic that is far stronger than it looks.

Porcelaneous stoneware, fired at lower temperatures, was known in China by the seventh century, but true porcelain was perfected during the Song dynasty. To create blue-and-white porcelain such as the flask in FIGURE 24–7, blue pigment was made from cobalt oxide, finely

ground and mixed with water. The decoration was painted directly onto the unfired porcelain vessel, then a layer of clear glaze was applied over it. (In this technique, known as **underglaze** painting, the pattern is painted beneath the glaze.) After firing, the piece emerged from the kiln with a clear blue design set sharply against a snowy white background.

Entranced with the exquisite properties of porcelain, European potters tried for centuries to duplicate it. The technique was finally discovered in 1709 by Johann Friedrich Böttger in Dresden, Germany, who tried—but failed—to keep it a secret.

24-7 • FLASK

Ming dynasty, 1426–1435. Porcelain with decoration painted in underglaze cobalt blue. Collection of the Palace Museum, Beijing.

Dragons have featured prominently in Chinese folklore from earliest times—Neolithic examples have been found painted on pottery and carved in jade. In Bronze Age China, dragons came to be associated with powerful and sudden manifestations of nature, such as wind, thunder, and lightning. At the same time, dragons became associated with superior beings such as virtuous rulers and sages. With the emergence of China's first firmly established empire during the Han dynasty, the dragon was appropriated as an imperial symbol, and it remained so throughout Chinese history. Dragon sightings were duly recorded and considered auspicious. Yet even the Son of Heaven could not monopolize the dragon. During the Tang and Song dynasties the practice arose of painting pictures of dragons to pray for rain, and for Chan (Zen) Buddhists, the dragon was a symbol of sudden enlightenment.

Emperor (ruled 1426–1435), such as the **FLASK** in **FIGURE 24–7**. The subtle shape, the refined yet vigorous decoration of dragons posturing above the sea, and the flawless glazing embody the high achievement of Ming artisans.

ARCHITECTURE AND CITY PLANNING

Centuries of warfare and destruction have left very few Chinese architectural monuments intact. The most important remaining example of traditional Chinese architecture is **THE FORBIDDEN CITY**, the imperial palace compound in Beijing, whose principal buildings were constructed during the Ming dynasty (**FIG. 24–8**).

THE FORBIDDEN CITY. The basic plan of Beijing was the work of the Mongols, who laid out their capital city according to traditional Chinese principles. City planning began early in China—in the seventh century, in the case of Chang'an (present-day Xi'an), the capital of the Sui and Tang emperors. The walled city of Chang'an was laid out on a rectangular grid, with evenly spaced streets that ran north–south and east–west. At the northern end stood a walled imperial complex.

Beijing, too, was developed as a walled, rectangular city with streets laid out in a grid. The palace enclosure occupied the center of the northern part of the city, which was reserved for the Mongols. Chinese lived in the southern third of the city. Later, Ming and Qing emperors preserved this division, with officials living in the northern or Inner City and commoners living in the southern or Outer City. Under the third Ming emperor, Yongle (ruled 1403–1424), the Forbidden City was rebuilt as we see it today.

The approach to the Forbidden City was impressive. Visitors entered through the Meridian Gate, a monumental gate with side wings (SEE FIG. 24–8). Inside the Meridian Gate a broad courtyard is crossed by a bow-shaped waterway that is spanned by five arched marble bridges. At the opposite end of the courtyard is the Gate of Supreme Harmony, opening onto an even larger courtyard that houses three ceremonial halls raised on a broad platform. First is the Hall of Supreme Harmony, where, on the most important state occasions, the emperor was seated on his throne,

24-8 • THE FORBIDDEN CITY
Now the Palace Museum, Beijing. Mostly Ming dynasty.
View from the southwest.

SEE MORE: View a simulation about the Forbidden City
www.myartslab.com

facing south. Beyond is the smaller Hall of Central Harmony, then the Hall of Protecting Harmony. Behind these vast ceremonial spaces, still on the central axis, is the inner court, again with a progression of three buildings, this time more intimate in scale. In its balance and symmetry the plan of the Forbidden City reflects ancient Chinese beliefs about the harmony of the universe, and it emphasizes the emperor's role as the Son of Heaven, whose duty was to maintain the cosmic order from his throne in the middle of the world.

THE LITERATI AESTHETIC

In the south, particularly in the district of Suzhou, literati painting, associated with the educated men who served the court as government officials, remained the dominant trend. One of the major literati figures from the Ming period is Shen Zhou (1427–1509), who had no desire to enter government service and spent most of his life in Suzhou. He studied the Yuan painters avidly and tried to recapture their spirit in such works as *Poet on a Mountaintop* (see "*Poet on a Mountaintop*," page 802). Although the style of the painting recalls the freedom and simplicity of Ni Zan (SEE FIG. 24–3), the motif of a poet surveying the landscape from a mountain plateau is Shen's creation.

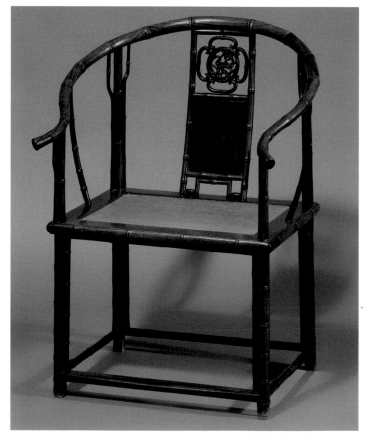

24-9 • ARMCHAIR
Ming dynasty, 16th–17th century. Huanghuali wood (hardwood), 39⅜ × 27¼ × 20″ (100 × 69.2 × 50.8 cm). The Nelson-Atkins Museum of Art, Kansas City, Missouri. Purchase, Nelson Trust (46-78/1)

24-10 • GARDEN OF THE CESSATION OF OFFICIAL LIFE (ALSO KNOWN AS THE HUMBLE ADMINISTRATOR'S GARDEN)

Suzhou, Jiangsu. Ming dynasty, early 16th century.

Early in the sixteenth century, an official in Beijing, frustrated after serving in the capital for many years without promotion, returned home. Taking an ancient poem, "The Song of Leisurely Living," for his model, he began to build a garden. He called his retreat the Garden of the Cessation of Official Life to indicate that he had exchanged his career as a bureaucrat for a life of leisure. By leisure, he meant that he could now dedicate himself to calligraphy, poetry, and painting, the three arts dear to scholars in China.

LITERATI INFLUENCE ON FURNITURE, ARCHITECTURE, AND GARDEN DESIGN. The taste of the literati came to influence furniture and architecture, and especially the design of gardens. Chinese furniture made for domestic use reached the height of its development in the sixteenth and seventeenth centuries. Characteristic of Chinese furniture, the chair in **FIGURE 24–9** is constructed without the use of glue or nails. Instead, pieces fit together based on the principle of the **mortise-and-tenon** joint, in which a projecting element (tenon) on one piece fits snugly into a cavity (mortise) on another. Each piece of the chair is carved, as opposed to being bent or twisted, and the joints are crafted with great precision. The patterns of the wood grain provide subtle interest unmarred by any

painting or other embellishment. The style, like that of Chinese architecture, is one of simplicity, clarity, symmetry, and balance. The effect is formal and dignified but natural and simple—virtues central to the Chinese view of proper human conduct as well.

The art of landscape gardening also reached a high point during the Ming dynasty, as many literati surrounded their homes with gardens. The most famous gardens were created in the southern cities of the Yangzi Delta, especially in Suzhou. The largest surviving garden of the era is the **GARDEN OF THE CESSATION OF OFFICIAL LIFE (FIG. 24–10)**. Although modified and reconstructed many times through the centuries, it still reflects many of the basic ideas of the original Ming owner. About a third of the garden is

Poet on a Mountaintop

In earlier landscape paintings, human figures were typically shown dwarfed by the grandeur of nature. Travelers might be seen scuttling along a narrow path by a stream, while overhead towered mountains whose peaks conversed with the clouds and whose heights were inaccessible. Here, the poet has climbed the mountain and dominates the landscape. Even the clouds are beneath him. Before his gaze, a poem hangs in the air, as though he were projecting his thoughts.

The poem, composed by Shen Zhou himself, and written in his distinctive hand, reads:

White clouds like a scarf enfold the mountain's waist;
Stone steps hang in space—a long, narrow path.
Alone, leaning on my cane, I gaze intently at the scene,
And feel like answering the murmuring brook with the music of my flute.

(Translation by Jonathan Chaves, *The Chinese Painter as Poet*, New York, 2000, p. 46.)

Shen Zhou composed the poem and wrote the inscription at the time he painted the album. The style of the calligraphy, like the style of the painting, is informal, relaxed, and straightforward—qualities that were believed to reflect the artist's character and personality.

The painting reflects Ming philosophy, which held that the mind, not the physical world, was the basis for reality. With its perfect synthesis of poetry, calligraphy, and painting, and with its harmony of mind and landscape, *Poet on a Mountaintop* represents the essence of Ming literati painting.

Shen Zhou POET ON A MOUNTAINTOP
Leaf from an album of landscapes; painting mounted as part of a handscroll. Ming dynasty, c. 1500.
Ink and color on paper, 15¼ × 23¾″ (40 × 60.2 cm). Nelson-Atkins Museum of Art, Kansas City, Missouri.
Purchase, Nelson Trust (46-51/2)

devoted to water through artificially created brooks and ponds. The landscape is dotted with pavilions, kiosks, libraries, studios, and corridors. Many of the buildings have poetic names, such as Rain Listening Pavilion and Bridge of the Small Flying Rainbow.

DONG QICHANG, LITERATI THEORIST. The ideas underlying literati painting found their most influential expression in the writings of Dong Qichang (1555–1636). A high official in the late Ming period, Dong Qichang embodied the literati tradition as poet, calligrapher, and painter. He developed a view of Chinese art history that divided painters into two opposing schools, northern and southern. The names have nothing to do with geography— a painter from the south might well be classed as northern—but reflect a parallel Dong drew with the northern and southern schools of Chan (Zen) Buddhism in China. The southern school of Chan, founded by the eccentric monk Huineng (638–713), was unorthodox, radical, and innovative; the northern school was traditional and conservative. Similarly, Dong's two schools of painters represented progressive and conservative traditions. In Dong's view the conservative northern school was dominated by professional painters whose academic, often decorative, style emphasized technical skill. In contrast, the progressive southern school preferred ink to color and free brushwork to meticulous detail. Its painters aimed for poetry and personal expression. In promoting this theory, Dong gave his unlimited sanction to literati painting, which he positioned as the culmination of the southern school, and he fundamentally influenced the way the Chinese viewed their own tradition.

Dong Qichang summarized his views on the proper training for literati painters in the famous statement "Read ten thousand books and walk ten thousand miles." By this he meant that one must first study the works of the great masters, then follow "heaven and earth," the world of nature. These studies prepared the way for greater self-expression through brush and ink, the goal of literati painting. Dong's views rested on an awareness that a painting of scenery and the actual scenery are two very different things. The excellence of a painting does not lie in its degree of resemblance to reality—that gap can never be bridged—but in its expressive power. The expressive language of painting is inherently abstract and lies in its nature as a construction of brushstrokes. For example, in a painting of a rock, the rock itself is not expressive; rather, the brushstrokes that suggest a rock are expressive.

With such thinking Dong brought painting close to the realm of calligraphy, which had long been considered the highest form of artistic expression in China. More than a thousand years before Dong's time, a body of critical terms and theories had evolved to discuss calligraphy in light of the formal and expressive properties of brushwork and composition. Dong introduced some of these terms—ideas such as opening and closing, rising and falling, and void and solid—to the criticism of painting.

Dong's theories are fully embodied in his painting **THE QING-BIAN MOUNTAINS (FIG. 24–11)**. According to his own inscription,

24-11 • Dong Qichang THE QINGBIAN MOUNTAINS
Ming dynasty, 1617. Hanging scroll, ink on paper, 21'8" × 7'4⅜" (6.72 × 2.25 m). Cleveland Museum of Art. Leonard C. Hanna, Jr., Fund

the painting was based on a work by the tenth-century artist Dong Yuan. Dong Qichang's style, however, is quite different from the styles of the masters he admired. Although there is some indication of foreground, middle ground, and distant mountains, the space is ambiguous, as if all the elements were compressed to the surface of the picture. With this flattening of space, the trees, rocks, and mountains become more readily legible in a second way, as semi-abstract forms made of brushstrokes.

Six trees arranged diagonally define the extreme foreground and announce themes that the rest of the painting repeats, varies, and develops. The tree on the left, with its outstretched branches and full foliage, is echoed first in the shape of another tree just across the river and again in a tree farther up and toward the left. The tallest tree of the foreground grouping anticipates the high peak that towers in the distance almost directly above it. The forms of the smaller foreground trees, especially the one with dark leaves,

are repeated in numerous variations across the painting. At the same time, the simple and ordinary-looking boulder in the foreground is transformed in the conglomeration of rocks, ridges, hills, and mountains above. This double reading, both abstract and representational, parallels the work's double nature as a painting of a landscape and an interpretation of a traditional landscape painting.

The influence of Dong Qichang on the development of Chinese painting of later periods cannot be overstated. Indeed, nearly all Chinese painters since the early seventeenth century have reflected his ideas in one way or another.

QING DYNASTY

In 1644, when the armies of the Manchu people to the northeast of China marched into Beijing, many Chinese reacted as though their civilization had come to an end. Yet, the Manchus had already

24-12 • Yun Shouping AMARANTH
Leaf from an album of flowers, bamboo, fruits, and vegetables. 1633–1690. Album of 10 leaves; ink and color on paper; each leaf 10 × 13″ (25.3 × 33.5 cm). Collection of Phoenix Art Museum. Gift of Marilyn and Roy Papp

The leaf is inscribed by the artist: "Autumn garden abounds in beauty, playfully painted by Ouxiangguan (Yun Shouping)." Translation by Momoko Soma Welch.

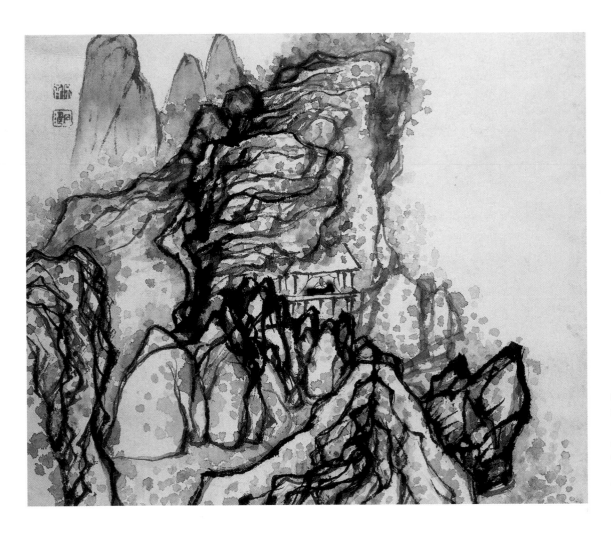

24–13 • Shitao
LANDSCAPE
Leaf from *An Album of Landscapes*. Qing dynasty, c. 1700. Ink and color on paper, 9½ × 11″ (24.1 × 28 cm). Collection C. C. Wang family

adopted many Chinese customs and institutions before their conquest. After gaining control of all of China, a process that took decades, they showed great respect for Chinese tradition. In art, all the major trends of the late Ming dynasty eventually continued into the Manchu, or Qing, dynasty (1644–1911).

ORTHODOX PAINTING

Literati painting had been established as the dominant tradition; it now became orthodox. Scholars followed Dong Qichang's recommendation and based their approach on the study of past masters, and they painted large numbers of works in the manner of Song and Yuan artists as a way of expressing their learning, technique, and taste.

The Qing emperors of the late seventeenth and eighteenth centuries were painters themselves. They collected literati painting, and their taste was shaped mainly by artists such as Wang Hui (SEE FIG. 24–1). Thus literati painting, long associated with reclusive scholars, ultimately became an academic style practiced at court. Imbued with values associated with scholarship and virtue, these paintings constituted the highest art form of the Qing court. The emperors also esteemed a style of bird-and-flower painting developed by Yun Shouping (1633–1690). Like the orthodox style of landscape painting, it was embraced by literati painters—many of them court officials themselves. The style, most often seen in

albums or fans, recalled aspects of Song- and Yuan-dynasty bird-and-flower painting, and artists cited their ancient models as a way to enrich both the meaning and the beauty of these small-format works. In a leaf from an album of flowers, bamboo, fruits and vegetables, which employs a variety of brush techniques (**FIG. 24–12**), Yun Shouping represents flowers of the autumn season.

INDIVIDUALIST PAINTING

The first few decades of Qing rule had been both traumatic and dangerous for those who were loyal—or worse, related—to the Ming. Some committed suicide, while others sought refuge in monasteries or wandered the countryside. Among them were several painters who expressed their anger, defiance, frustration, and melancholy in their art. They took Dong Qichang's idea of painting as an expression of the artist's personal feelings very seriously and cultivated highly original styles. These painters have become known as the individualists.

SHITAO.   One of the individualists was Shitao (1642–1707), who was descended from the first Ming emperor and who took refuge in Buddhist temples when the dynasty fell. In his later life he brought his painting to the brink of abstraction in such works as **LANDSCAPE (FIG. 24–13).** A monk sits in a small hut, looking out onto mountains that seem to be in turmoil. Dots, used for centuries to indicate vegetation on rocks, here seem to have taken on a life of their own. The rocks also seem alive—about to swallow up the monk and his hut. Throughout his life Shitao continued to identify himself with the fallen Ming, and he felt that his secure world had turned to chaos with the Manchu conquest.

THE MODERN PERIOD

In the mid and late nineteenth century, China was shaken from centuries of complacency by a series of humiliating military defeats at the hands of Western powers and Japan. Only then did the government finally realize that these new rivals were not like the Mongols of the thirteenth century. China was no longer at the center of the world, a civilized country surrounded by "barbarians." Spiritual resistance was no longer sufficient to solve the problems brought on by change. New ideas from Japan and the West began to filter in, and the demand arose for political and cultural reforms. In 1911 the Qing dynasty was overthrown, ending 2,000 years of imperial rule, and China was reconceived as a republic.

During the first decades of the twentieth century Chinese artists traveled to Japan and Europe to study Western art. Returning to China, many sought to introduce the ideas and techniques they had learned, and they explored ways to synthesize the Chinese and the Western traditions. After the establishment of the present-day Communist government in 1949, individual artistic freedom was curtailed as the arts were pressed into the service of the state and its vision of a new social order. After 1979, however, cultural attitudes began to relax, and Chinese painters again pursued their own paths.

WU GUANZHONG. One artist who emerged during the 1980s as a leader in Chinese painting is Wu Guanzhong (b. 1919). Combining his French artistic training and Chinese background, Wu Guanzhong developed a semiabstract style to depict scenes from the Chinese landscape. He made preliminary sketches on site, then, back in his studio, he developed these sketches into free interpretations based on his feeling and vision. An example of his work, **PINE SPIRIT**, depicts a scene in the Huang (Yellow) Mountains (**FIG. 24–14**). The technique, with its sweeping gestures of paint, is clearly linked to Abstract Expressionism, an influential Western movement of the post–World War II years (Chapter 32); yet the painting also claims a place in the long tradition of Chinese landscape as exemplified by such masters as Shitao.

Like all aspects of Chinese society, Chinese art has felt the strong impact of Western influence, and the question remains whether Chinese artists will absorb Western ideas without losing their traditional identity. Interestingly, landscape remains an important subject, as it has been for more than a thousand years, and calligraphy continues to play a vital role. Using the techniques and methods of the West, some of China's artists have joined an international avant-garde (see, for example, Wenda Gu in Chapter 32), while other painters still seek communion with nature through their ink brushstrokes as a means to come to terms with human life and the world.

24-14 • Wu Guanzhong PINE SPIRIT
1984. Ink and color on paper, 2′3⅝″ × 5′3½″ (0.70 × 1.61 m). Spencer Museum of Art, The University of Kansas, Lawrence. Gift of the E. Rhodes and Leonard B. Carpenter Foundation

ARTS OF KOREA: THE JOSEON DYNASTY TO THE MODERN ERA

In 1392, General Yi Seonggye (1335–1408) overthrew the Goryeo dynasty (918–1392), establishing the Joseon dynasty (1392–1910), sometimes called the Yi dynasty. He first maintained his capital at Gaeseong, the old Goryeo capital, but moved it to Seoul in 1394, where it remained through the end of the dynasty. The Joseon regime rejected Buddhism, espousing Neo-Confucianism as the state philosophy. Taking Ming-dynasty China as its model, the new government patterned its bureaucracy on that of the Ming emperors, even adopting as its own such outward symbols of Ming imperial authority as blue-and-white porcelain. The early Joseon era was a period of cultural refinement and scientific achievement, during which Koreans invented Han'geul (the Korean alphabet) and movable type, not to mention the rain gauge, astrolabe, celestial globe, sundial, and water clock.

JOSEON CERAMICS

Like their Silla and Goryeo forebears (see Chapter 10), Joseon potters excelled in the manufacture of ceramics, taking their cue from contemporaneous Chinese wares, but seldom copying them directly.

BUNCHEONG CERAMICS. Descended from Goryeo celadons, Joseon-dynasty stonewares, known as *buncheong* wares, enjoyed widespread usage throughout the peninsula. Their decorative effect relies on the use of white slip that makes the humble stoneware resemble more expensive white porcelain. In fifteenth-century examples, the slip is often seen inlaid into repeating design elements stamped into the body.

Sixteenth-century *buncheong* wares are characteristically embellished with wonderfully fluid, calligraphic brushwork painted in iron-brown slip on a white slip ground. Most painted *buncheong* wares have stylized floral décor, but rare pieces, such as the charming wine bottle in **FIGURE 24–15**, feature pictorial decoration. In fresh, lively brushstrokes, a bird with outstretched wings grasps a fish that it has just caught in its talons; waves roll below, while two giant lotus blossoms frame the scene.

Japanese armies repeatedly invaded the Korean peninsula between 1592 and 1597, destroying many of the *buncheong* kilns, and essentially bringing the ware's production to a halt. Tradition holds that the Japanese took many *buncheong* potters home with them to produce *buncheong*-style wares, which were greatly admired by connoisseurs of the tea ceremony. In fact, the spontaneity of Korean *buncheong* pottery has inspired Japanese ceramics to this day.

PAINTED PORCELAIN. Korean potters produced porcelains with designs painted in underglaze cobalt blue as early as the fifteenth century, inspired by Chinese porcelains of the early Ming period (SEE FIG. 24–7). The Korean court dispatched artists from the royal painting academy to the porcelain kilns—located some 30 miles southeast of Seoul—to train porcelain decorators. As a result, from the fifteenth century onward, the painting on the best Korean porcelains closely approximated that on paper and silk, unlike in China, where ceramic decoration followed a path of its own with but scant reference to painting traditions.

In another unique development, Korean porcelains from the sixteenth and seventeenth centuries often feature designs painted in underglaze iron-brown rather than the cobalt blue customary in Ming porcelain. Also uniquely Korean are porcelain jars with bulging shoulders, slender bases, and short, vertical necks, which

24-15 • HORIZONTAL WINE BOTTLE WITH DECORATION OF A BIRD CARRYING A NEWLY CAUGHT FISH

Korea. Joseon dynasty, 16th century. *Buncheong* ware: light gray stoneware with decoration painted in iron-brown slip on a white slip ground, 6¹⁄₁₀ × 9½" (15.5 × 24.1 cm). Museum of Oriental Ceramics, Osaka, Japan. Gift of the Sumitomo Group (20773)

24-16 • BROAD-SHOULDERED JAR WITH DECORATION OF A FRUITING GRAPEVINE

Korea. Joseon dynasty, 17th century. Porcelain with decoration painted in underglaze iron-brown slip, height 22⅛" (53.8 cm). Ewha Women's University Museum, Seoul, Republic of Korea.

Chinese potters invented porcelain during the Tang dynasty, probably in the eighth century. Generally fired in the range of 1300° to 1400° C, porcelain is a high-fired, white-bodied ceramic ware. Its unique feature is its translucency. Korean potters learned to make porcelain during the Goryeo dynasty, probably as early as the eleventh or twelfth century, though few Goryeo examples remain today. For many centuries, only the Chinese and Koreans were able to produce porcelains.

appeared by the seventeenth century and came to be the most characteristic ceramic shapes in the later Joseon period. Painted in underglaze iron-brown, the seventeenth-century jar shown in **FIGURE 24–16** depicts a fruiting grape branch around its shoulder. In typical Korean fashion, the design spreads over a surface unconstrained by borders, resulting in a balanced but asymmetrical design that incorporates the Korean taste for unornamented spaces.

JOSEON PAINTING

Korean secular painting came into its own during the Joseon dynasty. Continuing Goryeo traditions, early Joseon examples employ Chinese styles and formats, their range of subjects expanding from botanical motifs to include landscapes, figures, and a variety of animals.

Painted in 1447 by An Gyeon (b. 1418), **DREAM JOURNEY TO THE PEACH BLOSSOM LAND (FIG. 24–17)** is the earliest extant and dated Joseon secular painting. It illustrates a fanciful tale by China's revered nature poet Tao Qian (365–427), and recounts a dream about chancing upon a utopia secluded from the world for centuries while meandering among the peach blossoms of spring.

As with their Goryeo forebears, the monumental mountains and vast, panoramic vistas of such fifteenth-century Korean paintings, echo Northern Song painting styles. Chinese paintings of the Southern Song (1127–1279) and Ming periods (1368–1644) also influenced Korean painting of the fifteenth, sixteenth, and seventeenth centuries, though these styles never completely supplanted the imprint of the Northern Song masters.

THE SILHAK MOVEMENT. In the eighteenth century, a truly Korean style emerged, inspired by the *silhak* ("practical learning") movement, which emphasized the study of things Korean in addition to the Chinese classics. The impact of the movement is

24-17 • An Gyeon DREAM JOURNEY TO THE PEACH BLOSSOM LAND

Korea. Joseon dynasty, 1447. Handscroll, ink and light colors on silk, 15¼ × 41¾" (38.7 × 106.1 cm). Central Library, Tenri University, Tenri (near Nara), Japan.

萬二千峯皆骨山何人用
意寫眞頹衆香浮
而扶赤外
積氣雄諸
世界
間
岳帛

芙蓉之素
半林松
柏塗玄閣縱今脚
蹢頂今過事似枕邊者不慳

甲題
寅春

金剛全圖
謙齋

24-18 • Jeong Seon
PANORAMIC VIEW OF THE
DIAMOND MOUNTAINS
(GEUMGANG-SAN)
Korean. Joseon Dynasty, 1734. Hanging
scroll, ink and colors on paper,
40⅝ × 37″ (130.1 × 94 cm). Lee'um,
Samsung Museum, Seoul, Republic
of Korea.

exemplified by the painter Jeong Seon (1676–1759), who chose well-known Korean vistas as the subjects of his paintings, rather than the Chinese themes favored by earlier artists. Among Jeong Seon's paintings are numerous representations of the Diamond Mountains (Geumgang-san), a celebrated range of craggy peaks along Korea's east coast. Painted in 1734, the scroll reproduced in **FIGURE 24–18** aptly captures the Diamond Mountains' needlelike peaks. The subject is Korean, and so is the energetic spirit and the intensely personal style, with its crystalline mountains, distant clouds of delicate ink wash, and individualistic brushwork.

Among figure painters, Sin Yunbok (b. 1758) is an important exemplar of the *silhak* attitude. Active in the late eighteenth and early nineteenth centuries, Sin typically depicted aristocratic figures in native Korean garb. The album leaf entitled **PICNIC AT THE LOTUS POND (FIG. 24–19)** represents a group of Korean gentlemen enjoying themselves in the countryside on an autumn day in the company of several *gisaeng* (female entertainers). The figures are recognizably Korean—the women with their full coiffures, short jackets, and generous skirts, and the men with their beards, white robes, and wide-brimmed hats woven of horsehair and coated with black lacquer. The stringed instrument played by

24–19 • Sin Yunbok PICNIC AT THE LOTUS POND
Leaf from an album of genre scenes. Korea. Joseon dynasty, late 18th century. Album of 30 leaves;
ink and colors on paper, 11⅛ × 13⅞″ (28.3 × 35.2 cm). Kansong Museum of Art, Seoul, Republic of Korea.

the gentleman seated at lower right is a *gayageum* (Korean zither), the most hallowed of all Korean musical instruments.

MODERN KOREA

Long known as "the Hermit Kingdom," the Joseon dynasty pursued a policy of isolationism, closing its borders to most of the world, except China, until 1876. Japan's annexation of Korea in 1910 brought the Joseon dynasty to a close, but effectively prolonged the country's seclusion from the outside world. The legacy of self-imposed isolation compounded by colonial occupation (1910–1945)—not to mention the harsh circumstances imposed by World War II (1939–1945), followed by the even worse conditions of the Korean War (1950–1953)—impeded Korea's artistic and cultural development during the first half of the twentieth century.

A MODERNIST PAINTER FROM KOREA.   Despite these privations, some modern influences did reach Korea indirectly via China and

Japan, and beginning in the 1920s and 1930s a few Korean artists experimented with contemporary Western styles, typically painting in the manner of Cézanne or Gauguin, but sometimes trying abstract, nonrepresentational styles. Among these, Gim Hwangi (1913–1974) was influenced by Constructivism and geometric abstraction and would become one of twentieth-century Korea's influential painters. Like many Korean artists after the Korean War, Gim wanted to examine Western modernism at its source. He visited Paris in 1956 and then, from 1964 to 1974, lived and worked in New York, where he produced his best-known works. His painting **5-IV-71** presents a large pair of circular radiating patterns composed of small dots and squares in tones of blue, black, and gray **(FIG. 24–20)**. While appearing wholly Western in style, medium, concept, and even title—Gim Hwangi typically adopted the date of a work's creation as its title—*5-IV-71* also seems related to Asia's venerable tradition of monochrome **ink painting**, while suggesting a transcendence that seems Daoist or

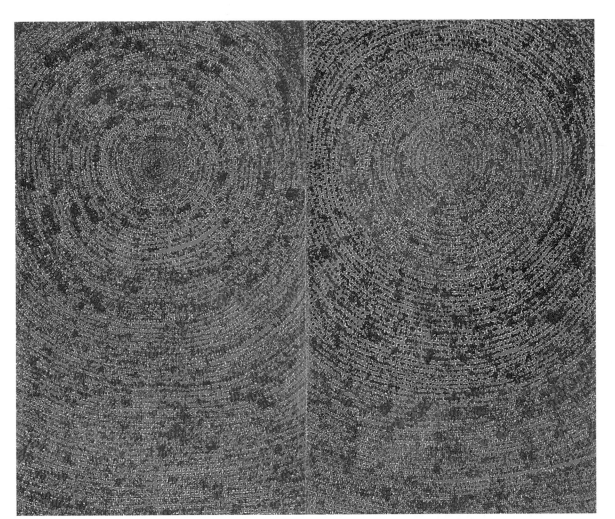

24-20 • Gim Hwangi 5-IV-71 Korea. 1971. Oil on canvas, 39½ × 39½″ (100 × 100 cm). Whanki Museum, Seoul, Republic of Korea.

Buddhist in feeling. Given that the artist was Korean, that he learned the Chinese classics in his youth, that he studied art in Paris, and that he then worked in New York, it is possible that his painting embodies all of the above. Gim's painting illustrates the paradox that the modern artist faces while finding a distinctive, personal style: whether to paint in an updated version of a traditional style, in a wholly international style, in an international style with a distinctive local twist, or in an eclectic, hybrid style that incorporates both native and naturalized elements from diverse traditions. By addressing these questions, Gim Hwangi blazed a trail for subsequent Korean-born artists, such as the renowned video artist Nam June Paik (1932–2006), whose work can be seen in FIGURE 32–57.

THINK ABOUT IT

24.1 Explain the role played by one of the following three ways of thought prevalent in Chinese society—Daoism, Confucianism, and Buddhism—and discuss the implications that it had for the visual arts. Make specific reference to works from this chapter.

24.2 Examine a work commissioned by the court at Beijing and distinguish which of its features are typical of court art.

24.3 Discuss the place that calligraphy held within Chinese society and in relation to other arts. Then, explain why Dong Qichang's *The Qingbian Mountains* (SEE FIG. 24–11) has elicited comparison with the art of calligraphy.

24.4 Discuss the culture of the literati, including their values and their system of art patronage, and distinguish the formats of painting that they used.

24.5 Theorize reasons for the emergence of individualist painting in China, using works such as Shitao's *Landscape* (SEE FIG. 24–13) to support your argument.

PRACTICE MORE: Compose answers to these questions, get flashcards for images and terms, and review chapter material with quizzes www.myartslab.com

25-1 • Suzuki Harunobu **THE FLOWERS OF BEAUTY IN THE FLOATING WORLD: MOTOURA AND YAEZAKURA OF THE MINAMI YAMASAKIYA**   Edo period, 1769.
Polychrome woodblock print on paper, 11⅜ × 8½″ (28.9 × 21.8 cm). Chicago Art Institute.
Clarence Buckingham Collection (1925.2116)

SEE MORE: View videos on *ukiyo-e* techniques **www.myartslab.com**

JAPANESE ART AFTER 1333

Lounging at a window seat, a young woman pauses from smoking her pipe while the young girl at her side peers intently through a telescope at boats in a bay below (FIG. 25–1). The scene takes place in the city of Edo (now Tokyo) in the 1760s, during an era of peace and prosperity that started some 150 years earlier when the Tokugawa shoguns unified the nation. Edo was then the largest city in the world, with over 1 million inhabitants: samurai-bureaucrats and working-class townspeople. The commoners possessed a vibrant culture centered in urban entertainment districts, where geisha and courtesans (licenced prostitutes), such as the lady and her young trainee portrayed in this woodblock print, worked.

In the 1630s, the Tokugawa shogunate banned Japanese citizens from traveling abroad and restricted foreign access to the country. Nagasaki became Japan's sole international port, which only Koreans, Chinese, and Dutch could enter (and they could not travel freely around the country). The government did this to deter Christian missionaries and to assert authority over foreign powers. Not until 1853, when Commodore Matthew Perry of the United States forced Japan to open additional ports, did these policies change. Even so, foreign influences could not be prevented, as the tobacco pipe and telescope in this print testify.

The Japanese had first encountered Westerners—Portuguese traders—in the mid sixteenth century. The Dutch reached Japan by 1600 and brought tobacco and, soon after that, the telescope and other exotic optical devices, including spectacles, microscopes, other curious objects, and books, many illustrated. The Japanese people eagerly welcomed these foreign goods and imitated foreign customs, which conferred an air of sophistication on the user. Looking through the telescopes like the one in this print was a popular amusement of prostitutes and their customers. It also conveyed sexual overtones, because of its phallic shape, and suggests the ribald humor then in vogue. Novel optical devices, all readily available by the mid eighteenth century, offered a new way of seeing, and impacted the appearance of Japanese pictorial art. Yet Chinese influences in the arts still remained strong and spread throughout the population as never before, due to new efforts to educate the broader populace in Chinese studies. In varying degrees, the intermingling of diverse native and foreign artistic traditions has continued to shape the arts of Japan up to the present.

LEARN ABOUT IT

25.1 Evaluate the importance of Zen Buddhism to Japan's visual arts.

25.2 Compare art created in Kyoto to art made in the city of Edo during the Edo period.

25.3 Appraise the role and significance of crafts in Japanese artistic culture.

25.4 Recognize foreign influences on Japanese art in the Muromachi and Edo periods.

25.5 Understand the changing role of patronage in the development of Japanese art.

HEAR MORE: Listen to an audio file of your chapter www.myartslab.com

MUROMACHI PERIOD

By the year 1333, Japanese art had already developed a long and rich history (see "Foundations of Japanese Culture," page 817). Very early, a particularly Japanese sensitivity to artistic production had emerged, including a love of natural materials, fondness for representing elements of the natural world, and an overriding attention to fine craftsmanship. Aesthetically, Japanese arts had come to feature a taste for asymmetry, abstraction, brevity or boldness of expression, and humor—characteristics that continue to distinguish Japanese art, appearing and reappearing in ever-changing guises.

Late in the twelfth century, the authority of the emperor had been supplanted by rule by powerful and ambitious warriors (samurai) under the leadership of the shogun, the general-in-chief. But in 1333, Emperor Go-Daigo attempted to retake power. He failed and was forced into hiding in the mountains south of Kyoto where he set up a "southern court." Meanwhile, the shogunal family then in power, the Minamoto, was overthrown by warriors of the Ashikaga clan, who placed a rival to the upstart emperor on the throne in Kyoto, in a "northern court," and had him declare their clan head as shogun. They ruled the country from the Muromachi district in Kyoto, and finally vanquished the southern court emperors in 1392. The Muromachi period, also known as the Ashikaga era (1392–1573), formally began with this event.

The Muromachi period is marked by the ascendance of Zen Buddhism, introduced into Japan in the late twelfth century, whose austere ideals particularly appealed to the highly disciplined samurai. While Pure Land Buddhism, which had spread widely during the latter part of the Heian period (794–1185), remained popular, Zen (which means meditation) became the dominant cultural force in Japan among the ruling elite.

ZEN INK PAINTING

During the Muromachi period, brightly colored narrative handscrolls depicting native themes continued to be produced, but monochrome ink painting in black ink and its diluted grays—which had just been introduced to Japan from the continent at the end of the Kamakura period (1185–1333)—reigned supreme. Muromachi ink painting was heavily influenced by the aesthetics of Zen, but unlike earlier Zen paintings that had concentrated on depictions of important individuals associated with the Zen monastic tradition, many artists also began painting Chinese-style ink landscapes. Traditionally, the monk-artist Shubun (active c. 1418–1463) is regarded as Japan's first great master of the ink landscape. Unfortunately, no works survive that can be proven to be his. Two landscapes by Shubun's pupil Bunsei (active c. 1450–1460) have survived, however. The one shown in **FIGURE 25–2** is closely modeled on Korean ink landscape paintings that themselves copied Chinese Ming period models (such as **FIG. 24–5**). It contains a foreground consisting of a spit of rocky land with an overlapping series of motifs—a spiky pine tree, a craggy rock, a poet seated in a hermitage, and a brushwood fence

MAP 25-1 • JAPAN

Japan's wholehearted emulation of myriad aspects of Chinese culture began in the fifth century and was challenged by new influences from the West only in the mid nineteenth century after Western powers forced Japan to open its treaty ports to international trade.

surrounding a small garden of trees and bamboo. In the middle ground is space—emptiness, the void. We are expected to "read" the empty paper as representing water. Beyond the blank space, subtle tones of gray ink delineate a distant shore where fishing boats, a small hut, and two people stand. The two parts of the painting seem to echo each other across a vast expanse. The painting illustrates well the pure, lonely, and ultimately serene spirit of the Zen-influenced poetic landscape tradition.

SESSHU. Another of Shubun's pupils, Sesshu (1420–1506), outshone his master, and has come to be regarded as one of the greatest Japanese painters of all time. Although they completed training to become Zen monks, at the monastery, Shubun and his followers specialized in art rather than in religious ritual or teaching, unlike earlier Zen monk-painters for whom art production was just one facet of their lives. By Shubun's day, temples had formed their own to head a small provincial Zen temple in western Japan, in his quest to concentrate on painting unencumbered by monastic duties and entanglements with the political elite. His new temple was patronized by a private and wealthy warrior clan that was engaged in trade with China. With funding from them, he had the opportunity to visit China in 1467 on a diplomatic mission. He traveled extensively there for three years, viewing the scenery, stopping at Zen (Chan in Chinese) monasteries, and studying Chinese paintings by professional artists rather than those by contemporary literati masters. When he returned from China, he remained in the provinces to avoid the turmoil in Kyoto, which was being devastated by civil warfare that would last for the next hundred years. Only a few paintings from Sesshu's years prior to his sojourn in China have recently come to light. These he painted in a style closer to Shubun and he signed them with another name. His paintings after his return demonstrate he consciously broke artistically with the refined landscape style of his teacher. These masterful paintings by Sesshu exhibit a bold, new spirit, evident in his **WINTER LANDSCAPE** **(FIG. 25–3)**. A cliff descending from the mist seems to cut the composition in two. Sharp, jagged brushstrokes delineate a series of

25-2 • Bunsei LANDSCAPE
Muromachi period, mid 15th century. Hanging scroll, ink and light colors on paper, 28¾ × 13″ (73.2 × 33 cm). Museum of Fine Arts, Boston. Special Chinese and Japanese Fund (05.203)

professional painting ateliers in order to meet demands for large numbers of paintings from warrior patrons. Sesshu trained as a Zen monk at Shokokuji, where Shubun had his studio. There, he worked in the painting atelier under Shubun for 20 years, but then left Kyoto

25-3 • Sesshu WINTER LANDSCAPE
Muromachi period, c. 1470s. Hanging scroll, ink on paper, 18¼ × 11½″ (46.3 × 29.3 cm). Collection of the Tokyo National Museum. National Treasure.

rocky hills, where a lone figure makes his way to a Zen monastery. Instead of a gradual recession into space, flat overlapping planes fracture the composition into crystalline facets. The white of the paper is left to indicate snow, while the sky is suggested by tones of gray. A few trees cling desperately to the rocky land, and the harsh chill of winter is boldly expressed.

THE ZEN DRY GARDEN

Zen monks led austere monastic lives in their quest for the attainment of enlightenment. In addition to daily meditation, they engaged in manual labor to provide for themselves and maintain their temple properties. Many Zen temples constructed dry landscape courtyard gardens, not for strolling in but for contemplative viewing. Cleaning and maintaining these gardens—pulling weeds, tweaking unruly shoots, and raking the gravel—was a kind of active meditation. It helped to keep their minds grounded.

The dry landscape gardens of Japan, *karesansui* ("dried-up mountains and water"), exist in perfect harmony with Zen Buddhism. The dry garden in front of the abbot's quarters in the Zen temple at Ryoanji is one of the most renowned Zen creations in Japan (**FIG. 25–4**). A flat rectangle of raked gravel, about 29 by 70 feet, surrounds 15 stones of different sizes in islands of moss. The stones are set in asymmetrical groups of two, three, and five. Low, plaster-covered walls establish the garden's boundaries, but beyond the perimeter wall maple, pine, and cherry trees add color and texture to the scene. Called "borrowed scenery," these elements are a considered part of the design even though they grow outside the garden. The garden is celebrated for its severity and emptiness.

Dry gardens began to be built in the fifteenth and sixteenth centuries in Japan. By the sixteenth century, Chinese landscape painting influenced the gardens' composition, and miniature clipped plants and beautiful stones were arranged to resemble famous paintings. Especially fine and unusual stones were coveted and even carried off as war booty, such was the cultural value of these seemingly mundane objects.

The Ryoanji garden's design, as we see it today, probably dates from the mid seventeenth century. By the time the garden was created, such stone and gravel gardens had become highly intellectualized, abstract reflections of nature. This garden has been interpreted as representing islands in the sea, or mountain peaks rising above the clouds, perhaps even a swimming tigress with her cubs, or constellations of stars and planets. All or none of these interpretations may be equally satisfying—or irrelevant—to a monk seeking clarity of mind through contemplation.

25-4 • ROCK GARDEN, RYOANJI, KYOTO
Muromachi period, c. 1480. Photographed spring 1993. Photograph by Michael S. Yamashita. UNESCO World Heritage Site, National Treasure.

The American composer John Cage once exclaimed that every stone at Ryoanji was in just the right place. He then said, "And every other place would also be just right." His remark is thoroughly Zen in spirit. There are many ways to experience Ryoanji. For example, we can imagine the rocks as having different visual "pulls" that relate them to one another. Yet there is also enough space between them to give each one a sense of self-sufficiency and permanence.

Foundations of Japanese Culture

With the end of the last Ice Age roughly 15,000 years ago, rising sea levels submerged the lowlands connecting Japan to the Asian landmass, creating the chain of islands we know today as Japan (MAP 25–1). Not long afterward, early Paleolithic cultures gave way to a Neolithic culture known as Jomon (c. 11,000–400 BCE) after its characteristic cord-marked pottery. During the Jomon period, a sophisticated hunter-gatherer culture developed. Agriculture supplemented hunting and gathering by around 5000 BCE, and rice cultivation began some 4,000 years later.

A fully settled agricultural society emerged during the Yayoi period (c. 400 BCE–300 CE), accompanied by hierarchical social organization and more centralized forms of government. As people learned to manufacture bronze and iron, use of those metals became widespread. Yayoi architecture, with its unpainted wood and thatched roofs, already showed the Japanese affinity for natural materials and clean lines, and the style of Yayoi granaries in particular persisted in the design of shrines in later centuries. The trend toward centralization continued during the Kofun period (c. 300–552 CE), an era characterized by the construction of large royal tombs, following the Korean practice. Veneration of leaders grew into the beginnings of the imperial system that has lasted to the present day.

The Asuka era (552–645 CE) began with a century of profound change as elements of Chinese civilization flooded into Japan, initially through the intermediary of Korea. The three most significant Chinese contributions to the developing Japanese culture were Buddhism (with its attendant art and architecture), a system of writing, and the structures of a centralized bureaucracy. The earliest extant Buddhist temple compound in Japan, Horyuji, which contains the oldest currently existing wooden buildings in the world, dates from this period.

The arrival of Buddhism also prompted some formalization of Shinto, the loose collection of indigenous Japanese beliefs and practices. Shinto is a religion that connects people to nature. Its rites are shamanistic and emphasize ceremonial purification. These include the invocation and appeasement of spirits, including those of the recently dead. Many Shinto deities are thought to inhabit various aspects of nature, such as particularly magnificent trees, rocks, and waterfalls, and living creatures such as deer. Shinto and Buddhism have in common an intense awareness of the transience of life, and as their goals are complementary—purification in the case of Shinto, enlightenment in the case of Buddhism—they have generally existed comfortably alongside each other to the present day.

The Nara period (645–794) takes its name from Japan's first permanently established imperial capital. During this time the founding works of Japanese literature were compiled and Buddhism became the most important force in Japanese culture. Its influence at court grew so great that in 794 the emperor moved the capital from Nara to Heian-kyo (present-day Kyoto), far from powerful monasteries.

During the Heian period (794–1185) an extremely refined court culture thrived, embodied today in an exquisite legacy of poetry, calligraphy, and painting. An efficient method for writing the Japanese language was developed, and with it a woman at the court wrote Japan's most celebrated fictional story, which some describe as the world's first novel: *The Tale of Genji*. Esoteric Buddhism, as hierarchical and intricate as the aristocratic world of the court, became popular.

The end of the Heian period was marked by civil warfare as regional warrior (samurai) clans were drawn into the factional conflicts at court. Pure Land Buddhism, with its simple message of salvation, offered consolation to many in troubled times. In 1185 the Minamoto clan defeated their arch rivals, the Taira, and their leader, Minamoto Yoritomo, assumed the position of shogun (general-in-chief). While paying respects to the emperor, Minamoto Yoritomo kept actual military and political power to himself, setting up his own capital in Kamakura. The Kamakura era (1185–1333) began a tradition of rule by shogun that lasted in various forms until 1868. It was also the time in which renewed contacts with China created the opportunity for Zen Buddhism, which was then flourishing in China (known there as Chan), to be introduced to Japan. By the end of the Kamakura period, numerous Zen monasteries had been founded in Kyoto and Kamakura, and Chinese and Japanese Chan/Zen monks were regularly visiting each others' countries.

MOMOYAMA PERIOD

The civil wars sweeping Japan laid bare the basic flaw in the Ashikaga system, which was that samurai were primarily loyal to their own feudal lord (*daimyo*), rather than to the central government. Battles between feudal clans grew more frequent, and it became clear that only a warrior powerful and bold enough to unite the entire country could control Japan. As the Muromachi period drew to a close, three leaders emerged who would change the course of Japanese history.

The first of these leaders was Oda Nobunaga (1534–1582), who marched his army into Kyoto in 1568 and overthrew the reigning Ashikaga shogun in 1573, initiating a new age of Japanese politics. A ruthless warrior, Nobunaga went so far as to destroy a Buddhist monastery because the monks refused to join his forces. Yet he was also a patron of the most rarefied and refined arts. Assassinated in the midst of one of his military campaigns, Nobunaga was succeeded by one of his generals, Toyotomi Hideyoshi (1537–1598), who soon gained complete power in Japan. He, too, patronized the arts when not leading his army, and he considered culture a vital adjunct to his rule. Hideyoshi, however, was overly ambitious. He believed that he could conquer both Korea and China, and he wasted much of his resources on two ill-fated invasions. A stable and long-lasting military regime

25-5 • HIMEJI CASTLE, HYOGO, NEAR OSAKA
Momoyama period, 1601–1609. Unesco World Heritage Site, National Treasure.

finally emerged soon after 1600 with the triumph of a third leader, Tokugawa Ieyasu (1543–1616), a former ally of Nobunaga who served as a senior retainer to Hideyoshi, and only asserted his power after Hideyoshi's death. But despite its turbulence, the era of Nobunaga and Hideyoshi, known as the Momoyama period (1573–1615), was one of the most creative eras in Japanese history.

Today the very word Momoyama conjures up images of bold warriors, luxurious palaces, screens shimmering with gold leaf, and, in contrast, rustic tea-ceremony ceramics. Europeans first made an impact in Japan at this time. After the arrival of a few wayward Portuguese explorers in 1543, traders and missionaries soon followed. It was only with the rise of Nobunaga, however, that Westerners were able to extend their activities beyond the ports of Kyushu, Japan's southernmost island. Nobunaga welcomed foreign traders, who brought him various products, the most influential of which were firearms.

ARCHITECTURE

European muskets and cannons quickly changed the nature of Japanese warfare and Japanese castle architecture. To protect castles from these new weapons, in the late sixteenth century they became heavily fortified garrisons. Some were eventually lost to warfare or torn down by victorious enemies, and others have been extensively altered over the years. One of the most beautiful of the few that have survived intact is Himeji, not far from the city of Osaka (**FIG. 25–5**). Rising high on a hill above the plains, Himeji has been given the name White Heron. To reach the upper fortress, visitors must follow angular paths beneath steep walls, climbing from one area to the next past stone ramparts and through narrow fortified gates, all the while feeling as though lost in a maze, with no sense of direction or progress. At the main building, a further climb up a series of narrow ladders leads to the uppermost chamber. There, the footsore visitor is rewarded with a stunning 360-degree view of the surrounding countryside.

DECORATIVE PAINTINGS FOR *SHOIN* ROOMS

Castles such as Himeji were sumptuously decorated, offering artists unprecedented opportunities to work on a grand scale. Interiors were divided into rooms by paper-covered sliding doors (**fusuma**), perfect canvases for large-scale murals. Free-standing folding screens (*byobu*) were also popular. Some had gold-leaf backgrounds, whose glistening surfaces not only conveyed light within the castle rooms but also displayed the wealth of the warrior leaders. Temples, too, commissioned large-scale paintings in these formats for grand reception rooms where the monks met with their wealthy warrior patrons (see "*Shoin* Design," opposite).

The Japanese tea ceremony and *shoin*-style interior residential architecture are undoubtedly the most significant and most enduring expressions of Japanese taste to emerge during the Momoyama period. **Shoin** combine a number of interior features in more-or-less standard ways, though no two rooms are ever the same. These features include wide verandas, walls divided by wood posts, floors covered with woven straw *tatami* mats, recessed panels in ceilings, sometimes painted and sometimes covered with reed matting, several shallow alcoves for prescribed purposes, *fusuma* (paper-covered sliding doors), and **shoji** screens—wood frames covered with translucent rice paper. The *shoin* illustrated here was built in 1601 as a guest hall, called Kojoin, at the Buddhist temple of Onjoji near Kyoto.

The *shoin* is a formal room for receiving important upper-class guests. With some variations due to differences in status, these rooms were designed for buildings used by samurai, aristocrats, and even well-to-do commoners. They are found in various types of buildings including private residences, living quarters at religious complexes (both Shinto shrines and Buddhist temples) and guesthouses or reception rooms at these places for use by high-ranking patrons, and at the finest houses of entertainment (such as seen in fig. 25–1) where geisha and courtesans entertained important guests. The owner of the building or the most important guest would be seated in front of the main alcove (*tokonoma*), which would contain a hanging scroll, an arrangement of flowers, or a large painted screen. Alongside that alcove was another that featured staggered shelves, often for displaying writing instruments. The veranda side of the room also contained a writing space fitted with a low writing desk.

The architectural harmony of a *shoin* is derived from standardization of its basic units, or modules. In Japanese carpentry, the common module of design and construction is the **bay**, reckoned as the distance from the center of one post to the center of another, which is governed in turn by the standard size of **tatami** floor mats. Although varying slightly from region to region, the size of a single *tatami* is about 3 by 6 feet. Room area in Japan is still expressed in terms of the number of *tatami* mats; for example, a room may be described as an eight-mat room.

shoji — veranda — writing alcove — *tokonoma* — *tatami* — staggered shelves — *fusuma*

ARTIST'S RENDERING OF THE KOJOIN GUEST HOUSE AT ONJOJI
Otsu, Shiga prefecture. Momoyama period, 1601. National Treasure.

SEE MORE: View a simulation of *Shoin* Design **www.myartslab.com**

Daitokuji, a celebrated Zen monastery in Kyoto, has a number of subtemples for which Momoyama artists painted magnificent *fusuma*. One, the Jukoin, possesses *fusuma* by Kano Eitoku (1543–1590), one of the most brilliant painters from the hereditary lineage of professional artists known as the Kano school. Eitoku headed this school, which was founded by his grandfather. The Kano school painted for the highest ranking warriors from the sixteenth century through 1868. They perfected a new style that combined the Muromachi ink-painting tradition with brightly colored decorative subjects. **FIGURE 25–6** shows two of the three walls of **FUSUMA** panels at Jukoin painted by Eitoku when was in his mid twenties. To the left, the subject is the familiar Kano school theme of cranes and pines, both symbols of long life; to the right is a great gnarled plum tree, symbol of spring. The trees are so massive they seem to extend far beyond the panels. An island rounding both walls of the far corner provides a focus for the outreaching trees. Ingeniously, it

25-6 • Kano Eitoku **FUSUMA**
Depicting pine and cranes (left) and plum tree (right) from the central room of the Jukoin, Daitokuji, Kyoto. Momoyama period, c. 1563–1573. *Fusuma* (sliding door panels), ink and gold on paper, height 5′9⅛″ (1.76 m). National Treasure.

belongs to both compositions at the same time, thus uniting them into an organic whole. Eitoku's vigorous use of brush and ink, his powerfully jagged outlines, and his dramatic compositions recall the style of Sesshu, but the bold new sense of scale in his works is a defining characteristic of the Momoyama period.

THE TEA CEREMONY

Japanese art is never one-sided. Along with castles and their opulent interior decoration, there was an equal interest during the Momoyama period in the quiet, the restrained, and the natural. This was expressed primarily through the tea ceremony.

The term "tea ceremony," a phrase now in common use, does not convey the full meaning of *chanoyu*, the Japanese ritual drinking of tea, which has no counterpart in Western culture. Tea had been introduced to Japan in the ninth century. Then, it was molded into cakes and boiled. However, the advent of Zen brought to Japan a different way of preparing tea, with the leaves crushed into powder and then whisked in bowls with hot water. Zen monks used such tea as a mild stimulant to aid meditation. Others found it had medicinal properties.

SEN NO RIKYU. The most famous tea master in Japanese history was Sen no Rikyu (1522–1591). He conceived of the tea ceremony as an intimate gathering in which a few people would enter a small rustic room, drink tea carefully prepared in front of them by their host, and quietly discuss the tea utensils or a Zen scroll hanging on the wall. He largely established the aesthetic of modesty, refinement, and rusticity that permitted the tearoom to serve as a respite from the busy and sometimes violent world outside. A traditional tearoom combines simple elegance and rusticity. It is made of natural materials such as bamboo and wood,

with mud walls, paper windows, and a floor covered with *tatami*. One tearoom that preserves Rikyu's design is named Taian **(FIG. 25–7)**. Built in 1582, it has a tiny door (guests must crawl to enter)

25-7 • Sen no Rikyu **TAIAN TEAROOM**
Myokian Temple, Kyoto. Momoyama period, 1582. National Treasure.

and miniature *tokonoma* for displaying a Zen scroll or a simple flower arrangement. At first glance, the room seems symmetrical. But a longer look reveals the disposition of the *tatami* does not match the spacing of the *tokonoma*, providing a subtle undercurrent of irregularity. The walls seem scratched and worn with age, but the *tatami* are replaced frequently to keep them clean and fresh. The mood is quiet; the light is muted and diffused through three small paper windows. Above all, there is a sense of spatial clarity. Nonessentials have been eliminated, so there is nothing to distract from focused attention. This tearoom aesthetic became an important element in Japanese culture.

THE TEA BOWL. Every utensil connected with tea, including the water pot, the kettle, the bamboo spoon, the whisk, the tea caddy, and, above all, the tea bowl, came to be appreciated for its aesthetic quality, and many works of art were created for use in *chanoyu*.

The age-old Japanese admiration for the natural and the asymmetrical found full expression in tea ceramics. Korean-style rice bowls made for peasants were suddenly considered the epitome of refined taste, and tea masters urged potters to mimic their imperfect shapes. But not every misshapen bowl would be admired. A rarified appreciation of beauty developed that took into consideration such factors as how well a tea bowl fitted into the hands, how subtly the shape and texture of the bowl appealed to the eye, and who had previously used and admired it. For this purpose, the inscribed storage box became almost as important as the ceramic that fitted within it, and if a bowl had been given a name by a leading tea master, it was especially treasured by later generations.

One of the finest tea bowls extant is named Mount Fuji after Japan's most sacred peak **(FIG. 25–8)**. (Mount Fuji is depicted in FIGURE 25–12.) An example of **raku** ware—a hand-built, low-fired ceramic developed for use in the tea ceremony—the bowl was crafted by Hon'ami Koetsu (1558–1637), a leading cultural figure of his day. Koetsu was most famous as a calligrapher, but he was also a painter, poet, lacquer designer, sword connoisseur, and potter. With its small foot, straight sides, irregular shape, and crackled texture, this bowl exemplifies tea taste.

EDO PERIOD

When Tokugawa Ieyasu gained control of Japan, he forced the emperor to proclaim him shogun, a title neither Nobunaga nor Hideyoshi had held. His reign initiated the Edo period (1615–1868), named after the city that he founded (present-day Tokyo) as his capital. This period is alternatively known as the Tokugawa era. Under the rule of the Tokugawa family, peace and prosperity came at the price of a rigid and repressive bureaucracy. The problem of a potentially rebellious *daimyo* was solved by ordering all feudal lords to spend either half of each year, or every other year, in Edo, where their families were required to live. Zen Buddhism was supplanted as the prevailing intellectual force by a

25-8 • Hon'ami Koetsu TEA BOWL, CALLED MOUNT FUJI
Momoyama-Edo period, early 17th century. *Raku* ware, height 3⅜″ (8.5 cm). Sakai Collection, Tokyo. National Treasure.

Connoisseurs developed a subtle vocabulary to discuss the aesthetics of tea. A favorite term was *sabi* ("loneliness"), which refers to the tranquility found when feeling alone. Other virtues were *wabi* ("poverty"), which suggests the artlessness of humble simplicity, and *shibui* ("bitter" or "astringent"), meaning elegant restraint. Tea bowls, such as this example, embody these aesthetics.

form of Neo-Confucianism, a philosophy formulated in Song-dynasty China that emphasized loyalty to the state, although the popularity of Buddhism among the commoner population surged at this time.

The shogunate officially divided Edo society into four classes. Samurai officials constituted the highest class, followed by farmers, artisans, and finally merchants. As time went on, however, merchants began to control the money supply, and in Japan's increasingly mercantile economy their accumulation of wealth soon exceeded that of the samurai, which helped, unofficially, to elevate their status. Reading and writing became widespread at all levels of society, and with literacy came intellectual curiosity and interest in the arts. All segments of the population—including samurai, merchants, townspeople, and rural peasants—were able to patronize artists. A rich cultural atmosphere developed unlike anything Japan had experienced before, in which artists worked in a wide variety of styles that appealed to these different groups of consumers.

RINPA SCHOOL PAINTING

During the Edo period, Edo was the shogun's city while life in Kyoto took its cues from the emperor and his court who resided there. Kyoto was also home to wealthy merchants, artists, and craftsmakers who served the needs of the courtiers and shared their interest in refined pursuits, such as the tea ceremony, and also their appreciation of art styles that recalled those perfected by aristocratic

Lacquer Box for Writing Implements

This lacquer box reflects the collaborative nature of Japanese artistic production and the fluidity with which artists worked in various media. It was designed by the Rinpa school painter Ogata Korin (1658–1716), who oversaw its execution, although he left the actual work to trained crafts specialists. He also frequently collaborated with his brother Kenzan, a celebrated potter. The upper tray housed writing implements, the larger bottom section stored paper (see "Inside a Writing Box," page 824). Korin's design sets a motif of irises and a plank bridge in a dramatic asymmetrical combination of mother-of-pearl, silver, lead, and gold lacquer. The subject was one he frequently also represented in painting because it was immensely popular with the educated Japanese of his day. They immediately recognized the imagery as an allusion to a famous passage from the tenth-century *Tales of Ise*, a classic of Japanese literature. A nobleman poet, having left his wife in the capital, pauses at a place called Eight Bridges, where a river branches into eight streams, each covered with a plank bridge. Irises are in full bloom, and his traveling companions urge the poet to write a *waka*—a five-line, 31-syllable poem—beginning each line with a syllable from the word for "iris": *Kakitsubata* (*ka-ki-tsu-ba-ta*). The poet responds (substituting *ha* for *ba*):

> **K**aragoromo
> **ki**tsutsu narenishi
> **tsu**ma shi areba
> **ha**rubaru kinuru
> **ta**bi o shi zo omou.
> When I remember
> my wife, fond and familiar
> as my courtly robe,
> I feel how far and distant
> my travels have taken me.
> (Translated by Stephen Addiss)

The poem in association with the scene became so famous that any image of a group of irises, with or without a plank bridge, immediately calls the episode to mind.

Lacquer is derived in Asia from the sap of the lacquer tree, *Rhus verniciflua*, indigenous to China but very early in history also grown commercially throughout east Asia. It is gathered by tapping into a tree and letting the sap flow into a container. It can be colored with vegetable or mineral dyes. Applied in thin coats to a surface of wood or leather, lacquer hardens into a glasslike protective coating that is waterproof, heat- and acid-resistant, and airtight. Its practical qualities made it ideal for storage containers, and vessels for food and drink. The creation of a piece of lacquer can take several years. First, the item is fashioned of wood and sanded smooth. Next, up to 30 layers of lacquer are thinly applied, each dried and polished before the next is brushed on.

Japanese craftsmakers exploited the decorative potential of lacquer to create expensive luxury items, such as this box, which was created when lacquer arts had been perfected. It features inlays of mother-of-pearl and precious metals in a style known as *makie* ("sprinkled design"), in which flaked or powdered gold or silver was embedded in a still-damp coat of lacquer.

Ogata Korin **LACQUER BOX FOR WRITING IMPLEMENTS**
Edo period, late 17th–early 18th century. Lacquer, lead, silver, and mother-of-pearl, 5⅝ × 10¾ × 7¾″ (14.2 × 27.4 × 19.7 cm). Tokyo National Museum, Tokyo. National Treasure.

DETAILS OF BOX INTERIOR AND LID
Left: interior of lid; center: top tray with ink stone and waterpot; right: exterior view of box lid.

25-9 • Tawaraya Sotatsu WAVES AT MATSUSHIMA
Edo period, 17th century. Pair of six-panel folding screens, ink, mineral colors, and gold leaf on paper; each screen 4'9⅞" × 11'8½" (1.52 × 3.56 m). Freer Gallery of Art, Smithsonian Institution, Washington, D.C. Gift of Charles Lang Freer (F1906.231 & 232)

The six-panel screen format was a triumph of scale and practicality. Each panel consisted of a light wood frame surrounding a latticework interior covered with several layers of paper. Over this foundation was pasted a high-quality paper, silk, or gold-leaf ground, ready to be painted by the finest artists. Held together with ingenious paper hinges, a screen could be folded for storage or transportation, resulting in a mural-size painting light enough to be carried by a single person, ready to be displayed as needed.

artists in the Heian period. The most famous and original Kyoto painter who worked for this group of patrons was Tawaraya Sotatsu (active c. 1600–40), who occasionally collaborated with the potter Koetsu (SEE FIG. 25–8). Sotatsu is considered the first great painter of the Rinpa school, the modern name given to a group of artists whose art reinterpreted ancient courtly-style arts. These artists are grouped together because of their shared interests and art styles,

and did not constitute a formal school, such as the Kano. Rinpa masters were not just painters, however: They sometimes collaborated with craftsmakers (see "Lacquer Box for Writing Implements," opposite).

One of Sotatsu's most famous pairs of screens depict the islands of Matsushima near the northern city of Sendai (FIG. 25–9). On the right screen (shown here on top), mountainous islands echo

Writing boxes hold tools basic for both writing and painting: ink stick, ink stone, brushes, and paper, which are beautiful objects in their own right.

Ink sticks are basically soot from burning wood or oil that is bound into a paste with resin, and pressed into small stick-shaped or cake-shaped molds to harden.

Fresh ink is made for each writing or painting session by grinding the hard, dry ink stick in water against a fine-grained stone. A typical ink stone has a shallow well at one end sloping up to a grinding surface at the other. The artist fills the well with water from a waterpot. The ink stick, held vertically, is dipped into the well to pick up a small amount of water, then is rubbed in a circular motion firmly on the grinding surface. Grinding ink is viewed as a meditative task, time for collecting one's thoughts and concentrating on the painting or calligraphy ahead.

Brushes are made from animal hair set in simple bamboo or hollow-reed handles. Brushes taper to a fine point that responds sensitively to any shift in pressure. Although great painters and calligraphers do eventually develop their own styles of holding and using the brush, all begin by learning the basic position for writing. The brush is held vertically, grasped firmly between the thumb and first two fingers, with the fourth and fifth fingers often resting against the handle for more subtle control.

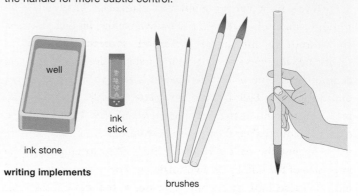

ink stone
well
ink stick
writing implements
brushes

the swing and sweep of the waves, with stylized gold clouds in the upper left. The left screen continues the gold clouds until they become a sand spit from which twisted pines grow. Their branches seem to lean toward a strange island in the lower left, composed of an organic, amoebalike form in gold surrounded by mottled ink. This mottled effect was a specialty of Rinpa school painters.

As one of the "three famous beautiful views of Japan," Matsushima was often depicted in art. Most painters showed the pine-covered islands that make the area famous from above. Sotatsu's genius was to portray them in an abbreviated manner and from a fresh vantage point, as though the viewer were passing the islands in a boat on the roiling waters. The artist's asymmetrical composition and use of thick mineral colors in combination with soft, playful brushwork and sparkling gold leaf create the boldly decorative effect that is the hallmark of the Rinpa tradition.

NATURALISTIC PAINTING

NAGASAWA ROSETSU.   By the middle of the eighteenth century, the taste of wealthy Kyoto merchants had shifted, influencing the styles of artists who competed for their patronage. The public was enthralled with novel imagery captured in magnifying glasses, telescopes, and an optical device that enhanced the three-

25–10 • Nagasawa Rosetsu BULL AND PUPPY
Edo period, late 18th century. Left of a pair of six-panel screens, ink and gold wash on paper, 5′7¼″ × 12′3″ (1.70 × 3.75 m). Los Angeles County Museum of Art, California. Joe and Etsuko Price Collection (L.83.45.3a)

dimensional effects of Western-style perspective pictures. Schools of independent artists emerged in Kyoto to satisfy demands for naturalistic-style paintings that reflected this fascination. The most influential was founded by Maruyama Okyo, who had perfected methods to incorporate Western shading and perspective into a more native Japanese decorative style, creating a sense of volume new to east Asian painting, while still retaining a sense of familiarity.

Okyo's most famous pupil was Nagasawa Rosetsu (1754–1799), a painter of great natural talent who added his own boldness and humor to his master's tradition. Rosetsu delighted in surprising his viewers with odd juxtapositions and unusual compositions. One of his finest works is a pair of screens, the left one depicting a bull and a puppy (FIG. 25–10). The bull is so immense that his mammoth body exceeds the borders of the screen, undoubtedly influenced by new optical devices. The puppy, white against the dark gray of the bull, helps to emphasize the huge size of the bull by its own smallness. The puppy's relaxed and informal pose, looking happily right out at the viewer, gives this powerful painting a humorous touch that increases its charm. In the hands of a master such as Rosetsu, plebeian subject matter became simultaneously delightful and monumental.

LITERATI PAINTING

Because the city of Kyoto was far from the watchful eyes of the government in Edo, and the emperor resided there with his court, it enjoyed a degree of privilege and independence not found in any other Japanese city. These conditions allowed for the creation of art in the new Rinpa and naturalistic styles. They also encouraged the emergence of new schools of philosophy based on interpretations of Chinese Confucianism that disagreed with those taught at schools sponsored by Tokugawa shoguns. These new interpretations incorporated ideas from Chinese Daoism, which promoted cultivation of a person's uniqueness, thus encouraging artistic creativity. Kyoto's intellectuals, who admired Chinese culture, even created a new, more informal tea ceremony of their own, featuring steeped tea called *sencha* because it was the tea drunk by Ming-dynasty Chinese literati. They did this as political protest—by then *chanoyu* had become encumbered by rules and was closely associated with the repressive shogunate. Influenced by the new ideas, a Chinese manner of painting arose in the mid eighteenth century in emulation of Chinese literati painting. Artists who embraced this style, both professionals who painted for paying clients and amateurs who painted for their own enjoyment, quickly grew to number hundreds as its popularity spread throughout Japan alongside increased interest in drinking *sencha*, as well as in other aspects of Chinese culture. They learned about Chinese literati painting from paintings and woodblock-printed painting manuals imported from China, and also from Chinese emigrant monks and merchants who lived in Japan.

The best and most successful of these artists took Chinese literati painting models as starting points for their original interpretations of literati themes. One of them was Ike Taiga (1723–1776),

admired as much for his magnetic personality as for his art. He was born into a poor farming family near Kyoto and showed innate talent for painting at a young age. Moving to Kyoto in his teens, he became friends with Chinese scholars there, including those who promoted drinking *sencha*. Taiga became a leader in this group, attracting admirers who were enamored of both his quasi-amateurish painting style and his quest for spiritual self-cultivation. His character and personal style are seen in the scintillating, rhythmic layering of strokes used to define the mountains in his TRUE VIEW OF KOJIMA BAY (FIG. 25–11) which blends Chinese

25-11 • Ike Taiga TRUE VIEW OF KOJIMA BAY
Edo period, third quarter of 18th century. Hanging scroll, ink and color on silk. 39¼ × 14⅝″ (99.7 × 37.6 cm). Hosomi Museum, Kyoto.

The production of woodblock prints combined the expertise of three people: the artist, the carver, and the printer. Coordinating and funding the endeavor was a publisher, who commissioned the project and distributed the prints to stores or itinerant peddlers, who would sell them.

The artist supplied the master drawing for the print, executing its outlines with brush and ink on tissue paper. Colors might be indicated, but more often they were understood or decided on later. The drawing was passed on to the carver, who pasted it face down on a hardwood block, preferably cherrywood, so that the outlines showed through the paper in reverse. A light coating of oil might be brushed on to make the paper more transparent, allowing the drawing to stand out clearly. The carver then cut around the lines of the drawing with a sharp knife, always working in the same direction as the original brushstrokes. The rest of the block was chiseled away, leaving the outlines in relief. This block, which reproduced the master drawing, was called the **key block**. If the print was to be **polychrome**, having multiple colors, prints made from the key block were in turn pasted face down on blocks that would be used as guides for the carver of the color blocks. Each color generally required a separate block, although both sides of a block might be used for economy.

Once the blocks were completed, the printer took over. Paper for printing was covered lightly with animal glue (gelatin). Before printing, the paper was lightly moistened so that it would take ink and color well. Water-based ink or color was brushed over the block, and the paper placed on top and rubbed with a smooth, padded device called a *baren*, until the design was completely transferred. The key block was printed first, then the colors one by one. Each block was carved with two small marks called **registration marks**, in exactly the same place in the margins, outside of the image area—an L in one corner, and a straight line in another. By aligning the paper with these marks before letting it fall over the block, the printer ensured that the colors would be placed correctly within the outlines. One of the most characteristic effects of later Japanese prints is a grading of color from dark to pale. This was achieved by wiping some of the color from the block before printing, or by moistening the block and then applying the color gradually with an unevenly loaded brush—a brush loaded on one side with full-strength color and on the other with diluted color.

Toshusai Sharaku ONOE MATSUSUKE AS MATSUSHITA MIKINOSHIN

Edo period, 1794–95. Polychrome woodblock print, ink and colors on mica ground paper, 14³⁄₁₆ × 9¹¹⁄₁₆″ (36.1 × 24.6 cm). British Museum, London. (1909,0618,0.42)

Much as people today buy posters of their favorite sports, music, or movie stars, so, too, in the Edo period people clamored for images of their idols, actors of the popular form of drama known as Kabuki. The artist of this print was renowned for capturing the personality of his subjects. The actor has his eyes crossed, in what was a frozen, tension-filled moment in an action-packed play. The print has a shiny mica background, made of crushed shells, painstakingly applied by printers.

SEE MORE: View a video about the printmaking process of woodcut www.myartslab.com

models, Japanese aesthetics, and personal brushwork. The gentle rounded forms of the mountains intentionally recall the work of famous Chinese literati painters, and Taiga utilizes a stock landscape composition that separates foreground and background mountains with a watery expanse (SEE FIG. 25–2). However, he did not paint an imaginary Chinese scene but a personal vision of an actual Japanese place that he had visited—Kojima Bay—as a document accompanying the painting explains. Still, in deference to his admiration for Chinese literati, Taiga places two figures clad in Chinese robes on the right, midway up the mountain.

UKIYO-E: PICTURES OF THE FLOATING WORLD

Edo served as the shogun's capital as well as the center of a flourishing popular culture associated with tradespeople. Deeply Buddhist, commoners were acutely aware of the transience of life, symbolized, for example, by the cherry tree which blossoms so briefly. Putting a positive spin on this harsh realization, they sought to live by the mantra: Let's enjoy it to the full as long as it lasts. This they did to excess in the restaurants, theaters, bathhouses, and brothels of the city's pleasure quarters, named after the Buddhist phrase *ukiyo* ("floating world"). Every major city in Japan had these

25–12 • Katsushika Hokusai THE GREAT WAVE
From *Thirty-Six Views of Mt. Fuji*. Edo period, c. 1831. Polychrome woodblock print on paper, 9⅞ × 14⅝"
(25 × 37.1 cm). Honolulu Academy of Arts, Honolulu, Hawaii. James A. Michener Collection (HAA 13, 695)

EXPLORE MORE: Gain insight from a primary source related to *The Great Wave* www.myartslab.com

quarters, and most were licensed by the government. But those of Edo were the largest and most famous. The heroes of the floating world were not famous samurai or aristocratic poets. Instead, swashbuckling Kabuki actors and beautiful courtesans were admired. These paragons of pleasure soon became immortalized in paintings and—because paintings were too expensive for common people—in woodblock prints known as *ukiyo-e* ("pictures of the floating world"; see "Japanese Woodblock Prints," opposite). Most prints were inexpensively produced by the hundreds and not considered serious fine art. Yet when first imported to Europe and America, they were immediately acclaimed and strongly influenced late nineteenth- and early twentieth-century Western art (see Chapter 30).

HARUNOBU. The first woodblock prints had no color, only black outlines. Soon artists added colors by hand to make them more resemble paintings. But to produce colored prints more rapidly they gradually devised a system to print colors using multiple blocks. The first artist to design prints that took advantage of this new technique,

known as **nishiki-e** ("brocade pictures"), was Suzuki Harunobu (1724–1770), famous for his images of courtesans (SEE FIG. 25–1).

HOKUSAI. During the first half of the nineteenth century, the heyday of popular travel, pictures of famous sights of Japan grew immensely popular. The two most famous *ukiyo-e* printmakers, Utagawa Hiroshige (1797–1858) and Katsushika Hokusai (1760–1849), specialized in this genre. Hiroshige's *Fifty-Three Stations of the Tokaido* and Hokusai's *Thirty-Six Views of Mt. Fuji* became the most successful sets of graphic art the world has known. The woodblocks were printed, and printed again, until they wore out. They were then recarved, and still more copies were printed. This process continued for decades, and thousands of prints from the two series are still extant.

THE GREAT WAVE (FIG. 25–12) is the most famous of the scenes from *Thirty-Six Views of Mt. Fuji*. The great wave rears up like a dragon with claws of foam, ready to crash down on the figures huddled in the boats below. Exactly at the point of imminent disaster, but far in the distance, rises Japan's most sacred peak, Mount Fuji, whose slopes, we suddenly realize, swing up like waves and whose snowy crown is like foam—comparisons the artist makes clear in the wave nearest us, caught just at the moment of greatest resemblance. In the late nineteenth century when Japonisme, or *japonism*, became the vogue in the West, Hokusai's art was greatly appreciated, even more so than it had been in Japan: The first book on the artist was published in France.

ZEN PAINTING: BUDDHIST ART FOR RURAL COMMONERS

Outside Japan's urban centers, art for commoners also flourished, much of it tied to their devotion to Buddhism. Deprived of the support of the samurai officials who now favored Confucianism, Buddhism nevertheless thrived during the Edo period through patronage from private individuals, many of them rural peasants. In the early eighteenth century, one of the great monks who preached in the countryside was the Zen master Hakuin Ekaku (1685–1769), born in a small village near Mount Fuji. After hearing a fire-and-brimstone sermon in his youth he resolved to become a monk and for years he traveled around Japan seeking out the strictest Zen teachers. He became the most important Zen master of the last 500 years, and invented many *koan* (questions posed to novices by Zen masters to guide their progression towards enlightenment during meditation), including the famous "What is the sound of one hand clapping?" He was also, in his later years, a self-taught painter and calligrapher, who freely gave away his scrolls to admirers (who included not only farmers but also artisans, merchants, and even samurai) as a way of spreading his religious message.

Hakuin's art differed from that of Muromachi period monk-painters like Bunsei and Sesshu (SEE FIGS. 25–2, 25–3). His work featured everyday Japanese subjects or Zen themes that conveyed his ideas in ways his humble followers could easily understand. He often painted Daruma (Bodhidharma in Sanskrit) (FIG. 25–13), the semilegendary Indian monk who founded Zen (see Chapter 11). Hundreds of Zen monks of the Edo period and later created simply brushed Zen ink paintings. Hakuin largely set the standards that subsequent Zen artists followed.

CRAFTS

The ingenuity and technical proficiency that contributed to the development of *ukiyo*-prints came about because of Japan's long history of fine crafts production. Textiles, ceramics, lacquer, woodwork, and metalwork were among the many crafts in which Japanese artisans excelled. In pre-modern Japan, unlike the West, no separate words distinguished fine arts (painting and sculpture) from crafts. (The Japanese word for fine art and corresponding modern Japanese language words for various types of craft were not coined until 1872.) This was largely because professional Japanese artist and crafts studios basically followed the same hereditary, hierarchical structure. A master artist directed all activity in a workshop of trainees, who gradually gained seniority through years of apprenticeship and innate talent. Sometimes, such as when a pupil was not chosen to succeed the master, he would go off and start his own studio. This teamwork approach to artistic production is characteristic of the way most traditional Japanese arts were created.

25-13 • Hakuin Ekaku GIANT DARUMA
Edo period, mid 18th century. Hanging scroll, ink on paper 4'3½" × 1'9¾" (130.8 × 55.2 cm). Manyo'an Collection, New Orleans 1973.2

As a self-taught amateur painter, Hakuin's painting style is the very antithesis of that of consummate professionals, such as painters of the Kano or Rinpa schools. The appeal of his art lies in its artless charm, humor, and astonishing force. Here Hakuin has portrayed the wide-eyed Daruma during his nine years of meditation in front of a temple wall in China. Intensity, concentration, and spiritual depth are conveyed by a minimal number of broad, forceful brushstrokes. The inscription is the ultimate Zen message, attributed to Daruma himself: "Pointing directly to the human heart, see your own nature and become Buddha."

Kosode Robe ➤ With design of waves and floral bouquets. Edo period, second half of 18th century to early 19th century. White figured satin ground with silk and metallic thread embroidery, stencil tie-dyeing, brush painting; indigo blue dyed silk lining, height 64¾″ (163 cm), width 24½″ (61.5 cm) below sleeve, 50″ (127 cm) sleeve top. The Nelson-Atkins Museum of Art, Kansas City, Missouri. Gift of Mrs. Harold J. Owens (57-45)

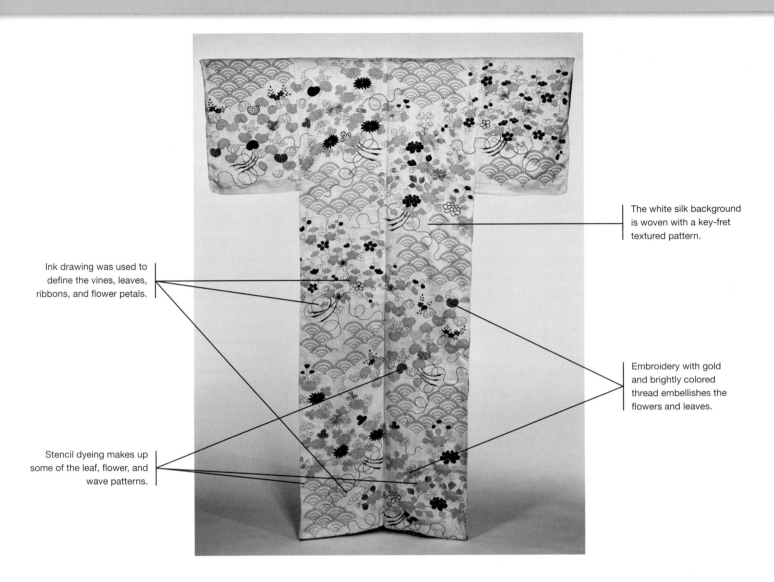

The white silk background is woven with a key-fret textured pattern.

Ink drawing was used to define the vines, leaves, ribbons, and flower petals.

Embroidery with gold and brightly colored thread embellishes the flowers and leaves.

Stencil dyeing makes up some of the leaf, flower, and wave patterns.

SEE MORE: View the Closer Look feature for *Kosode* Robe **www.myartslab.com**

KOSODE ROBES. The kimono is as much a symbol of Japanese culture as is the tea ceremony. Before the late nineteenth century, it was known as *kosode*. These loose, unstructured garments that wrap around the body and are cinched with a sash were the principal outer article of clothing of both men and women, beginning in the Muromachi period. *Kosode* ("small sleeves") refers to the vertical length of the sleeves (in contrast, young, unmarried women wore robes with long, flowing sleeves). Because of their fragility, few *kosode* prior to the Edo period survive. But those from the eighteenth century reveal the opulent tastes of affluent merchant-class women of the day (see "A Closer Look," page 830). In the example shown, ribbons and flower bouquets float above abstract waves and scalloped-edged clouds in a playful, asymmetrical composition. Artisans used many techniques to create the rich interplay of textures and designs on this gorgeous robe, made in the country's premier textile center of Kyoto. Its design elements resemble those found in paintings of the period.

25-14 • LARGE PLATE WITH LEAF DESIGN
Edo period, early 18th century. Arita ware, *Ko*-Imari type. Porcelain with underglaze blue decoration, diameter 15⅜″ (39.1 cm). Nelson-Atkins Museum of Art, Kansas City. Purchase: Nelson Trust (63-4)

JAPANESE PORCELAIN.   While the history of ceramic production dates to the earliest days of Japanese civilization, production of glazed, high-fired stoneware ceramics proliferated in Japan only from the sixteenth century, encouraged largely by the tea ceremony. The industry thrived in southern Japan, where, around 1600, influxes of more highly skilled Korean potters helped native artisans to learn new continental technologies that allowed them to manufacture porcelain for the first time. One town, Arita, became the center for the production of porcelain, created for export to the West and for domestic use. While tea ceremony aesthetics still favored rustic wares such as Koetsu's tea bowl (SEE FIG. 25–8), porcelain was more widely adopted for everyday use in response to a growing fashion for Chinese arts. Porcelains made in Arita are known by various names according to their dating and decorative schemes. Those ornamented exclusively with underglaze cobalt blue, the first porcelains made in Japan, are generally known as Imari, the name for the port city from which some of them were exported to Europe. However, the piece shown in **FIGURE 25–14** must have been made for domestic use, as the audaciously abstracted design would not have appealed to Europeans, who preferred more recognizable natural forms. Complementing the strong, vertical stylized leaves are small, half-round forms resembling chestnuts.

THE MODERN PERIOD

The tensions that resulted from Commodore Matthew Perry's forced opening of trade ports in Japan in 1853 precipitated the downfall of the Tokugawa shogunate. In 1868 the emperor was formally restored to power, an event known as the Meiji Restoration. The court soon moved from Kyoto to Edo, which was renamed Tokyo ("Eastern Capital"). After a period of intense industrialization in the first two decades after the Meiji Restoration, influential private individuals and government officials, sometimes working cooperatively, created new arts institutions including juried exhibitions, artists' associations, arts universities, and cultural heritage laws. These rekindled appreciation for the art of the past, encouraged

25-15 • Yokoyama Taikan FLOATING LIGHTS
Meiji period, 1909. One of a pair of hanging scrolls, ink, colors, and gold on silk, 56½ × 20½″ (143 × 52 cm). The Museum of Modern Art, Ibaraki.

perpetuation of artistic techniques threatened by adoption of Western ways, and stimulated new artistic production. Many of these arts institutions still exist today.

MEIJI-PERIOD NATIONALIST PAINTING

The Meiji period (1868–1912) marked a major change for Japan. Japanese society adapted various aspects of Western education, governmental systems, clothing, medicine, industrialization, and technology in efforts to modernize the nation. Teachers of sculpture and oil painting came from Italy, while adventurous Japanese artists traveled to Europe and America to study.

A MEIJI PAINTER. Ernest Fenollosa (1853–1908), an American who had recently graduated from Harvard, traveled to Japan in 1878 to teach philosophy and political economy at Tokyo University. Within a few years, he and a former student, Okakura Kakuzo (1862–1913), began urging artists to study traditional Japanese arts rather than to focus exclusively on Western art styles and media, but infuse them with a modern sensibility. Yokoyama Taikan (1868–1958) subsequently developed his personal style within the Nihonga (modern Japanese painting) genre promoted by Okakura. Encouraged by Okakura, who had gone there before him, Taikan visited India in 1903. He embraced Okakura's ideals of pan-Asian cultural nationalism, expressed in the first line of Okakura's book, *Ideals of the East* (1903), with the words "Asia is One." This outlook later contributed to fueling Japan's imperialist ambitions. Taikan's **FLOATING LIGHTS** (FIG. 25–15) was inspired by a visit to Calcutta, where he observed women engaged in divination on the banks of the Ganges. The naturalism of their semitransparent robes and the flowing water reveal his indebtedness to Western art. In contrast, the lightly applied colors, and graceful branches with delicate, mottled brushwork defining the leaves, recall techniques of Rinpa-school artists.

JAPAN AFTER WORLD WAR II

In the aftermath of World War II (1941–1945), Japan was a shambles, her great cities ruined. Nevertheless, under the U.S.-led Allied Occupation (1946–1952), the Japanese people immediately began rebuilding, unified by a sense of national purpose. Within ten years, Japan established nascent automobile, electronics, and consumer goods industries. Rail travel, begun in 1872, expanded and improved significantly after the war and by the time of the Tokyo Olympics in 1964 the capital had an extensive commuter rail system, and Japan was the world leader in city-to-city high-speed rail transit with its new Shinkansen (bullet train). As the rest of the world came to know Japan, foreign interest in its arts focused especially on the country's still thriving crafts traditions. Not only were these a source of national pride and identity, the skills and attitudes they fostered also served as the basis for Japan's national revival.

POSTWAR ARCHITECTURE. The Hiroshima Peace Memorial Museum and Park (FIG. 25–16) was one of the first monuments constructed after World War II. A memorial to those who perished on August 6, 1945, and an expression of prayers for world peace, it attests to the spirit of the Japanese people at this difficult juncture in history. Tange Kenzo (1913–2005), who would eventually become one of the masters of Modernist architecture, designed the complex after winning an open competition as a young, up-and-coming architect.

The building's design befits the solemnity of its function. Concrete piers raise its stripped concrete form 20 feet off the ground. The wood formwork of the concrete recalls the wooden forms of traditional Japanese architecture. But the use of concrete is also inspired by Le Corbusier's 1920s Modernist villas. Evenly spaced vertical concrete fins lining the façade afford light shade. They suggest both the regular spacing of elements present in modular *shoin* architecture (see "*Shoin* Design," page 819) and the values of Modernist architects who advocated that structure should

25-16 • Tange Kenzo HIROSHIMA PEACE MEMORIAL MUSEUM
Showa period, 1955. Main building (center) repaired in Heisei period, 1991. East building (right), the former Peace Memorial Hall, which first opened in 1955, was rebuilt in June 1994 and attached to the main building. Designated UNESCO World Heritage site in 1996.

This exquisite wooden box was crafted by Eri Sayoko (1945–2007). In 2002, the government designated her a Living National Treasure for her accomplishment in the art of cut-gold leaf (*kirikane*), traditionally used to decorate Buddhist sculpture and paintings (as in FIG. 11–15). The National Treasure designation originated in Japanese laws of 1897 that were intended to safeguard the nation's artistic heritage at a time when art was being bought by Western collectors but suffering neglect at home. In 1955 the government added provisions to honor living individuals who excel in traditional craft techniques with the title Living National Treasure. This historic preservation system is the most complex of its type in the world.

Eri was the third person awarded the title for cut-gold-leaf decoration and the first woman. In its encouragement of traditional crafts, the Living National Treasure system has greatly assisted women in gaining much-deserved recognition. In pre-modern Japan (encompassing the prehistoric era up to the start of the Meiji period in 1868), women mostly operated in the private sphere of the home where they created crafts for their own enjoyment or for devotional purposes. By the eighteenth century, this situation had begun to change, so that women could be poets, calligraphers, and painters; the wives or daughters of famous male artists gained the most recognition. Among the most famous was Gyokuran, wife of the literati painter Ike Taiga (SEE FIG. 25–11). However, the conservative nature of traditional Japanese crafts workshops meant women could not hold leadership positions in them, and until the postwar period they were seldom recognized for their achievements in crafts. Eri Sayoko flourished in the new climate, as one of the first women to work in the medium of cut-gold, which she took up via an unorthodox route.

Eri specialized in Japanese painting in high school and in design-dyeing in junior college. After marriage to a traditional Buddhist sculptor she started producing Buddhist paintings and began an apprenticeship with a master *kirikane* craftsman. She was so talented that after only three years she was able to exhibit her work professionally. Her art is informed by her deep study of the history of the technique, and her marvelous sensitivity for color betrays her training in dyeing. Eri's elegant, functional objects, typified by this box, are infused with modern sensibilities, although her designs have a basis in traditional *kirikane* patterns. Her art reveals that adherence to a craft tradition can still result in artistic originality.

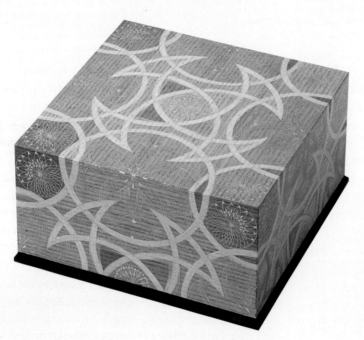

Eri Sayoko **ORNAMENTAL BOX: DANCING IN THE COSMOS**
Heisei period, 2006. Wood with polychrome and cut gold, height 33⅞″ (86 cm), width 6½″ (16.5 cm), depth 6½″ (16.5 cm). Collection of Eri Kokei

dictate form. In this commission Tange infuses Modernist tendencies and materials with a Japanese sense of interval and refinement, characteristics also seen in the work of most younger contemporary Japanese architects active today.

POSTWAR CRAFTS. Throughout their history, the Japanese have displayed a heightened sensitivity toward the surface quality of things, for polish, for line, for exquisiteness and stylishness. Their appreciation of craft has continued to the present (see "Craftsmakers as Living National Treasures," above). Some crafts are made for use in the tea ceremony, which remains popular today. Others are produced as functional objects for use in the home, as high-fashion apparel, or simply as decoration. Many combine diverse influences, native and foreign, that the maker integrates uniquely, often using novel techniques invented to achieve the desired results. In this way, the traditions of fine crafts in Japan, among the signature achievements of Japanese culture, continue to be enriched.

A MODERN CERAMICIST. Perhaps because the arts of tea ceremony and flower arrangement both require ceramic vessels,

25–17 • Fukami Sueharu SKY II
Heisei period, c. 1990. Celadon-glazed porcelain with wood base 3 × 44⅛ × 9½" (7.7 × 112.1 × 24.2 cm).
Helen Foresman Spencer Museum of Art, University of Kansas, Lawrence, Kansas.
Museum purchase: R. Charles and Mary Margaret Clevenger Fund (1992.0072)

the Japanese have a particular love for pottery. While some ceramicists continue to create *raku* tea bowls and other traditional wares, others experiment with new styles and innovative techniques.

Fukami Sueharu (b. 1947) is among the most innovative clay artists in Japan today. Yet his art has roots in the past—in his case, in Chinese porcelains with pale bluish-green glazes (*seihakuji*). Even so, his forms and fabrication methods, typified by his **SKY II**, are ultramodern (**FIG. 25–17**). He created the piece using a slip casting technique, in which he injected liquid clay into a mold using a high-pressure compressor. Although he sometimes makes functional pieces, mainly cylinders that could hold flower arrangements, *Sky II* shows his mastery of pure form. The title suggests sources of his abstract sculptural form: a wing or a blade of an aircraft slicing through the heavens. The pale blue sky-colored glaze enhances this allusion.

A plurality of artistic styles and media reflects Japan's long history and idiosyncratic worldview. While maintaining a strong sense of national identity, it has been able to absorb techniques and ideas from other lands, improve them, polish and refine them, and paradoxically make them its own. Deeply influenced by the Shinto and Buddhist religions, benefiting from a rich topography and mild climate, with citizens' lives revolving around a complex and hierarchical social structure, and reflecting a well-educated population curious about the rest of the world yet self-consciously different from it, the arts of Japan share common aesthetic principles that make them distinctively Japanese.

THINK ABOUT IT

25.1 Discuss the unique characteristics of Japanese Zen gardens, and explain how the rock garden at Ryoanji embodies the ideals of Zen Buddhism.

25.2 Explain how differences between pictorial styles of artists from the cities of Kyoto and Edo reflect the variations in the social status, and cultural and intellectual interests of the residents. Build your discussion upon a comparison of a painting or lacquer box by a Rinpa-school artist from Kyoto with a woodblock print that was made in Edo.

25.3 Discuss how the Japanese tea ceremony works and observe the role that craft arts play within it. Explore the unique aesthetics of the tearoom and craft arts associated with the ceremony, making reference to at least one work from this chapter.

25.4 Discuss Chinese influences on Japanese art styles and techniques in the Muromachi and Edo periods; for your answer, look back to Chapter 24 and draw specific comparisons between two works from each chapter.

25.5 Distinguish at least three different patron groups for Japanese arts and architecture in the Muromachi, Momoyama, and Edo periods. Discuss the kinds of arts and architecture each group preferred and how they were used by these patrons.

PRACTICE MORE: Compose answers to these questions, get flashcards for images and terms, and review chapter material with quizzes
www.myartslab.com

26-1 • Julia Jumbo TWO GREY HILLS TAPESTRY WEAVING   Navajo, 2003.
Handspun wool, 36 × 24½″ (91.2 × 62.1 cm). Wheelwright Museum of the American Indian,
Santa Fe, New Mexico.